HOMOSEXUALITY
AND WORLD RELIGIONS

HOMOSEXUALITY AND WORLD RELIGIONS

Edited by Arlene Swidler

Trinity Press International
Valley Forge, Pennsylvania

First Edition 1993

Trinity Press International
P.O. Box 851
Valley Forge, PA 19482

Cover design by Jim Gerhard

Library of Congress Cataloging-in-Publication Data

Homosexuality and world religions : edited by Arlene Swidler.
    p.   cm.
    Includes bibliographical references.
    ISBN 1-56338-051-X
    1. Homosexuality—Religious aspects—Comparative studies.
I. Swidler, Arlene.
BL65.H64H65   1993
291.1'7835766—dc20   93-6848
                                                            CIP

Printed in the United States of America

93 94 95 96 97 98 6 5 4 3 2 1

Contents

Preface

When the idea of a volume collecting the data on homosexuality and the world's major religions first occurred to me, I immediately began to check with other people: publishers of both books and periodicals, gay activists, owners of specialized bookstores, and academics teaching sexuality courses. There was unanimous agreement: nothing like this had yet been done.

On whether such a project should actually be undertaken there was slightly less agreement. Most people were extremely enthusiastic; this would be a significant contribution to knowledge. But a few were reluctant to encourage me. They asked: Do we really need to have more bad news? Don't gays have enough problems without your documenting them? The correlation between pessimism about the project's eventual value and a negative attitude toward religion in general was usually quite obvious.

Our research into the various religious traditions has turned up a wide spectrum of differences not only between religions but also within individual traditions over time. Such diversity suggests that, because the attitudes of religion toward homosexuality are not fixed, the traditions have much to learn from one another's reflections and history. Our findings, then, are not simply "bad news" and more "problems," but rather a basis and, we hope, a stimulus for dialogue.

Whenever possible I have found scholars who could write from within their own faith tradition: our essay on Buddhism is written by a Buddhist, our essay on Islam by a Muslim. But even within a specific culture material is often not easily available. On a trip to China a few years back I queried some scholars about the status of homosexual people there. Were there any laws discriminating against gays? No. Were there perhaps laws that by protecting the family worked to the detriment of gays? After some consultation, the consensus was "No problem. No homosexuals in China."

Some contributors thus discovered that, even when working within their own religion and area of expertise, they found far less published research and scholarship to build upon and draw upon than did others of our group. Some had larger amounts of legal and historical documentation to work with than did others. Some could depend more on direct personal knowledge of attitudes toward and understanding of homosexuality. Some were able to draw upon field research or pastoral work. The collection thus includes a variety of approaches and perspectives.

Under these circumstances, it is not surprising that this volume is more a product of collaboration than are many such collections. The writers sent data and possible sources on to one another. They were able to suggest other competent authors who could contribute to the collection.

Many of us working on this volume have previously been involved in interfaith dialogue and research and have been grateful for the insights and empathy that have resulted. We share a hope that the essays in this volume will raise questions, suggest new ways of looking at homosexuality, and initiate fruitful interfaith discussions on a topic too long relegated to the closet.

ARLENE SWIDLER

1

Homosexuality and the Traditional Religions of the Americas and Africa

Robert M. Baum

In conducting a survey of attitudes toward homosexuality in the traditional religions of the Americas and Africa, one must keep in mind that many of these traditions have not been carefully analyzed, that there are more whose general attitudes toward sexuality have not been studied, and that there are still more whose attitudes toward homosexuality have not been examined. The studies that do exist have been conducted primarily by ethnographers, travelers, government officials linked to alien political systems, and Christian missionaries. All of these groups are composed primarily of outsiders both to the religious traditions being described and to the network of social relations that shape the community under study. In sharp contrast to the other religious traditions being examined in this book, few works written by adherents of the religions themselves will be discussed. Existing evidence about attitudes toward homosexuality has been gathered by observations of behaviors by these outsiders, by participant observation in rituals, and through interviews. Given the human tendency toward privacy in intimate relations, however, these methods often fail to provide detailed information about homosexual relations. The limitations of such research methods are further reinforced by the awareness of African and Native American communities that European and Euro-American outsiders were often hostile to many forms of homosexual relations and therefore should be kept ignorant of such practices in the culture being studied. Finally, much of the more specialized knowledge of traditional religions is kept hidden from the uninitiated and from outsiders because religious knowledge provides power, and the ability to use that power responsibly must be demonstrated before being taught. This can be done, in predominantly oral cultures, only when strong personal ties gradually develop with one's teachers.[1]

Despite these limitations, there is at least fragmentary evidence about attitudes toward homosexuality in over two hundred of the several thousand different ethnic groups of the Americas and Africa. In the last fifteen years there has been a marked increase in the number of in-depth studies of homosexual relations in these culture areas. Gilbert Herdt's pioneering study of Melanesian ritual homosexuality, *Guardians of the Flutes*, has encouraged anthropologists to study the religious and social importance of homosexual relations in many different societies. Walter Williams' recent work on North American Indians has drawn on often fragmentary data to forge an important analysis of the berdache tradition.[2] There still is no book-length work, however, that focuses on similar issues in an African context.

An examination of the place of homosexuality within American and African religions reveals an importance in homosexual relations that goes far beyond ethical judgments about sin and propriety to include revelations about the nature of spiritual beings, religious authorities, and the psychosexual development of peoples in these communities. In contrast to the patriarchal or asexual image of the godhead in Western religions and the nontheistic focus of most schools of Buddhism, traditional religions of the Americas and Africa often see spiritual power in a sexual dimension, with different types of spiritual power associated with each biological sex. In many instances spiritual beings and their religious specialists in the human community are seen as androgynous, or of an intermediate gender, and thereby provide an importance for a diversity of sexual orientations that remain peripheral to many other religious systems. Mircea Eliade saw androgyny as

> an archaic and universal formula for the expression of **wholeness,** the co-existence of the contraries, or *coincidentia oppositorum*. More than a state of sexual completeness and autarchy, androgyny symbolizes the perfection of a primordial, non-conditioned state. . . . But **androgyny extends even to divinities who are pre-eminently masculine or feminine.** This means that androgyny has become a general formula signifying **autonomy, strength, wholeness;** to say of a divinity that it is androgyne is as much as to say that it is the ultimate being, the ultimate reality.[3]

Just as spiritual beings may draw on both masculine and feminine powers, so may the religious specialists who communicate with them or perform their rituals. Similarly, in some sacred traditions the gods manifest their androgynous natures through sexual relations with beings of the same sex; so may some of their adepts, who seek to act according to the model of their spiritual benefactors.

Those traditional religions that are linked to various types of homosexual relations manifest concerns with sex-based concepts of spiritual power that lead to very different formulations of genders than do religious traditions that see sex roles as primarily linked to reproduction and that marginalize concepts of gender that are not essentially geared to that end.[4] Furthermore, these religions tend to reject the tendency in many cultures to equate homosexual relations with being "homosexual." Bisexuality is condoned in some traditional religions. In others, various types of homosexual relations may have religious importance during certain life phases and lose importance in others. Humans, like gods, may display different sexual orientations in different contexts. In some traditions homosexual relations in one's youth are seen as essential to the physical and spiritual development of heterosexual adults.

In trying to detect patterns in the diversity of religious attitudes toward homosexuality, I will draw on the important work of David Greenberg, who has analyzed attitudes toward homosexuality in all the major culture areas of the globe and, where possible, from ancient times to the present. He has proposed a fourfold system of classification of the types of homosexual relations that are socially sanctioned in various cultures, based on the relationships between the people who are involved. Three of these are common in the Americas and Africa. The first of these, transgenerational homosexuality, is found primarily among males and involves an older, more assertive man and a younger male partner. A second type he describes as transgenderal homosexuality. This involves people assuming a gender role that does not correspond to the one normally associated with one's biological sex. This could be viewed as an intermediate or cross-gender role in which the person draws on opposite sex characteristics to enter a gender that is neither male nor female. Only one of the partners in a transgenderal relationship assumes an intermediate gender role; the other retains the gender role associated with his or her biological sex. A third type of homosexuality, according to Greenberg, involves an egalitarian relationship between two people of the same sex. This is often associated with a particular life phase, is not universal within the community, and has less religious significance than the others. The last of Greenberg's categories, a class-distinguished homosexuality, appears to be less important in these culture areas, though there is some hint of it in Meso-America and among the Azande of East Africa.[5]

In this essay I will examine each culture area, beginning with the Americas and concluding with Africa. In each section I will examine the three types of homosexual relations described above as well as their place within the religious systems of a particular region. Given the cultural and historical differences as well as the uneven quality and quantity of available sources, different issues are stressed in each section.

I

In examining homosexuality within Native American religions, I will focus primarily on North America, where ethnographers and other observers have documented various types of homosexual relations existing in 113 different Indian nations. There are specific references to female homosexuality in thirty-three of them.[6] The vast majority of these descriptions are of transgendered relationships, mostly among men-women called berdache by early European observers, but also among women-men. Some incidences of egalitarian and transgenerational relationships are also mentioned. Much of the evidence is drawn from ethnographic fieldwork conducted in the late nineteenth and early twentieth centuries and from travelers' and missionaries' descriptions beginning in the sixteenth century. These sources tend to be highly judgmental, reflecting either religious or psychoanthropological theories that assume that homosexuality is either sinful or pathological. At least until the eighteenth century, English accounts were relatively reticent about homosexuality, though it figures far more prominently in early accounts by French and Spanish observers. Indeed, the social acceptance of homosexual relations in many Indian societies was often cited by Spanish officials in order to justify their conquest.[7]

Egalitarian homosexual relationships have been described within Indian communities of the Great Plains, the Southwest, central and southern Mexico, and Brazil. In most cases these relationships developed between adolescent boys or adolescent girls and were not seen as indicative of an "exclusive" sexual orientation. Because women tended to marry at an earlier age than men, these relationships were more common among males, though they did occur in societies where women did not marry until after puberty. Adolescent homosexual relations are often described as play, or as Claude Lévi-Strauss describes it, as "sham love."[8] Rather than being a threat to the normal sexual development of young people, they are seen as useful, even if sometimes amusing, ways for young people to explore their sexuality without entering into the complex struggle over the control of reproductive resources. Among the Mohave of the Southwest and some Mexican Indians, these relationships may continue among adults. Some Mohave men whose relationships became long-term and exclusive referred to each other as wives, thereby indicating a very different type of relationship than a marriage between a berdache and a male, which will be discussed shortly. The Lakota Sioux also distinguished relationships between male-gendered men from relationships between berdaches and male-gendered men. Only the former were regarded as homosexual.[9]

Transgenerational relationships are most common among males in Meso-America and northwestern South America. Spanish conquistadores and missionaries described such relationships among the Mayas, Aztecs, and Indians of northwest South America. Among the Mayas of the sixteenth and seventeenth centuries, parents would seek out young boys to give to their adolescent sons to serve as receiving partners in anal intercourse prior to marriage. According to Father Bartolomé de Las Casas, these relationships were justified by a tradition concerning a god who came to earth and taught men about homosexuality:

> It was always held [among them] as a great and nefarious sin until a demon appeared under the disguise of an Indian, named Cu, and in another language Chin . . . who induced them to commit it, as he himself executed it with another demon; from there it happened that some of them did not consider it sinful, saying that if that demon or god had committed it [sodomy] he had persuaded them that it was not a sin. Due to this fact some parents provided their youngsters with a boy to use him for a woman.[10]

The age difference between the adolescent who played the more active role and his younger partner appears to have been significant because egalitarian sexual relationships between boys were, according to Las Casas, vigorously condemned. The emphasis on parents giving a young boy to their son suggests that the younger partner had little choice in the manner. If he was drawn from a lower class, as well as a younger age group, this could indicate a class-based form of forced homosexual relations. Unfortunately, there is little additional material about this god who introduced men to homosexual relations, though there are similar myths in other cultures of the region.[11]

Among the Aztecs and some peoples of northwestern South America, transgenerational relations took on some of the characteristics of transgendered relations as well. Some Aztec priests were forbidden to marry but had sexual relations with boys who dressed as women and who served the temple. According to de Sahagún, these priests may have been associated with the powerful creator god, Tezcatlipoca, though Greenberg suggests that they were associated with Xochipila, "patron of male homosexuality and male prostitution."[12] Gonzalo Fernandez de Oviedo described similar types of relationships:

Headmen or principal[s] who sin in this way have youths with whom they use this accursed sin, and those consenting youths, as soon as they fall into this guilt wear *naguas* [skirts] like women . . . and they wear strings of beads and bracelets and the other things used by women as adornment; and they do not exercise in the use of weapons, nor do anything proper to men, but they occupy themselves in the usual chores of the house such as to sweep and wash and other things customary for women.[13]

In these descriptions of transgenerational relations there seems to be an emphasis on the power of the active partner. In contrast to the Melanesian and African forms, there appears to be little concern with the social or physical mentoring of the younger partners in these relationships. Aztec transgenerational relationships' close association with the priestly class, who were not allowed to marry, may indicate some priestly ambivalence about women and ritual authority.

The most widespread form of homosexual relations among Native Americans and the one with the greatest significance within their religions is the transgenderal relationship. The male form of this relationship has become known as *berdache,* a term first applied to transgendered men by French missionaries and explorers. In their attempt to categorize an unfamiliar institution in terms of their own society, French commentators used a word of Arabic or Persian origin, with the misleading meaning of "kept boys" or "male prostitutes."[14] A far more accurate description of the North American berdache has been offered by Charles Callender and Lee Kochems, for whom a berdache was

a person, usually male, who was anatomically normal but assumed the dress, occupations, and behavior of the other sex to effect a change in gender status. This shift was not complete; rather it was a movement toward a somewhat intermediate status that combined social attributes of males and females. The terminology for berdaches defined them as a distinct gender status, designated by special terms rather than by the words "man" or "woman."[15]

As used in this essay, the term *berdache* refers to people who are biologically of one sex but assume an intermediate gender that draws heavily on opposite-sex gender characteristics. They are not considered to have become the opposite sex nor are they seen as "homosexuals." Rather, they are regarded as people who occupy a third gender and enter into sexual relationships only with people of male or female gender.

Native American concepts of intermediate gender are rooted in many of their sacred traditions about divinities and the creation of the world. According to Navajo tradition, transgendered people existed in the third world of creation. Because the Navajo think we are presently living in a fifth world, the berdache (nadle) tradition is thus regarded as an enduring legacy from a primordial past. A pair of twin culture heroes, Turquoise Boy and White Shell Girl, lived there as the first berdaches, introduced pottery making and a variety of tools, and led people into the fourth world when the third world became no longer habitable. Despite these benefits, these nadle also introduced death into the world.[16] The Kamia of California also trace transgendered individuals back to the creation of the world and associate them with the introduction of agriculture. The Ojibwa and Arapaho have traditions about trickster culture heroes who introduce certain economic activities, transform themselves into females (or symbols of women), and become a source of disorder. Among the Zuni of the Southwest, a transgendered kachina spirit, known as Ko'lhamana, mediates the ongoing disputes between farmers and nomadic hunters.[17]

People assume this intermediate gender status in a variety of ways. In some instances it is believed that individuals are born transgendered. Among the Tlingit of the Northwest Coast, berdache are thought to be the reincarnated descendants of a woman who married the Sun. According to myth, her eighth child was born "half-girl and half-boy" and "always comes back in the tribe." Tlingit berdaches are seen as spiritually powerful because they are descended from the Sun and from a woman powerful enough to marry him.[18] Among some tribes of the Great Basin and the Southwest, parents and elders test young children to see if they have a transgendered orientation. These tests tend to focus on tools and toys associated with a particular sex. Ruth Underhill described one such test of a Papago youth:

> His parents suspected it when he was very young because he never wanted to play with boys, always with girls. So they thought they would test him. They built a little enclosure and in it they put a bow and arrow and some basketry materials. They

told the boy to go in there and play, and when he was busy they set fire to the enclosure. They thought they would see which things he saved. Out he came, carrying the basketry materials. They tried the same thing again and again after that, and it was always the same.[19]

By choosing the objects associated with women's work in a time of crisis, the young boy demonstrated his preference for an intermediate gender. Similar tests were done for girls. In many of these cases, it was assumed that the children's gender orientations had developed in the womb; the tests merely confirmed their intermediate status.[20]

In some communities parents determined the gender of their children. Among the Alaskan Aleut and the Californian Laché, parents chose boys they felt were feminine or would make good women and raised them as girls. This was particularly true when there was a shortage of women in the family and women performed vital tasks in the tribal economy. Sometime during their adolescence, their parents would arrange their marriages to men, usually as second wives. Among the Kaska Indians of western Canada, some parents would decide to raise a daughter as a son, tie dried bear ovaries around her belt to prevent her from becoming fertile, and train her in the arts of war and hunting.[21]

More frequently, young people would begin to have dreams or visions that were seen as requiring them to become berdache. These experiences often began during puberty. The Mohave think that these berdache dreams begin in the womb, thereby effecting a gender transformation that begins to manifest itself in small children. Both the Yuma and the Maricopa link the assumption of berdache status to excessive dreaming.[22] A dream was often seen as a summons by a god or goddess who commanded the dreamer to assume an intermediate gender. Dreams were often associated with a moon goddess or other deities linked with women's work and fertility, like the Hidatsa goddesses Holy Woman, Village Old Woman, or Woman Above.[23] Alfred Bowers described the power of Village Old Woman to pursue a young man:

The customs of the berdache were based on native concepts that for a man to dream of Village-Old-Woman or a loop of sweetgrass was an instruction to dress as a woman and to behave as a special class of "female." It was believed that when a man saw a coil of sweetgrass in the brush he should look away, otherwise the Village-Old-Woman or the female deities whom she created would cause his mind to weaken so that he would have no relief until he "changed his sex." Often a man would tell of his experiences, how everywhere he looked he would see the coiled sweetgrass and how hard he was trying to keep from changing over.[24]

Divine summonses to assume berdache status could not be ignored. The Mystic Lake Sioux believed that a man who refused a dream summons to become a berdache would die, whereas the Ojibwa believed that it was essential to his coming to peace with his "manitou," a sacred life force.[25]

Although dreams were an important way of commanding people to assume an intermediate gender, visions were also important. This was particularly true among Plains Indians, where the vision quest was a central part of the rites of passage of young people into adulthood.[26] Visions that were associated with berdache were seen as divine commands to assume a transgendered status. Among the Osage, the Lakota, and the Omaha, a goddess appeared to the young visionary and offered him or her a choice between a male object and a female object. In some instances the vision seekers chose objects associated with the opposite sex, but in others they thought they were choosing same-sex objects, only to find that they had been tricked. James Dorsey describes this type of vision:

> The Omaha believe that the unfortunate beings, called Minqugua, are mysterious or sacred because they have been affected by the Moon Being. When a young Omaha fasted for the first time on reaching puberty, it was thought that the Moon Being appeared to him, holding in one hand a bow and arrows and in the other a pack strap, such as the Indian women use. When the youth tried to grasp the bow and arrows the Moon Being crossed his hands very quickly, and if the youth was not very careful he seized the pack strap instead of the bow and arrows, thereby fixing his lot in after-life. In such a case he could not help acting the woman, speaking, dressing, and working just as Indian women do.[27]

This vision illustrates the linkage between trickster deities and the transgenderal relationship, but central to such visions are the symbols of a sexual division of labor. Visions of choosing work implements associated with the opposite sex are seen as commands to assume transgendered status not only in the area of sexual relations but in economic production as well. This linkage is shared by the Lakota, Santee, and Teton Sioux, who believe that male berdache are summoned by visions of Double Woman, a goddess associated with women's crafts.[28]

In many cases dreams and visions confirm behaviors that have already been manifested. According to Williams, Lakota parents bring their twelve-year-old sons, if they think they are likely to become berdache (*winkte*), "to a ceremony to communicate with past *winktes* who had power, to verify if it is just a phase or a permanent thing for his lifetime. If the proper vision takes place, and communication with a past *winkte* is established, then everyone accepts him as a *winkte*." This differs from an ordinary vision quest in its emphasis on communication with deceased *winktes* rather than with a wider array of spiritual guides.[29]

Among the Yuma, the dream experience is so profound that it transforms the dreamer. "When he [i.e., the transvestite] came out of the dream, he put his hand to his mouth and laughed four times. He laughed with a woman's voice and his mind was changed from male into female. Other young people noticed this and began to feel toward him as a woman."[30] Dreams and visions are seen as capable of transforming people's body language, speech patterns and pitch, and, of most importance, their spirits.

Among the Mohave, dreams are important not only to adolescents who enter a transgender status but also to those who initiate them. Before a Mohave boy can be initiated into *alyha* (berdache) status, four men must dream about the ceremony, thereby providing independent confirmations of this major change in his life. The four men play a central role in the ritual preparations on the eve of a boy's initiation. Throughout the night they sing songs associated with the *alyha* and weave the bark skirts that he will wear. These songs refer to the god Mastamba, who is said to have created the *alyha* ritual. The ceremony, which includes ritual bathing, painting of the body, and the initiate's public dancing in a feminine style, lasts four days. Should he refuse to perform any of the rituals, he would not become an *alyha*. The boy has four full days of ritual to ponder the implications of his new status. Should he complete the ritual, he is given a new name and assumes his role as a man-woman in his community.[31]

Transgendered men and women often married people of the same sex. Such marriages have been described as early as the midsixteenth century.[32] Their spouses were considered heterosexual, because they had married people of a different gender. There appears to have been little stigma attached to such marriages. For example, the distinguished Lakota warrior and religious leader, Crazy Horse, had two *winkte* wives. Usually male berdache became second wives of their husbands, because reproduction was an essential part of most households. As second wives, berdache engaged in sexual relations with their husbands and assisted the women in household work. They were also allowed to adopt children. Female berdaches were more likely to enter into monogamous marriages. They fulfilled the male role in the family economic unit and were usually the only sexual partners of their wives. Among the Lakota, it was important that the transgendered woman, *koskalaka* ("young man" or "woman who does not want to marry"), be ritually bound to her mate with the blessing of the goddess Double Woman:

> They do a dance in which a rope is twined between them and coiled to form a "rope baby." The exact purpose or result of this dance is not mentioned, but its significance is clear. In a culture that values children and women because they bear them, two women who don't want to marry [a man] become united by the power of *wiya numpa* (Double Woman) and their union is validated ["legitimized," in Malinowski's sense] by the creation of a rope baby. That is, the rope baby signifies the potency of their union in terms that are comprehensible to their society.[33]

One could interpret the rope baby as symbolically tying off the fertility of the women who perform the ritual. Transgendered individuals did not marry others of intermediate gender, though in rare instances they did marry members of the opposite sex.[34]

Among many Indian groups of the northern Plains, berdache marriages were actively discouraged or even forbidden. In such cases male berdache were expected to be sexually promiscuous, sharing their sexual favors with many of the men of their communities. Berdache did not, however, engage in sex with other berdache and they were careful to observe their community's rules against incest.[35] Among the Sauk and the Fox of the Midwest, sexual relations with a berdache were a prerequisite for entrance into one of the ritual societies. Sex with a berdache was not seen as homosexual, but as sexual relations between people of different genders.[36] In some communities, including the Ingalik, Pima, Creek, Chiricahua Apache, and the Bella Coola, berdache were considered undersexed in a physical sense. Their importance as transgendered individuals stemmed more from their economic and religious position than from their sexual activities.[37]

In most Indian communities, berdache assumed the economic role associated with the opposite sex. Male berdache cleaned Indian homes, sewed garments, did quillwork, tanned hides, and cooked. Female berdache engaged in hunting and warfare, participated in tribal councils, and occasionally became chiefs. Indeed, a preadolescent interest in opposite-sex economic activities was often seen as evidence of berdache status.[38] This emphasis on changing economic roles is central to an Omaha account of an experience that led a young man to become a berdache:

> Once a young man went to fast, and was gone many days. He started home, not having had any dreams or visions, and on his way home he met a matronly woman who addressed him as "daughter." She said to the young man: "You are my daughter, and you shall be as I am. I give to you this hoe. With it you shall cultivate ground, raise corn, beans, and squash, and you shall be skilled in braiding buffalo hair and in embroidering moccasins, leggings, and robes." In speaking to the woman the young man discovered that he had been unconsciously using the feminine terminals of speech. He tried to recover himself and use the speech of man, but he failed. On his return to his people he dressed himself as a woman, and took upon himself the avocations of a woman.

As a result of this extraordinary experience, a boy returning from a vision quest is told that he will take on women's work. Among the Yuma, girls who dream of weapons become female berdache and assume the economic role of hunters and warriors.[39] It is this change in economic activity, more than in the sexual realm, that is transformative.

Among the Navajo, berdache (*nadle*) appear in creation myths as the source of knowledge of pottery making and basket weaving and are closely associated with the acquisition of wealth:

> If there were no *nadle*, the country would change. They are responsible for all the wealth in the country. If there were no more left, the horses, sheep, and Navaho would all go. They are leaders just like President Roosevelt. A *nadle* around the hogan will bring good luck and riches. They have charge of all the riches. It does a great deal for the country if you have *nadle* around.[40]

The berdache attract wealth, not only because they are skilled at both men's and women's work but also because they are seen as sacred. It is their sacred nature which makes them especially helpful in war. In many communities male berdache accompany warriors on raids but perform rituals to assist in battle rather than engage in the fighting themselves. According to E. A. Hoebel, the berdache represented "stored-up unexpended virility" that would bring them success in battle. Their assistance to warriors was recognized, at least by the Cheyenne, through the berdache's prominent role in the Scalp Dance after battle. Among the Omaha, the Osage, the Illinois, and the Miami, male berdache could still fight and even lead war parties. Certain restrictions applied, however. The Illinois insisted that berdache could not use bows and arrows, symbols of maleness, whereas the Miami made them wear male dress in combat.[41]

Female berdache often participated in battle, occasionally rising to the position of war leaders. Pedro de Magalhaes de Gandavo described Tupinamba transgendered warriors in 1576:

> There are some Indian women who determine to remain chaste: these have no commerce with men in any manner, nor would they consent to it even if refusal meant death. They give up all the duties of women and imitate men, and follow men's pursuits as if they were not women. They wear the hair cut in the same way as the men, and go to war with bows and arrows and pursue game, always in company with men; each has a woman to serve her, to whom she says she is married, and they treat each other and speak with each other as man and wife.[42]

Women warriors are also described among the Lakota, Chero-kee, Apache, Kaska, Winnebago, Cocopa, Blackfoot, and Snake.[43] Perhaps the most famous transgendered woman warrior was Kauxuma Nupika, "Gone to the Spirits," a Kutenai woman who lived in the early nineteenth century. After a failed marriage to a Canadian scout, she returned to the Kutenai claiming that the whites had used their spiritual powers to transform her into a man. While changing her sex she also claimed to have received special powers from spirits that she had encountered in her vi-sions. She became a Kutenai war leader and took a wife. She also became a shaman and prophesised that a time would come when the Indians would receive as many of the material goods of the whites as they desired. She attracted a substantial follow-ing, but the movement died out.[44]

In many Native American communities, berdache were regarded as sacred people, chosen by gods and given special powers that could benefit the community. This was particu-larly true among Plains and Southwest Indians. As early as 1673, Father Marquette described the revered position of the Illinois berdache:

> There is some mystery in this, for they never marry and glory in demeaning themselves to do everything that the women do. . . . They are present at all the juggleries, and the solemn dances in honor of the Calumet; at these they sing, but must not dance. They are summoned to the Councils, and nothing can be decided without their advice. Finally, through their profession of leading an Extraordinary life, they pass for Manitous,—That is to say, for Spirits—or persons of Consequence.[45]

In Algonkian-speaking communities, manitous can refer either to gods or to a life-enhancing force. Rather than "Spirits" as Marquette suggests, they were probably seen as repositories of manitou force that enhanced the positive life force of the com-munity. Among the Hidatsa of the northern Plains, such sacred powers were given to berdache by various goddesses who were associated with women's work and fertility and who provided them with detailed instruction about rituals of the Holy Woman society, a society that also included postmenopausal women.[46]

Given the berdaches' sacred status in many Indian commu-nities, it is not surprising that they often played a leadership role in rituals. Among the Papago, Kiowa, and Cheyenne, berdache played a central role in the scalp dances that followed battles.[47] Among the Hidatsa, they played an active role in the preparation of ritual areas for the Sunset Wolf Ceremony, the Earth Naming Ritual, and the Sun Dance. In the Sun Dance, male berdache worked with a group of postmenopausal women to prepare the Sun Dance space and erect the Sun Dance pole. They combined the purity associated with women with the absence of the polluting qualities associated with menstruation. This combination of qualities would also explain their role as cooks in rituals where women were not active participants. Among the Zuni of the Southwest, berdache impersonated androgynous gods in ritual dances.[48] In many communities, berdache were known as powerful healers. Berdache healers were especially associated with the healing of venereal diseases and insanity. They also assisted at childbirths. Among the Navajo, they were seen as powerful Blessingway singers.[49] They also played an important role in funeral rites. Among the Yokut of California, berdache were the only ones who could prepare the dead for burial, and they led the songs and dances associated with mourning rituals.[50]

Many male berdache did not leave their communities on long hunting or warrior expeditions and could become an important source of social continuity. Stephen Powers described this role among the Yuki and Pomo of California: "They are set apart as a kind of order of priests or teachers. . . . [They] devote themselves to the instruction of the young by the narration of legends and moral tales . . . spending the whole time in rehearsing the tribal history in a sing-song monotone to all who choose to listen." Matilda C. Stevenson described a similar teaching role for transgendered Zunis.[51] As liminal individuals, spared the long trips associated with men's work as well as the difficulties of childbirth experienced by women and with access to the knowledge associated with both sexes, berdache could become the conservators of religious and historical knowledge for the entire community.

Lakota berdache (*winkte*) gave special names to boys in order to protect them against illness and to enhance their sacred power (*wakan*). Such a name was not given lightly. The *winkte* fasted and went on a vision quest before giving someone a *winkte* name. Once having done so, according to Williams, the *winkte* "will work with the boy and his family for the entire year, making spiritual preparations and offering close guidance to the boy. After the ceremony is over, it is the *winkte's* responsibility to help look after that child for life. He makes a medicine bag for the child to carry with him always."[52] The objects within the bag carried the protective power of the *winkte* with the boy wherever he went.

Transgendered individuals were particularly associated with shamanism. The Yurok of California, the Mohave, and the Lakota associated shamanic powers with the sacred qualities of the berdache, though many berdache did not claim such powers. Transgendered shamans were seen as able to predict the future.[53] This association was particularly true of the Araucanians or Mapuche of Chile who, until the nineteenth century, had only transgendered shamans. Alfred Métraux suggests that Araucanian shamans were recruited less for their visionary experience than for their feminine characteristics. Once chosen, young boys would wear girl's clothes and begin their training as shamans. As a result of Spanish and mestizo persecutions of "transvestites," the institution of the shamanic berdache was seriously undermined and replaced by women shamans. As Williams explained: "So strong was the association of femininity with spiritual power, that if the androgynous males could not fulfill the role, then the Indians would use the next most spiritually powerful persons."[54] By the nineteenth century, shamans who drew on both masculine and feminine spiritual powers had been replaced by shamans who could draw on the spiritual resources of only a single gender.

The European conquest of the Americas, beginning in the sixteenth century, led to the destruction of entire Indian communities and a precipitous population decline that began to reverse itself only in the twentieth century. Accompanying the imposition of foreign rule and forced removals, Native Americans had to endure what Europeans regarded as their "civilizing mission." Most European nations made reference to the need to civilize and convert the barbaric peoples of the Americas in the royal charters that allowed conquistadores and trading companies to establish themselves in the Americas. One of the important elements in the Spanish image of barbarism in the Americas was the Native Americans' acceptance of various types of homosexual relations. As early as Hernando Cortes' conquest of Mexico, there are records of conquistadores urging rulers and priests to eliminate sodomy from the palaces and temples. Vasco Nunez de Balboa went even further, putting "a large number of them to death by setting wild dogs upon them."[55] Although various types of homosexual relationships endured, Native Americans learned quickly to keep them concealed from Spanish authorities.

In the western United States, attacks on the berdache tradition became effective once Native Americans were confined to reservations. Indian agents often saw their role as far more than serving as a liaison between the government and white settlers on one hand and the reservation Indians on the other. They were active in banning many religious rituals, most notably the Sun Dance, and spiritual forms of healing. On many reservations they also tried to ban berdache transgenderism by forcing berdache to wear male clothes. This was reinforced by the Indian boarding schools, which attempted to sharply define sex roles in a European fashion, exalting patriarchy and condemning any form of androgynous behavior.[56] Missionaries openly condemned all forms of homosexual relations, excluding berdaches from church and from burial in church cemeteries and insisting that Christian Indians have nothing to do with berdache in their community. A Lakota healer described the way that such teachings were internalized:

> When the people began to be influenced by the missions and the boarding schools, a lot of them forgot the traditional ways and the traditional medicine. Then they began to look down on the *winkte* and lose respect. The missionaries and the government agents said *winktes* were no good, and tried to get them to change their ways. Some did, and put on men's clothing. But others, rather than change, went out and hanged themselves.[57]

As Native American communities moved away from the communitywide practice of traditional religions, the religious role of the berdache declined. A similar shift occurred with the decline of hunting and warfare and the prohibition of Native American healing techniques in the late nineteenth century. Those who converted to Christianity or who decided to engage in the Euro-American dominated economic sector often adopted concepts of gender from these newcomers to their communities. Within communities dominated by assimilated Indians, the berdache confronted increasing amounts of scorn.

By the 1930s, when the policy of active government interference in Native American customs was eased, there were many communities that had abandoned the berdache tradition entirely. The reaffirmation of Native American traditions that became increasingly important in the 1960s, the growing influence of feminist critiques of gender roles, and a growing toleration of homosexual relations in the Euro-American culture of the 1970s all contributed to renewed interest in the berdache tradition. In 1978, 250 *nadle* (Navajo berdache) held a meeting to discuss their role in Navajo religious and community life.[58] The future of berdache traditions appears to be closely linked to the ability of Native American religions to be able to command the adherence of a significant portion of their communities and shape their communities' definitions of gender relations.

II

In examining the relationship between homosexuality and African religions, one must keep in mind that there are very few studies of African sexuality and that these studies have tended to focus on heterosexual sexual expression. Given the predominantly oral character of African traditional religions and the tendency to privacy in sexual matters that is characteristic of most societies, there has been very little opportunity for anthropologists or other observers to acquire a systematic understanding of African attitudes about homosexuality. The difficulty of acquiring data has been compounded by Western stereotypes of African male sexual prowess and of African women's strong heterosexual desires. This has led researchers who have inquired about African attitudes about sexuality to focus on heterosexual relations and, because most researchers were male, to focus on male perspectives. By analyzing ethnographies of African communities, I have managed to obtain information about homosexuality in about fifty different African societies.[59] For most African societies, there are no published sources that discuss homosexual relations.

In a number of descriptions of African societies, ethnographers have included a blanket statement that "sexual perversions," sodomy, and homosexuality do not exist or are unknown. A description by Paul Parin, Fritz Morgenthaler, and Goldy Parin-Matthey is typical of this perspective:

> Manifest homosexuality does not seem to occur among the Dogon men. A number of older, worldly-wise men whom we questioned about this had never heard of homosexuality. When we explained to them what it was they said it might be good if there were something like that among the Dogon, then the young men would not be kept away from their work by thinking about amorous adventures with girls; they would satisfy their sexual needs with their comrades at work and then could immediately go back to work. A few Dogon had heard that homosexuality occurs among Muslim peoples.[60]

Three things could be underlying such a response to questions about homosexuality. First, they may be sufficiently "worldy-wise" to be aware that many Europeans do not approve of homosexuality and that information on such matters should be concealed from European inquirers. This is quite plausible, for Geneviève Calame-Griaule mentions the existence of homosexual relations among Dogon adolescent males, though it is both rare and socially condemned.[61] Second, as David Greenberg has suggested, questions by ethnographers about homosexuality often assume Western definitions of the phenomena. Greenberg has found that many researchers ask questions about men or women who sleep only with members of the same sex. This would exclude people who are bisexual or who at various phases of their lives have engaged in homosexual relations.[62] There are several African societies in which an exclusively homosexual orientation is not socially recognized but homosexual physical relationships are important. Finally, there is the possibility that these elders are being quite straightforward with the researchers. There could be a number of African societies where any form of homosexual relations is unknown.

This was exactly the image of the Diola of Senegambia that was presented to me. Louis Vincent Thomas, the dean of Diola ethnographers, states that there is no term for homosexuality in the Diola language and that such practices did not exist.[63] During the three years that I spent living in a Diola community, I found no manifest examples of homosexual relations among either males or females. Nor were there any examples of homophobic behavior in social interactions between individuals of the same sex, though young Diola men did joke about the neighboring Wolof and Lebou peoples who have a tradition of transvestite men. The only example of possible homosexual behavior that was reported also came from young men joking that when unmarried men shared a bed, a fairly common phenomenon due to a shortage of space in urban areas and the high cost of beds in rural areas, sometimes one of the men would have a dream about his girlfriend and caress his bedmate while he was asleep. Such incidents were reported as a subject of amusement and were not seen as indicating anything about the sexual preferences of the participants. Whether there was any conscious homosexual attraction involved in such actions remains unclear.[64] There were no visible signs that the dream idiom was a euphemism for ongoing sexual relations. Still, one cannot assume that this lack of evidence demonstrates the absence of homosexual practices among the Diola or in other African societies. Such statements are premature.

Despite the difficulties of acquiring accurate data about African sexuality, it appears that all three types of homosexual relations exist in some African communities and have widely varying degrees of religious significance. One finds African societies that see egalitarian homosexual relations as a natural part of human existence, usually during adolescence, but sometimes continuing throughout the lives of adults. These relationships tend to be neither exclusive of heterosexual relations nor of major ritual significance. Transgenderal and transgenerational homosexual relations appear to be far more important to religious life in African societies. Transgenerational relations are important to the growth of children into adults, whereas transgenderal relationships are linked to the attainment of certain types of religious authority. Some African societies have developed intermediate genders of men-women or women-men who, like their Native American counterparts, are seen as sacred and as spiritually powerful individuals. For the most part, the men and women involved in these relationships are not defined as "homosexual" because the activities that they engage in either are not exclusive or are not defined within the societies as same-sex physical activity.

Egalitarian homosexual relationships exist in 20 percent of the African societies analyzed in this study. In most cases, these relationships develop during adolescence and are abandoned at the time of marriage. Among the !Kung of southern Africa, small boys "play at sex and teach themselves, just as baby roosters teach themselves."[65] Sexual relations between boys involving manual stimulation and anal intercourse are regarded as a form of sexual education that will be extended into heterosexual relations as boys physically and emotionally mature. Among the nearby Naman of the Namib desert, sexual play among boys is regarded in a similar light. Some Naman boys will enact a ritual in which they drink water or coffee from the same bowl and pledge themselves to a lasting friendship. Such a ritual need not entail a continued physical relationship, but it was often used in that way.[66]

Among the Fon of Benin and the Nyakyusa of Tanzania, egalitarian relationships among adolescent males developed during their rites of passage from childhood to adulthood when they were isolated from females. Nyakyusa boys, sometime between the ages of ten and fourteen, leave their natal villages and become cattle herders living in separate settlements. Monica Wilson describes the relationships that develop in the cattle camps: "They begin among boys of ten to fourteen, herding cows, and continue among young men until marriage, but they are said never to continue after that, and are regarded simply as a substitute for heterosexual pleasure. 'A man never dreams of making love to another man'—only of making love to a woman." One of her informants suggests that these relationships are a part of a normal adolescence: "But when they have agreed and dance together, then even if people find them they say it is adolescence (luk ulilo), all children are like that. And they say that sleeping together and dancing is also adolescence."[67]

Normally, homosexual relations cease with marriage. Among the Nyakyusa, adult males who continue to be sexually involved with men are seen as irrational, and their actions are seen as a sign of witchcraft. Forced sexual relationships between males are also likened to witchcraft, that is, as spiritual assaults on the life force of the victims.[68] Although there are reports of homosexual relationships among adult men in other communities, they tend to be socially condemned and fairly rare. In societies that encourage egalitarian homosexual relationships among boys, such relationships are seen as assisting, or at least not impeding, the sexual formation of the adult male father. Forced sexual relations or sexual relations with men during a phase of life when one should be fathering children are seen as lessening the procreative power not only of the individuals involved but of their families as well.

In sharp contrast with men, women tend to enter into reciprocal relationships with other women as adults more frequently than as adolescents. Within those societies where such relationships develop, this seems to have two causes: girls are often married at a younger age than boys, and they often marry into polygynous households where they might have little attention from their husbands but considerable interaction with other women. Among the Nyakyusa, the Mongo, the Nupe of Nigeria, the Tswana of southern Africa, and the Azande of the southern Sudan, reciprocal relationships between adult women are particularly common among the wives of chiefs and kings who live in households with a large number of co-wives.[69] E. E. Evans-Pritchard sees this as a major factor in the creation of Azande women's reciprocal relationships in the late nineteenth century. He sees this

> as a product, like male homosexuality, of polygamy on a large scale; for if this precluded young men from normal sex, so in large polygamous homes it prevented the wives, or some of them, from receiving the amount of sexual attention they wished for from their common husband, who, moreover, might well have been elderly and not at the height of his sexual vigor.[70]

Although his theory of neglect from males as the primary cause of Azande women's desire for same sex relations may explain some women's motivations, it does not explain them all. The predominantly female environment of the wives of the Azande nobility, who were isolated from most men and had infrequent contact with their husbands whose affections they had to share, led many wives to establish deep and long-lasting relationships with other women in their husband's court. These friendships involved pledges of mutual assistance and support. Such relationships were recognized by the husband as well as the rest of the household and cemented by the *baghuru* ritual. The performance of this ritual required the permission of the husband, but "a husband finds it difficult to refuse his consent for it would not normally mean that any sexual element was involved. One of the women makes a small gift to the other and the other makes a return gift. They then take a maize cob and divide it, and each plants the seeds of her half in her garden."[71] The corn of the cob is described as blood red, symbolically paralleling the blood exchanged in men's rites of blood brotherhood.

The sexual dimension of *baghuru,* as it often developed, had to be kept hidden from the husband. According to Evans-Pritchard, princes killed wives who had sex with other women; commoners only beat their wives for the same offense. Sexual relations between women were seen as akin to witchcraft and could prove fatal to a husband if he actually saw his wife making love with another woman. Evans-Pritchard reported Azande oral traditions that "some of the great kings of the past— Basingbi, Gbudwe, Wando, and others—died on account of lesbian practices between their wives."[72]

Although Evans-Pritchard argues that homosexual acts by a man's wife could prove fatal to him, I am not convinced that lesbian sex was the problem; rather it was adultery. A wife's heterosexual adultery could also carry a spiritual pollution that could kill her husband. Evans-Pritchard noted this in a different context:

> It is also thought that adultery may cause misfortune, though it is only one participating factor, and witchcraft is also believed to be present. Thus it is said that a man may be killed in warfare or in a hunting accident as a result of his wife's infidelities. Therefore, before going to war or on a large-scale hunting expedition a man might ask his wife to divulge the names of her lovers.[73]

The claim that the danger to men was not lesbianism but adultery is further supported by evidence that chiefs sometimes provided slave girls to their daughters: "A ruler might give a girl slave to one of his daughters, who would anoint and paint the girl to make her attractive and then lie with her." This was a rare example of Greenberg's category of class-distinguished relations.[74]

Egalitarian relationships among wives of the Azande nobility appear to have been a way for women to build an alternative network of support and intimacy independent of the few men with whom they were allowed to interact. Such autonomy was seen as a threat to the authority of men, their spiritual well-being, and their sexual control of wives. Evans-Pritchard noted the fear that Azande men had of the consequences of sexual relations among women: "Azande further say that once a woman has started homosexual intercourse she is likely to continue it because she is then her own master and may have gratification when she pleases and not just when a man cares to give it to her, and the gratification may also last as long as she pleases."[75] This would explain the attempts of King Gbudwe, in the late nineteenth century, to suppress *baghuru* friendships among court wives.

One unintended effect of colonialism was the undermining of these relationships among elite women. With the radical diminution of the wealth and authority of the Azande chiefs, they had to become accustomed to smaller households with fewer wives. Wives of the nobility became more visible to husbands and villagers alike and less able to maintain secret relationships. Evans-Pritchard claimed that by the 1930s, when he conducted fieldwork, the incidence of egalitarian homosexual relationships among women had declined dramatically.

Transgenerational homosexual relations appear to be quite rare in Africa. I have found only two documented cases of such relationships among men, except in South Africa where the migrant labor system imposed through apartheid has led to the development of single-sex mine compound communities. African forms of transgenerational relations among males are described in terms of marriages between men and boys. Such relationships are not seen as physically forming the adult male, as one finds in Melanesia. Rather, there is an emphasis on the adult partner offering social and spiritual guidance to his companion in his transition to adulthood. In many oral cultures, knowledge is passed from elders to younger people through personal instruction that is an integral part of a long-term friendship or romantic involvement. Vinigi Grottanelli described these relationships among the Nzema of coastal Ghana as "*Agyale* or 'friendship marriage,' usually between a man and a male teenager, more rarely between two women, in which preliminaries partly similar to those of real marriage are performed, partners cohabit for short periods, exchange presents, and share the same bed or mat."[76] In these relationships the younger partner normally is the less assertive one, perhaps exchanging sexual pleasure for his elder's knowledge of their community.

Among the Azande of the Sudan, these marriages form part of a transition from boyhood to adulthood. The youngest boys in the Azande military age regiments—the *aparanga*, or bachelors—became "wives" of older boys in the same regiment. These marriages required the permission of the father of the younger boy and the payment of bridewealth to the father. Evans-Pritchard described these relationships: "If this boy was a good wife to his husband five spears might be paid for him, and for another as many as ten might be paid. . . . They did for their husbands everything a wife does for her husband." This included fetching water, cooking, and sharing a sleeping mat. Some married men also took boy wives to sleep with when ritual responsibilities to consult a poison oracle or military duties prohibited them from sleeping with women.[77] Although the junior partners in bachelor marriages were referred to as "wives," they were not considered to be women but men in training. Like many Melanesian youth, Azande boys accompanied their elders to battle and learned the ways of the warriors. As their "husbands" married women, they took younger boys as wives. Older boys often married the sisters of their boy wives, particularly when the family was pleased with the education the older boy had provided the younger in the bachelors' regiment. With the Anglo-Egyptian conquest of the Azande in the late nineteenth century and the subsequent disarming of age regiments, bachelor marriages declined in importance. Although age-differentiated relationships among men still exist, they do so in a less formal structure.

In southern Africa a new age-differentiated type of marriage has developed as a result of male migrant labor to diamond, gold, and coal mines to which men were not permitted to bring their wives. Senior miners would take new miners as wives, teach them the ways of the mine and the nature of its work, and offer them protection in exchange for cooking and sexual favors. Dunbar Moodie suggests that this type of trans-generational relationship represents the extension of traditional southern African forms of gerontocracy to the mine compounds, though he does not see the strong pedagogic element of this relationship, which helps to socialize the junior partner to the radically different environment of the mines.[78] Although social pressures and the threat of physical force did compel some young men to enter into such compound marriages, it is important to note that the senior partner in the relationship frequently had to pay bridewealth (*lobola*) to the boy whom he wished to marry.[79]

It appears that neither anal sex nor oral sex was socially acceptable in such relationships. Rather, the active partner placed his penis between the thighs of his more passive partner and reached orgasm through genital friction. This is the same sexual technique used by Zulu and Xhosa bachelors (called *metsha* in Xhosa and *hlobonga* in Zulu) to avoid impregnating girls they were courting in the rural areas.[80] In sexual relationships in the mine compound, as in rural areas, social custom encouraged forms of sexual expression that would not have lasting effects; some worried that a penetrating form of intercourse might lead to the impregnation of mine compound "wives." This fear had led the Ila of Zambia to prohibit pederasty and to impose stiff fines, comparable to those for fornication, against those who sought to have sexual relations with boys.[81] The mine compound "wives" often saved the bridewealth they received to help them pay bridewealth to marry women in the rural areas.

Transgenerational relationships among women are similarly rare in Africa. I have found only two African societies where such relationships are important, and one of these is contemporary Lesotho, which has been radically affected by apartheid. As previously mentioned, the Nzema have a form of same-sex marriage in which women marry girls and live together temporarily. In Lesotho, where Christian evangelization, Western education, and labor migration to South Africa have disrupted traditional puberty rituals for both boys and girls, new types of relations have developed to take their place. Pre-colonial Basotho female initiation included instruction on both the spiritual and sexual aspects of womanhood, using a collective ritual setting to evade prohibitions on sexual discussions between mothers and daughters. Part of that initiation involved groups of initiates getting together and engaging in manual stimulation and the stretching of each other's labia. This was done to increase the "heat" of sex in marriage.[82] With the establishment of a "protectorate" over Lesotho in the late nineteenth century and the rapid growth of Christianity and Western schooling, initiation rituals gradually lost participants. By 1977, 91.1 percent of girls attended Western schools, and by the same year only about one tenth of young women (aged twenty to thirty-nine) had participated in puberty rituals. Neither Western schools nor churches provided an arena where important guidance could be provided about the nature of womanhood in contemporary Lesotho. Judith Gay described the institution of "mummies and babies," young married women or older girls with younger girls, which provided an effective alternative to puberty rituals and to the alienating environment of the Lesotho schools or South African towns:

> Young girls in the modern schools develop close relationships, called "mummy-baby," with slightly older girls. Sexual intimacy is an important aspect of these relationships. Mummy-baby relationships not only provide emotional support prior to marriage, but also a network of support for married and unmarried women in new towns or schools, either replacing or accompanying heterosexual bonds.[83]

Mummies provided their younger companions with advice about heterosexual relationships, schools, and the town environments in which they found themselves. They also helped them materially by providing them with food and gifts, though that did not seem to be a major factor in initiating a relationship:

> The most frequently given reason for initiating a particular relationship was that one girl felt attracted to the other by her looks, her clothes, or her actions. When I suggested that girls might approach an older girl or woman as a patron, thinking of the gifts or material help they can gain from the relationship, some informants expressed shock, saying that such an attitude would

spoil the relationship, which should be based on sincere love, not on selfish calculation.[84]

In the increasingly atomized environment of southern Africa, Lesotho adolescent girls were brought through the transition from girlhood to adulthood and from village school to town school through a personalized form of initiation, a romantic relationship with a more experienced girl or young woman who could steer her toward a proper understanding of the role of women in contemporary Lesotho.

Transgenderal forms of homosexual relations are fairly common among the peoples of southern and central Africa. I have found descriptions of biological men who assume a gender role as men-women in six societies in that region and in two societies in northeast Africa. For the Otoro of the Nuba hills in the Sudan and among Khoisan peoples of southern Africa, certain men assume a transgender role: wearing women's clothes and hairstyles, performing women's work, and marrying men. In neither of these cases are there any descriptions of the religious significance of these men-women.[85]

Among the four Bantu-speaking societies, however, the transgender role is closely associated with various types of religious authority, ranging from prophets to spiritual healers. Within many African religions male spiritual power and female spiritual power are seen as separate and distinct. Men-women are seen as spiritually powerful precisely because they combine these powers, drawing on both a masculine power and a feminine power, as did the creator god who is the ultimate origin of life. Central to the religion of the Ila of Zambia is the institution of the *mwaami,* or prophet. Prophets are said to become possessed by ancestor spirits or by the creator god. *Mwaami* can be either men or women, but they can also be men-women, who are said to wear women's clothes, do women's work, and sleep "among, but not with, the women."[86] Although there is no indication that they had sexual relations with men, it is clear that they did not have sexual relations with women. Among the Ovimbundu of Angola there are similar descriptions of healers who dress as women, perhaps in an effort to tap the life-enhancing powers associated with female fertility.[87] For the Tonga of Zambia, the Zulu of South Africa, the

Ambo of Angola, and the Nilotic-speaking Lugbara of Uganda, one finds similar cases of transvestite diviners and healers. In each case the religious leader is commanded to assume a transgendered role as a result of a dream, vision, or an incident of spiritual possession. Ancestral spirits or other spirits order them to take on a new social role that opens them to the heightened power necessary to communicate in the realm of the spirit. Among the Zulu most diviners are women, so men who become diviners become like women. They wear women's clothes, learn to speak in high-pitched voices associated with women, and become apprentices to female diviners.[88] Harriet Ngubane describes the association of feminine roles and divination:

> Divination is a woman's thing, and if a man gets possessed he becomes a transvestite, as he is playing the role of a daughter rather than that of a son. For the special and very close contact with the spirits is reserved in this society for women only—women who are thought of as marginal, and can thus fulfill the important social role of forming a bridge between the two worlds.[89]

If marginality enhances individual receptivity to the world of the spirits, then the dual marginality of transgendered individuals provides an especially powerful type of religious specialist. This is recognized by the Ambo of Angola, who recognize the existence of both male and female spiritual healers and diviners. Certain types of diviners, usually female, use a musical instrument known as an *omakola* to assist them in diagnosing illness and in initiating other religious specialists. Those men who also make use of the *omakola* were described by Carlos Estermann as

> passive homosexuals (*omasenge*) who dressed like women, did women's work, and "contracted marriage"—not monogamous marriage, of course—with other men. In a general way this aberration is to be interpreted by the spiritism or spiritist belief of these people. An *esenge* is essentially a man who has been possessed since childhood by a spirit of female sex, which has been drawing out of him little by little the taste for everything that is masculine and virile.[90]

In both societies biological men who receive a spiritual calling to assume an intermediate gender role are seen as powerful religious leaders. Their authority arises from their isolation from important social institutions controlled by men and from their ability to combine the spiritual power of the masculine and the feminine.[91]

In certain Muslim African societies, there appears to be a similar role for transgendered men. Among the Hausa of Nigeria and the Wolof and Lebou of Senegambia, all of which are overwhelmingly Muslim societies, men who assume women's role are closely associated with cults whose origins are associated with their non-Islamic traditional religions. Within both the Hausa's *bori* cults and the Senegambian *Ndoep*, women are seen as the most likely people to become possessed by spirits, and, in the case of *bori*, it is particularly common among widowed or divorced women who choose not to remarry. They are known as *karuwai*, a term that has often been translated as prostitute, but which refers to a wider range of sexual transactions outside of marriage. Most of the men who attend *bori* on a regular basis are transgendered men who dress as women, cook for the *karuwai*, and live in the *karuwai*'s compounds.[92] Although they regularly attend *bori* and dance in a woman's style during the rituals, they are less likely to become possessed than women adepts. At Lebou and Wolof *Ndoep* rituals, one finds men and women participants cross-dressing as a way of encouraging spiritual possession. For men, however, the fact that they attend earns them the reputation of being effeminate. The male cross-dressers who attend *Ndoep* seem to carry their gender role beyond ritual settings. They are known as *gor-digen*, men-women, and are regarded as skilled dancers and conversationalists. Unlike other *Ndoep* participants, they are excluded from burial in Muslim cemeteries.[93]

Within African communities one finds that homosexual relations exist in a variety of forms. Egalitarian relations exist among men primarily during adolescence and are seen as part of the sexual transition from boyhood to marriage and parenthood. Egalitarian relations among women are more common among married women who live in polygynous households who seek to create supportive relationships. Transgenerational homosexual relations tend to be viewed as a bond between a more experienced elder, who may still be an adolescent, and a younger person who needs a teacher about the responsibilities of his or her gender as adults. It is closely linked to other forms of education through initiation schools and student-teacher relationships that are the most common form of instruction in African traditional religions. Still, the most significant form of homosexual relations in connection with religious institutions is of the transgenderal type. In response to visions or dreams, certain men assume women's dress and live like women, often marrying men, and become powerful diviners, healers, or shamans. It is their ability to draw on the distinctive powers of the feminine as well as the masculine that gives them their unusual spiritual powers. In most of Africa, European colonization and missionary evangelization have sharply reduced the frequency of homosexual relations by lessening their religious and social importance within African societies. Only in southern Africa, where apartheid and other forms of racial labor control of Africans have led to the exclusion of African women from towns where their men are working, has European colonization created new areas for socially important homosexual relations.

III

This brief examination of attitudes toward homosexual relations in traditional religions has indicated certain regional differences as well as some important similarities across the two cultural regions. Both Africa and the Americas have cultures that practice egalitarian, transgenerational, and transgenderal forms of homosexual relations. In each area egalitarian relations appear to be less central to the religious life of the communities. Religious authorities' primary concerns about egalitarian relations seem to focus on the appropriate life phases in which such relationships develop and the assurance that they will not interfere with the reproduction of the community's population. There are no special ritual offices for people who develop egalitarian homosexual relations, nor are there any for similar relations among heterosexuals.

Transgenerational homosexual relations in Africa, however, are seen as vital to the physical, emotional, and/or spiritual development of adolescent boys. In Africa such relationships are seen more as a form of mentoring and instruction, while including an important sexual element. As in Melanesia, however, it is important for males to break away from what is regarded as a female-dominated childhood to enter into an intensely male form of education as part of their transition to manhood.[94] Furthermore, they must experience the more passive gender role associated with women before they exert an active and often dominant role over wives. Such an experience would reinforce their tendency to identify with other men while having some degree of empathy with women.[95]

Transgenderal homosexual relations are of greatest importance among Native Americans but are also important in some African cultures. Within many Native American religions and a smaller number of African religions, transgendered individuals are seen as embodying the spiritual powers associated with both maleness and femaleness. These powers may have been given before birth, before adulthood through dreams and visions, or, rarely, through dreams and visions by adults. Often these summonses are regarded as direct communications from deities or ancestors who are seen as androgynous, who seek similar types of humans to serve them in human society. In other cases the power of women is seen as more oriented toward certain religious practices such as divination or shamanic trance, and men must assume feminine roles in order to tap into women's paths to spiritual authority.

Most of Africa and all of the Americas have had to endure the imposition of European or Euro-American rule, and in South Africa and all of the Americas the loss of most of their lands. Entire ethnic groups ceased to exist, while many others were moved onto reservations far from their precolonial homelands. Because of the length of time that has passed, the degree of disruption, and the scarcity of well-informed written sources for that period, we know little about preconquest religious attitudes toward homosexuality. Nor can we detect the type of changes that might have occurred in religious attitudes toward homosexuality before contact with Europeans. It is clear, however, that the first explorers and settlers became aware that certain forms of homosexual relations were morally sanctioned and that such relations played an important role in their forms of religious expression.[96]

European expansion into the Americas and Africa was accompanied by direct challenges to indigenous religions and social relations as well as indigenous political and economic activities. To the extent that conquered peoples embraced Christianity, they moved into a tradition that did not see a special religious role for people who engaged in homosexual relations. On the contrary, missionaries attacked them for tolerating any form of homosexuality. Where traditional religions could not sustain their vitality, ritual reliance on people who engaged in transgenderal and transgenerational relations ceased, and transgenderal homosexuality and transgenerational homosexuality lost most of their religious significance. Where traditional religions continued to command adherence, they often incorporated some of the values of a hegemonic European culture and undermined the values attached to homosexual relations. Only in southern Africa, where African migrant workers were forbidden to bring their families to the mining compounds, did the colonial conquest lead to an intensification of homosexual relations. Although these new forms of relations built upon traditional models of transgenerational mentoring, they were usually peripheral to traditional religious life and incorporated many aspects of the unequal distribution of power that characterizes contemporary South Africa. In all cases, however, in Africa and the Americas, the influence of European values tended to undermine the concept that homosexual relations could be important sources of spiritual power and religious education.

Notes

1. This creates a serious obstacle to the profound understanding of many traditional religions. Most researchers are funded for too short a time to establish such bonds and, as a result, receive only superficial religious instruction, which is often mistaken for an exposition of an entire religious system. For a discussion of this problem in studies of African religions, see Robert M. Baum, "Graven Images: Scholarly Representations of African Religions," *Religion* 20 (1990): 355–360.

2. Gilbert H. Herdt, *Guardians of the Flutes: Idioms of Masculinity* (New York: Columbia University Press, 1981). Walter L. Williams, *The Spirit and the Flesh: Sexual Diversity in American Indian Culture* (Boston: Beacon Press, 1986).

3. Mircea Eliade, *Myths, Dreams, and Mysteries* (New York: Harper & Row, 1975), pp. 174–175, and *Patterns of Comparative Religion* (New York: New American Library, 1974), pp. 420–421.

4. Barry D. Adam, "Age, Structure, and Sexuality: Reflections on the Anthropological Evidence on Homosexual Relations," *Journal of Homosexuality* 11, no. 1 (1985): 19.

5. Herdt has suggested a different type of classification: age-structured, gender-reversed, and role-specialized homosexuality. Although his first category is basically the same as Greenberg's, his second category seems to foreclose the possibility of intermediate genders, and his third category shifts from a focus on relationships between the participants to their social and religious roles. He does not mention egalitarian relations as a category. David F. Greenberg, *The Construction of Homosexuality* (Chicago and London: University of Chicago Press, 1988), pp. 25–26. Gilbert Herdt, "Homosexuality," in Mircea Eliade, ed., *The Encyclopedia of Religion* (New York: Macmillan, 1987), vol. 6, p. 446.

6. Williams, pp. 3–4. Charles Callender and Lee Kochems also conducted a survey of the berdache tradition and found eighty-eight documented traditions in North America. See Charles Callender and Lee Kochems, "The North American Berdache," *Current Anthropology* 24, no. 4 (1983): 444. Evelyn Blackwood, "Sexuality and Gender in Certain Native American Tribes: The Case of Cross-Gender Females," *Signs: Journal of Women in Culture and Society* 10, no. 1 (1984): 29.

7. Juan Gines de Sepulveda, in his famous debate at Valladolid, cited the acceptance of sodomy among Native Americans as important evidence of their barbaric natures and the civilizing benefits of Spanish domination. Francisco Guerra, *The Pre-Columbian Mind: A Study into the Aberrant Nature of Sexual Drives, Drugs Affecting Behaviour, and the Attitudes Towards Life and Death, with a Survey of Psychotherapy in Pre-Columbian America* (London: Semina Press, 1971), p. 80.

8. Claude Lévi-Strauss, "The Social Use of Kinship Terms Among Brazilian Indians," in Paul Bohannan and John Middleton, eds., *Marriage, Family, and Residence* (Garden City, N.Y.: Natural History Press, 1968), p. 172. Dorothy Eggan, "The General Problem of Hopi Adjustment," *American Anthropologist* 45 (1943): 368. Thomas Gregor, *Mehinaku: The Drama of Daily Life in a Brazilian Indian Village* (Chicago: University of Chicago Press, 1977), p. 254. Greenberg, p. 68. Napoleon Chagnon, *Yanomamö: The Fierce People* (New York: Holt, Rinehart & Winston, 1968), p. 76.

9. Williams, pp. 93, 194–195. George Devereux, "Institutionalized Homosexuality of the Mohave Indians," *Human Biology* 9, no. 4 (1937): 499.

10. Father Bartolomé de Las Casas (1542), quoted in Guerra, p. 70. This is confirmed by Friar Juan de Torquemada in 1615, quoted in Williams, p. 90.

11. Guerra describes a tradition in the Puerto Viejo area of the Incan Empire where giants were said to have been the source of male knowledge of homosexual relations. Guerra, p. 90. Greenberg, pp. 25–26.

12. Greenberg, p. 165. Guerra, p. 112. Tezcatlipoca was one of the Aztec's major creator gods, associated with the acquisition of wealth and with the power of sorcery. For a description of Tezcatlipoca, see David Carrasco, "Tezcatlipoca," in Mircea Eliade, ed., *The Encyclopedia of Religion* (New York: Macmillan, 1987), vol. 14, pp. 415–416.

13. Gonzalo Fernandez de Oviedo (1526), quoted in Guerra, p. 55.

14. Although this might apply to transgenerational/transgendered relationships between Aztec priests and temple boys, most transgendered relationships do not focus on a commercial exchange as in prostitution, nor are berdache controlled or supported by their partners in the sense that "kept" implies. Henry Angelino and Charles Shedd, "A Note on Berdache," *American Anthropologist* 57 (1955): 121. Williams, p. 9.

15. Callender and Kochems, p. 443.

16. Gladys Reichard, *Navaho Religion: A Study of Symbolism* (New York: Pantheon Books, 1950), pp. 146, 387. Williams, pp. 19–20.

17. Edward Gifford, cited in Jonathan Katz, *Gay American History: Lesbians and Gay Men in the U.S.A.* (New York: Thomas Crowell, 1976), p. 324. Devereux, p. 501. A. Irving Hallowell, *Culture and Experience* (New York: Schocken Books, 1971 [1955]), p. 304. Williams, pp. 12, 18.

18. Frederica de Laguna, *Under Mount Saint Elias: The History and Culture of the Yakutat Tlingit* (Washington, D.C.: Smithsonian Institution Press, 1972), vol. 2, p. 499.

19. Ruth Underhill, *Papago Woman* (New York: Holt, Rinehart & Winston, 1979), 64. Williams, p. 24. Callender and Kochems, p. 451. W. W. Hill, "Note on the Pima Berdache," *American Anthropologist* 40 (1938): 340.

20. This is true of the Mohave, Pima, Papago, Ute, and Shoshone. Devereux, p. 502.

21. Williams, pp. 45–46; Paula Gunn Allen, *The Sacred Hoop: Recovering the Feminine in American Indian Traditions* (Boston: Beacon Press, 1986), p. 196. Judy Grahn, "Strange Country This: Lesbianism and North American Indian Tribes," *Journal of Homosexuality* 12, no. 3 (1985): 53. Katz, p. 323.

22. Blackwood, p. 30. Leslie Spier, *Yuman Tribes of the Gila River* (Chicago: University of Chicago Press, 1933), p. 242.

23. Devereux, p. 502; Allen, *Sacred Hoop*, p. 196. Alice Fletcher and Francis La Flesche, *The Omaha Tribe, U.S. Bureau of American Ethnology Annual Report*, vol. 27, 1905–1906, p. 132. Williams, p. 26. Katz, p. 303. Raymond DeMallie, "Male and Female in Traditional Lakota Culture," in Patricia Albers and Beatrice Medicine, eds., *The Hidden*

Half: Studies of Plains Indian Women (Washington, D.C.: University Press of America, 1983), p. 243. Callender and Kochems, p. 451. Alfred Bowers, *Hidatsa Social and Ceremonial Organization, U.S. Bureau of American Ethnology Bulletin* (Washington, D.C.: Smithsonian Institution Press, 1965), pp. 132, 165.

24. Bowers, p. 326.

25. Ruth Landes, *The Mystic Lake Sioux: Sociology of the Medewakantonwan Santee* (Madison: University of Wisconsin Press, 1968), p. 207. Thomas A. McKenney, cited in Katz, p. 299.

26. Many of the ethnographies and travelers' accounts did not carefully distinguish between dreams and visions. I would regard visions as limited to spiritual experiences that occur in a waking state. Ruth Landes, *The Prairie Potawatomi: Tradition and Ritual in the Twentieth Century* (Madison: University of Wisconsin Press, 1970), p. 183. Williams, p. 54.

27. James O. Dorsey, *A Study of Siouan Cults, U.S. Bureau of American Ethnology Annual Report,* vol. 11, 1889–1890, p. 378. Williams, p. 29. DeMallie, p. 243.

28. DeMallie, p. 241. Landes, *Mystic Lake Sioux,* p. 57. There were individuals who resisted summons to assume berdache status. Some tried to conceal their dreams and visions; others tried suicide. Callender and Kochems, p. 453. Fletcher and La Flesche, p. 132. Dorsey, p. 378.

29. Williams, p. 54.

30. Daryl Forde, cited in Devereux, p. 502.

31. Devereux, pp. 503–508.

32. Guerra, p. 67.

33. Paula Gunn Allen, "Lesbians in American Indian Cultures," *Connections* 7 (1981): 82.

34. Williams, pp. 56, 111, 112, 120, 121. Callender and Kochems, p. 450. Angelino and Shedd, p. 122. Katz, p. 314.

35. Landes, *Mystic Lake Sioux,* p. 31. Callender and Kochems, p. 449. Williams, p. 101. de Laguna, p. 896.

36. Homosexual relations did occur among people of the same gender. This, unlike relations with a berdache, was considered homosexual. Williams, pp. 93, 101.

37. Callender and Kochems, p. 450.

38. Royal Hassrick, *The Sioux: Life and Customs of a Warrior Society* (Norman: University of Oklahoma Press, 1964), p. 123. John Fire/Lame Deer and Richard Erdoes, *Lame Deer Seeker of Visions* (New York: Simon & Schuster, 1972), p. 149. S. C. Simms, "Crow Indian Hermaphrodites," *American Anthropologist* 5 (1903): 586. Callender and Kochems, pp. 447–448. Fletcher and La Flesche, p. 136. Guerra, p. 55. Blackwood, p. 31.

Grahn, pp. 43, 53. Katz, pp. 308–310, 325. Beverly Hungry Wolf, *The Ways of My Grandmothers* (New York: Quill, 1982), p. 69.

39. The story is related by an Omaha named Black Dog. Fletcher and La Flesche, p. 132. Carolyn Niethammer, *Daughters of the Earth: The Lives and Legends of American Indian Women* (New York: Macmillan, 1977), p. 231.

40. W. W. Hill cited in Williams, pp. 63–64, 19.

41. E. Adanson Hoebel, *The Cheyennes: Indians of the Great Plains* (New York: Holt, Rinehart & Winston, 1978) p. 83. Callender and Kochems, p. 449. De Laguna, p. 864. Fletcher and La Flesche, p. 133. Williams, pp. 68–69.

42. Williams, p. 233.

43. It is unclear whether or not Apache and Cherokee women warriors were seen as transgendered. There is a curious silence about their sexual lives. Allen, "Lesbians," p. 67. Charles Hudson, *The Southeastern Indians* (Knoxville: University of Tennessee Press, 1976), p. 269. Kimberly Moore Buchanan, *Apache Women Warriors* (El Paso: Texas Western Press, 1986), passim. Katz, p. 325. Hungry Wolf, pp. 59, 62–63.

44. Her brother eventually discovered that she had not had a physical sex change, and this, together with the absence of the promised cargo, undermined her influence. Williams, pp. 236–238. Katz, pp. 293–298.

45. Father Marquette, cited in Katz, p. 287. Williams, pp. 17, 22, 36, 107, 167. Callender and Kochems, p. 452. Dorsey, p. 378. De-Mallie, p. 244. Landes, *Mystic Lake Sioux*, p. 66. William K. Powers, *Oglala Religion* (Lincoln: University of Nebraska Press, 1977), p. 58. Greenberg, p. 48.

46. Bowers, pp. 167, 326.

47. Mildred Mayhall, *The Kiowas* (Norman: University of Oklahoma Press, 1984), p. 33. Harriet Whitehead, "The Bow and the Burden Strap: A New Look at Institutionalized Homosexuality in Native North America," in Sherry Ortner and Harriet Whitehead, eds., *Sexual Meanings: The Cultural Construction of Gender and Sexuality* (Cambridge: Cambridge University Press, 1981), p. 89. Greenberg, p. 49.

48. Williams, pp. 32, 36. Bowers, pp. 320, 427, 438. Elsie Clews Parson, "The Zuñi La'Mana," *American Anthropologist* 18 (1916): 525. Ruth Benedict, *Patterns of Culture* (New York: New American Library, 1949), p. 243. Callender and Kochems, p. 453. Katz, p. 314.

49. Benedict, p. 243. Williams, p. 35. Mayhall, pp. 33, 164. Whitehead, p. 88.

50. This was also true of the Navajo, Lakota, and Creek. A. L. Kroeber, *Handbook of the Indians of California* (Berkeley: California Book Company, 1953), p. 497. Greenberg, p. 49. Williams, p. 36.

51. Stephen Powers (1877), quoted in Williams, p. 55. Matilda Coxe Stevenson (1896–1897), quoted in Katz, p. 314.

52. Williams, p. 37.

53. Kroeber, p. 46. Devereux, p. 500. Landes, *Mystic Lake Sioux,* p. 66. Lame Deer, p. 149.

54. Williams, p. 141. Alfred Métraux, "Religion and Shamanism," in Julian Steward, ed., *Handbook of South American Indians* (Washington, D.C.: Smithsonian Institution Press, 1949), vol. 5, p. 589.

55. Katz, p. 289. Guerra, pp. 48, 80, 123–124.

56. Katz, pp. 318–319. Simms, p. 581. Allen, *Sacred Hoop,* p. 196.

57. Williams, p. 182.

58. Ibid., p. 199.

59. Most ethnographies have relatively little information on sexuality, though they may have extensive materials on marriage and kinship. Of those that do discuss sexuality, there is a tendency to overlook homosexuality. Isaac Schapera's *Married Life in an African Tribe* (Harmondsworth, Eng.: Penguin, 1940, 1971), and Pierre Hanry's *Erotisme Africain: Le Comportement Sexuel des Adolescents Guinéens* (Paris: Payot, 1970) are typical. Between the two books, there are a total of five brief references to anything related to homosexual relations.

60. Paul Parin, Fritz Morgenthaler, and Goldy Parin-Matthey, *Les Blancs pensent trop: Treize entretiens psychologiques avec les Dogon,* cited in the Human Relations Area Files, FA16. See also Walter Goldschmidt, *Sebei Law* (Berkeley: University of California Press, 1967), p. 136; Jomo Kenyatta, *Facing Mount Kenya* (New York: Random House, 1965), p. 156; and Gerhard Lindblom, *The Akamba in British East Africa* (New York: Negro Universities Press, 1969 [1920]), p. 158.

61. Geneviève Calame-Griaule, trans. Dierdre LaPin, *Words and the Dogon World* (Philadelphia: ISHI, 1986), p. 409. There is a similar example among the !Kung of southern Africa. Elizabeth Thomas claims that there are no incidences of homosexual sex in that community, whereas Marjorie Shostak provides detailed descriptions of adolescent homosexual experimentation among the !Kung. Elizabeth Thomas, *The Harmless People* (New York: Random House, 1958), p. 89. Marjorie Shostak, *Nisa: The Life and Words of a !Kung Woman* (New York: Random House, 1983), pp. 31, 114–115.

62. Greenberg, p. 79.

63. Louis Vincent Thomas, *Les Diola* (Dakar: IFAN, 1958–1959), p. 570.

64. J. H. Driberg described a similar phenomenon among the Lango of Uganda. He was asked to investigate several complaints about "sexual aberrations" among young men in the bachelors' huts. He found that in several cases whatever sexual contact transpired was done while the young men were asleep and that this was a form of nocturnal

emission brought on by "the close proximity of the sleepers." Again, we know little of their conscious intentions. J. H. Driberg, *The Lango: A Nilotic Tribe of Uganda* (London: T. Fisher Unwin, 1923), pp. 209–210. Colin Turnbull found similar accounts for the Bambuti Pygmies. Colin Turnbull, *Wayward Servants: The Two Worlds of the African Pygmies* (Westport, Conn.: Greenwood Press, 1976 [1968]), p. 122.

65. Shostak, p. 114.

66. Isaac Schapera, *The Khoisan Peoples of South Africa* (London: Routledge & Kegan Paul, 1930), p. 243.

67. Monica Wilson, *Good Company: A Study of Nyakyusa Age Villages* (Boston: Beacon Press, 1971 [1951]), pp. 87–88, 196. Adam, p. 21.

68. I am using the term *witchcraft* in its anthropological sense and not in reference to European witchcraft. In much of Africa, witches are people whose souls travel in the night attacking the life force of other human beings. Wilson, pp. 88, 196.

69. Wilson, p. 88. Human Relations Area Files, "The Nupe" FF52. Human Relations Area Files, "The Mongo" F032. Schapera, *Married Life*, pp. 163–164.

70. E. E. Evans-Pritchard, "Sexual Inversion Among the Azande," *American Anthropologist* 72 (1970): 1432.

71. Ibid.

72. Ibid. E. E. Evans-Pritchard, *Witchcraft, Oracles and Magic Among the Azande* (Oxford: Clarendon Press, 1972 [1937]), pp. 123–125. E. E. Evans-Pritchard, ed., *Man and Woman Among the Azande* (London: Faber & Faber, 1974), p. 56.

73. Evans-Pritchard, *Witchcraft*, p. 77.

74. Evans-Pritchard, "Sexual Inversion," p. 1432. Greenberg, pp. 25–26.

75. Evans-Pritchard, "Seuxal Inversion," p. 1432.

76. Vinigi Grottanelli, *The Python Killer: Stories of Nzema Life* (Chicago: University of Chicago Press, 1988), p. 210.

77. Evans-Pritchard, *Man and Woman*, pp. 36–37.

78. T. Dunbar Moodie, "Migrancy and Male Sexuality on the South African Gold Mines," *Journal of Southern African Studies*, 14, no. 2 (1988): 228–242.

79. Henri Junod, *The Life of a South African Tribe* (New Hyde Park, N.Y.: University Books, 1962), vol. 1, pp. 492–495.

80. Moodie, pp. 228–256. Junod, pp. 492–495. Charles Van Onselen, *Chibaro: African Mine Labour in Southern Rhodesia 1900–1933* (London: Pluto, 1976).

81. Edwin Smith and Andrew Dale, *The Ila-Speaking Peoples of Northern Rhodesia* (New Hyde Park, N.Y.: University Books, 1968), vol. 2, p. 74.

82. Judith Gay, "Mummies and Babies and Friends and Lovers in Lesotho," *Journal of Homosexuality* 11 (1985): 101.

83. Ibid., pp. 97–99.

84. Ibid., pp. 102–103.

85. S. F. Nadel, "Two Nuba Religions: An Essay in Comparison," *American Anthropologist* 57 (1955): 677. Schapera, *Khoisan Peoples*, p. 243.

86. Smith and Dale, p. 74.

87. Wilfrid Hambly, *The Ovimbundu of Angola* (Chicago: Field Museum of Natural History, 1934), vol. 21, p. 181.

88. S. G. Lee, "Spirit Possession Among the Zulu," quoted in John Beattie and John Middleton, eds., *Spirit Mediumship and Society in Africa* (New York: Africana Publishing Company, 1969), p. 143. For a more general discussion of the relationship between transgendered roles and divination, see Beattie and Middleton, op.cit., p. xxv.

89. Harriet Ngubane, *Body and Mind in Zulu Medicine* (New York: Academic Press, 1977). Cited in Human Relations Area Files, "Zulu" FX20. For materials on the Tonga, see Elizabeth Colson, *Marriage and Family Among the Plateau Tonga of Northern Rhodesia* (Manchester: Manchester University Press, 1958), pp. 139–140.

90. Carlos Estermann, *The Ethnography of Southwestern Angola* (New York: Holmes & Meier, 1976 [1957]), vol. 1, p. 197.

91. There does not appear to be a comparable need for women to acquire the ability to tap masculine spiritual power, either because that brings the female religious leader closer to the distractions of male control over temporal power or because of the strong social emphasis on procreation. Unlike the Native American examples, there appear to be no cases of transgendered women in sub-Saharan Africa.

92. Mary Smith, *Baba of Karo: A Woman of the Muslim Hausa* (London: Faber & Faber, 1954), pp. 64–65. Fremont Besmer, *Horses, Musicians, and Gods: The Hausa Cult of Possession Trance* (Zaria: Ahmadu Bello University Press, 1983), p. 18. Renée Pittin, "Houses of Women: A Focus on Alternative Life-Styles in Katsina City," in Christine Oppong, ed., *Female and Male in West Africa* (London: George Allen & Unwin, 1983), p. 296. There appear to be certain parallels between transgendered men who associate with *bori* and *ndoep* and similar men who are leaders in Afro-Brazilian cults. The liminality of the gender role and the liminality of the religious experience appear to be closely linked. See Peter Fry, "Male Homosexuality and Spirit Possession in Brazil," *Journal of Homosexuality* 11 (1985): 137–153.

93. Geoffrey Gorer, *Africa Dances: A Book About West African Negroes* (London: John Lehmann, 1949), pp. 36, 45. Vincent Monteil, *L'Islam Noir* (Paris: Editions du Seuil, 1971), p. 53.

94. Girls' experience growing up in a family where women have primary control over child care may be an important reason for the rarity of female transgenerational relationships.

95. This parallels the humbling aspects of the ritual installation of kings in many African communities. Before becoming king, they spend a period of time, often several days, as the abused and powerless victims of religious authorities and court officials, with the dual purpose of generating empathy for their less powerful subjects and reinforcing their identification with royalty. Victor Turner, *The Ritual Process* (Ithaca: Cornell University Press, 1977), pp. 100–101.

96. Most travelers' accounts about Africa during the period of the trans-Atlantic slave trade, beginning in the late fifteenth century, did not describe life in the interior of the continent. Only when Europeans began to settle or establish trading and administrative posts in the interior, in the mid-nineteenth century, does one begin to obtain detailed descriptions of social relations in African communities other than the slave trading ports.

Bibliography

Adam, Barry D. 1985. "Age, Structure, and Sexuality: Reflections on the Anthropological Evidence on Homosexual Relations." *Journal of Homosexuality* 11, 1:19–33.

Allen, Paula Gunn. 1981. "Lesbians in American Indian Cultures." *Connections* 7, 1:67–86.

———. 1986. *The Sacred Hoop: Recovering the Feminine in American Indian Traditions.* Boston: Beacon Press.

Angelino, Henry, and Charles Shedd. 1955. "A Note on Berdache." *American Anthropologist* 57:121.

Baum, Robert M. 1990. "Graven Images: Scholarly Representations of African Religions." *Religion* 20:355–360.

Beattie, John, and John Middleton, eds. 1969. *Spirit Mediumship and Society in Africa.* New York: Africana Publishing Company.

Benedict, Ruth. 1949. *Patterns of Culture.* New York: New American Library.

Besmer, Fremont. 1983. *Horses, Musicians, and Gods: The Hausa Cult of Possession Trance.* Zaria: Ahmadu Bello University Press.

Blackwood, Evelyn. 1984. "Sexuality and Gender in Certain Native American Tribes: The Case of Cross-Gender Females." *Signs: Journal of Women in Culture and Society* 10, 1:27–42.

Bowers, Alfred. 1965. *Hidatsa Social and Ceremonial Organization, U.S. Bureau of American Ethnology Bulletin.* Washington, D.C.: Smithsonian Institution Press.

Buchanan, Kimberly Moore. 1986. *Apache Women Warriors.* El Paso: Texas Western Press.

Calame-Griaule, Geneviève. 1986. *Words and the Dogon World.* Translated by Deirdre LaPin. Philadelphia: ISHI.

Callender, Charles, and Lee Kochems. 1983. "The North American Berdache." *Current Anthropology* 24, 4:443–470.

Carrasco, David. 1987. "Tezcatlipoca." In *The Encyclopedia of Religion,* edited by Mircea Eliade, 14:415–416. New York: Macmillan.

Chagnon, Napoleon. 1968. *Yanomamö: The Fierce People.* New York: Holt, Rinehart & Winston.

Colson, Elizabeth. 1958. *Marriage and Family Among the Plateau Tonga of Northern Rhodesia.* Manchester: Manchester University Press.

de Laguna, Frederica. 1972. *Under Mount Saint Elias: The History and Culture of the Yakutat Tlingit.* Vol. 2. Washington, D.C.: Smithsonian Institution Press.

DeMallie, Raymond. 1983. "Male and Female in Traditional Lakota Culture." In *The Hidden Half: Studies of Plains Indian Women,* edited by Patricia Albers and Beatrice Medicine, 237–266. Washington, D.C.: University Press of America.

Devereux, George. 1937. "Institutionalized Homosexuality of the Mohave Indians." *Human Biology* 9, 4:498–527.

Dorsey, James O. 1889–1890. *A Study of Siouan Cults, U.S. Bureau of American Ethnology Annual Report* 11:351–548.

Driberg, J. H. 1923. *The Lango: A Nilotic Tribe of Uganda.* London: T. Fisher Unwin.

Eggan, Dorothy. 1943. "The General Problem of Hopi Adjustment." *American Anthropologist* 45:368.

Eliade, Mircea. 1974. *Patterns of Comparative Religion.* New York: New American Library.

———. 1974. *Shamanism: Archaic Techniques of Ecstasy.* Princeton: Princeton University Press.

———. 1975. *Myths, Dreams, and Mysteries.* New York: Harper & Row.

Estermann, Carlos. 1976. *The Ethnography of Southwestern Angola.* Vol. 1. New York: Holmes & Meier.

Evans-Pritchard, E. E. 1970. "Sexual Inversion Among the Azande." *American Anthropologist* 72:1428–1434.

———. 1972. *Witchcraft, Oracles, and Magic Among the Azande.* Oxford: Clarendon Press.

———. ed. 1974. *Man and Woman Among the Azande.* London: Faber & Faber.

Fletcher, Alice, and Francis La Flesche. 1905–1906. *The Omaha Tribe, U.S. Bureau of American Ethnology Annual Report,* Vol. 27.

Fry, Peter. 1985. "Male Homosexuality and Spirit Possession in Brazil." *Journal of Homosexuality* 11:137–153.

Gay, Judith. 1985. "Mummies and Babies and Friends and Lovers in Lesotho." *Journal of Homosexuality* 11:97–116.

Goldschmidt, Walter. 1967. *Sebei Law.* Berkeley: University of California Press.

Gorer, Geoffrey. 1949. *Africa Dances: A Book About West African Negroes.* London: John Lehmann.

Grahn, Judy. 1985. "Strange Country This: Lesbianism and North American Indian Tribes." *Journal of Homosexuality* 12, 3:43–57.

Greenberg, David F. 1988. *The Construction of Homosexuality.* Chicago and London: University of Chicago Press.

Gregor, Thomas. 1977. *Mehinaku: The Drama of Daily Life in a Brazilian Indian Village.* Chicago: University of Chicago Press.

Grottanelli, Vinigi. 1988. *The Python Killer: Stories of Nzema Life.* Chicago: University of Chicago Press.

Guerra, Francisco. 1971. *The Pre-Columbian Mind: A Study into the Aberrant Nature of Sexual Drives, Drugs Affecting Behaviour, and the Attitudes Towards Life and Death, with a Survey of Psychotherapy in Pre-Columbian America.* London: Semina Press.

Hallowell, A. Irving. 1971. *Culture and Experience.* New York: Schocken Books.

Hambly, Wilfrid. 1934. *The Ovimbundu of Angola.* Vol. 21. Chicago: Field Museum of Natural History.

Hanry, Pierre. 1970. *Erotisme Africain: Le Comportement Sexuel des Adolescents Guinéens.* Paris: Payot.

Hassrick, Royal. 1964. *The Sioux: Life and Customs of a Warrior Society.* Norman: University of Oklahoma Press.

Herdt, Gilbert. 1981. *Guardians of the Flutes: Idioms of Masculinity.* New York: Columbia University Press.

———. 1987. "Homosexuality." In *The Encyclopedia of Religion,* edited by Mircea Eliade, 6:445–453. New York: Macmillan.

Hill, W. W. 1938. "Note on the Pima Berdache." *American Anthropologist* 40:338–340.

Hudson, Charles. 1976. *The Southeastern Indians.* Knoxville: University of Tennessee Press.

Human Relations Area Files.

Hungry Wolf, Beverly. 1982. *The Ways of My Grandmothers.* New York: Quill.

Junod, Henri. 1962. *The Life of a South African Tribe.* Vol. 1. New Hyde Park, N.Y.: University Books.

Katz, Jonathan. 1976. *Gay American History: Lesbians and Gay Men in the U.S.A.* New York: Thomas Crowell.

Kenyatta, Jomo. 1965. *Facing Mount Kenya.* New York: Random House.

Kroeber, A. L. 1953. *Handbook of the Indians of California.* Berkeley: California Book Company.

Lame Deer/John Fire, and Richard Erdoes. 1972. *Lame Deer Seeker of Visions.* New York: Simon & Schuster.

Landes, Ruth. 1968. *The Mystic Lake Sioux: Sociology of the Medewakantonwan Santee.* Madison: University of Wisconsin Press.

———. 1970. *The Prairie Potawatomi: Tradition and Ritual in the Twentieth Century.* Madison: University of Wisconsin Press.

Lévi-Strauss, Claude. 1968. "The Social Use of Kinship Terms Among Brazilian Indians." In *Marriage, Family, and Residence,* edited by Paul Bohannan and John Middleton, 169–183. Garden City, N.Y.: Natural History Press.

Lindblom, Gerhard. 1969. *The Akamba in British East Africa.* New York: Negro Universities Press.

Mayhall, Mildred. 1984. *The Kiowas.* Norman: University of Oklahoma Press.

Métraux, Alfred. 1949. "Religion and Shamanism." In *Handbook of South American Indians,* edited by Julian Steward, 5:559–599.

Monteil, Vincent. 1971. *L'Islam Noir.* Paris: Editions du Seuil.

Moodie, T. Dunbar. 1988. "Migrancy and Male Sexuality on the South African Gold Mines." *Journal of Southern African Studies* 14, 2:228–256.

Nadel, S. F. 1955. "Two Nuba Religions: An Essay in Comparison." *American Anthropologist* 57:661–679.

Needham, Rodney. 1973. "The Left Hand of the Mugwe: An Analytical Note on the Structure of Meru Symbolism." In *Right and Left: Essays on Dual Symbolic Classification,* edited by R. Needham, 109–127. Chicago: University of Chicago Press.

Ngubane, Harriet. 1977. *Body and Mind in Zulu Medicine.* New York: Academic Press.

Niethammer, Carolyn. 1977. *Daughters of the Earth: The Lives and Legends of American Indian Women.* New York: Macmillan.

Parin, Paul, Fritz Morgenthaler, and Goldy Parin-Matthey. *Les Blancs pensent trop: Treize entretiens psychologiques avec les Dogon.* In Human Relations Area Files, FA16.

Parsons, Elsie Clews. 1916. "The Zuñi La'Mana." *American Anthropologist* 18:521–528.

Pittin, Renée. 1983. "Houses of Women: A Focus on Alternative Life-Styles in Katsina City." In *Female and Male in West Africa,* edited by Christine Oppong, 291–302. London: George Allen & Unwin.

Powers, William K. 1977. *Oglala Religion*. Lincoln: University of Nebraska Press.

Reichard, Gladys. 1950. *Navaho Religion: A Study of Symbolism*. New York: Pantheon Books.

Schapera, Isaac. 1930. *The Khoisan Peoples of South Africa*. London: Routledge & Kegan Paul.

———. 1971. *Married Life in an African Tribe*. Harmondsworth, Eng.: Penguin.

Shostak, Marjorie. 1983. *Nisa: The Life and Words of a !Kung Woman*. New York: Random House.

Simms, S. C. 1903. "Crow Indian Hermaphrodites." *American Anthropologist* 5:580–586.

Smith, Edwin, and Andrew Dale. *The Ila-Speaking Peoples of Northern Rhodesia*. Vol. 2. New Hyde Park, N.Y.: University Books.

Smith, Mary. 1954. *Baba of Karo: A Woman of the Muslim Hausa*. London: Faber & Faber.

Spier, Leslie. 1933. *Yuman Tribes of the Gila River*. Chicago: University of Chicago Press.

Thomas, Elizabeth. 1958. *The Harmless People*. New York: Random House.

Thomas, Louis Vincent. 1958–1959. *Les Diola: Essai d'analyse fonctionnelle sur une population de Basse Casamance*. Dakar: IFAN.

Turnbull, Colin. 1976. *Wayward Servants: The Two Worlds of the African Pygmies*. Westport, Conn.: Greenwood Press.

Turner, Victor. 1977. *The Ritual Process*. Ithaca: Cornell University Press.

Underhill, Ruth. 1979. *Papago Woman*. New York: Holt, Rinehart & Winston.

Van Onselen, Charles. *Chibaro: African Mine Labour in Southern Rhodesia 1900–1933*. London: Pluto, 1977.

Whitehead, Harriet. 1981. "The Bow and the Burden Strap: A New Look at Institutionalized Homosexuality in Native North America." In *Sexual Meanings: The Cultural Construction of Gender and Sexuality*, edited by Sherry Ortner and Harriet Whitehead, 80–115. Cambridge: Cambridge University Press.

Williams, Walter L. 1986. *The Spirit and the Flesh: Sexual Diversity in American Indian Culture*. Boston: Beacon Press.

Wilson, Monica. 1971. *Good Company: A Study of Nyakyusa Age Villages*. Boston: Beacon Press.

2

Homosexuality and Hinduism

Arvind Sharma

In the discussion of homosexuality and Hinduism, the first problem is presented by the term *homosexuality* itself. Apparently the term etymologically means sexual activity among members of the same (*homo*) sex[1] and thus should include both male and female homosexuality. Conventionally, however, through phonetic confusion between the Greek *homo* ("same") and Latin *homo* ("human," but sometimes erroneously thought to mean "male"), the term sometimes acquires the sense of *male* homosexuality, and the term *lesbianism*[2] is then reserved for female homosexuality. This convention will be observed in this essay, where required, for the sake of clarity.

The next problem is to identify the Sanskrit term for homosexuality.[3] The problem lies in the fact that homosexuality covers a whole range of sexual activity: (1) copulation between (a) men or (b) women; (2) anal intercourse; and (3) oral-genital contact. The problem is that although there are clear expressions for 1a and 1b, the words for cases 2 and 3 can be applied to both males and females. Thus the word *adhorata*[4] can mean anal intercourse among men as well as between a man and a woman, and *auparistaka*,[5] or mouth-congress (also called *maukhyā*), could similarly be applied to both cases.

It seems that homosexuality as a specific sexual mode of behavior was not differentiated from sodomy or pederasty in India, unlike the case in Greece[6] and in modern times.[7] In addition to this difficulty of definition, there is the further problem of paucity of evidence as to its prevalence. The well-known Indologist A. L. Basham remarks:

> The erotic life of ancient India was generally heterosexual. Homosexualism of both sexes was not wholly unknown; it is condemned briefly in the lawbooks, and the *Kāmasūtra* treats of it, but cursorily, and with little enthusiasm. Literature ignores it. In this respect ancient India was far healthier than most other ancient cultures.[8]

It is possible to maintain in the light of some fresh considerations that although Basham may still be right in regarding the emphasis on homosexuality as being relatively less in India than in other religions and cultures, nevertheless its incidence may have been underestimated.[9] And the limited practice of castration in India raises another point significant for the rest of the discussion, namely, whether rendering a word such as *klība* as *eunuch* regularly is correct or whether *impotent* would be a better rendering. This leads to the further point regarding the semantic accuracy of a whole range of words of this type that may or may not have been inclusive of deviant, or perhaps one should say variant, behavior.[10] Finally, the value judgment involved in Basham's remark is obvious. One may concur with his judgment and share his values, but perhaps this is the right place to state Erich Bethe's observation that the intrusion of moral evaluation is "the deadly enemy of science" and may therefore be bracketed for the duration of this essay.[11]

Nevertheless, it must be admitted that though homosexuality was not unknown, there is very little evidence available to show that it was widely practiced. Vern L. Bullough claims that "some medieval writers regarded the practice as quite common and in no way perverse, but others claimed that men who engaged in it with other men were reborn as men incapable of begetting."[12] He cites J. J. Meyer as his authority.[13] It is interesting that hitherto not a single case of homosexuality proper, to the best of my knowledge, has been identified in the vast range of Tantrika literature assigned to the medieval period despite the profusion of variant practices therein, nor is it evident in the erotic art of India. The statement that "some medieval writers speak of it as quite common and do not regard it as perverse" is found virtually verbatim in Benjamin Walker;[14] it is made by Geoffrey Parrinder[15] as well, and no evidence is cited by either. It is not found in Johann Jakob Meyer; only the latter half of the sentence about the rebirth of the homosexual as an impotent is found therein.[16] The Mahābhārata seems to know of it, but it is difficult to identify a clear case of homosexuality in that text itself.[17] This situation seems to be confirmed by the fact that even a medical text such as that of Suśruta (III.2.47) seems to entertain the fanciful idea that copulation between two females led to the birth of a child without any bones, an idea also alluded to in the Padmapurāṇa.[18]

But even though not widely practiced, homosexuality was certainly known in ancient India. This is clear from the fact that in both Hindu canonical and secular law specific punishment is provided for it. Its prevalence in medieval India could easily be postulated as a continuance of earlier practices as well as discerned through the observations in commentarial literature on the canonical law books. For more modern times again there are hints of its practice—though only hints—provided by Western observers. Yet it is interesting that even when the French Jesuit Abbé J. A. Dubois accused—or complimented—the Hindus of South India in the early decades of the nineteenth century in having "surpassed all the other nations of the world, both ancient and modern, in the unconscionable depravity of . . . their religious rites,"[19] there is no reference to homosexuality, unless the passing allusion to the depravity of the *cultus* that prevailed in Greece is supposed to signify it.

The discussion of homosexuality in Hinduism is therefore beset with difficulties. First, there is the terminological problem: how is homosexuality referred to? In this essay I have taken the term in its austere sense, dissociating it as far as possible from transvestism, hermaphroditism, and so forth. Such limitation may have narrowed the scope but sharpened the focus. Then there is the problem of the limited nature of the evidence available.[20] Despite these constraints, however, it seems possible to suggest a conceptual framework within which the issue of homosexuality in Hinduism could be fruitfully addressed.

Such a conceptual framework can be developed on the basis of a clue provided by Hindu axiology.[21] Classical Hinduism articulated the concept of the four ends of "man" called the *Puruṣārthas*. In fact:

> One of the main concepts which underlies the Hindu attitude to life and daily conduct is that of the four ends of man (purushārtha). The first of these is characterized by considerations of righteousness, duty, and virtue. This is called *dharma*. There are other activities, however, through which a man seeks to gain something for himself or pursue his own pleasure. When the object of this activity is some material gain, it is called *artha;* when it is love or pleasure, it is *kāma*. Finally, there is the renunciation of all these activities in order to devote oneself to religious or spiritual activities with the aim of liberating oneself from the worldly life; this is *mokṣa*. These four are referred to as "the tetrad" (*caturvarga*).[22]

It seems that the Hindu perspective on homosexuality is profoundly affected by the axiological angle through which it is perceived. Hence it is best to proceed by surveying the attitude to homosexuality as revealed in the literature dealing with these *Puruṣārthas*.

The texts that deal with *dharma* are called the *dharmasūtra* in their aphoristic form and *dharmaśāstra* when composed in language of normal discourse; those that deal with *artha* are called *arthaśāstra*. Although there are numerous *dharmaśāstras*, the most prominent being that of Manu, one *arthaśāstra*, that of Kauṭilya, enjoys such preeminence in the field that it alone will be referred to in this essay. Just as the texts that deal with *dharma* are called *dharmaśāstras* and those that deal with *artha, arthaśāstras*, predictably the texts that treat of *kāma* are called *kāmaśātras*. Of these, however, one particular work, called *Kāmasūtra* rather than *Kāmaśāstra* on account of its aphoristic style, and composed by Vātsyāyana, so dominates the field that our inquiry will be restricted to it.

If the class of works on *dharma, artha,* and *kāma* are called *dharma-, artha-* and *kāma-śāstras* respectively, then one would expect the texts belonging to the last category of *mokṣa* to be called *mokṣaśāstras*. The word was occasionally used but never caught on; the vast body of literature dealing with the salvific dimension of life is instead spoken of as *darśana* (the literature

of the various philosophical schools) or *tantra*—a body of literature that focuses more concretely on religious practices. Despite its limited currency, I will use the term *mokṣaśāstra* as an
umbrella term to subsume such—and similar—literature.[23]

Homosexuality and Dharma

The most authoritative Hindu text dealing with dharma is the
Mānavadharmaśāstra, more briefly known as the Manusmṛti
and usually ascribed to the second century A.D. There are references to homosexuality in the Manusmṛti, as is clear from
the mention of the committing of what has been translated as
an "unnatural offence with a male" in XI.175. Several interesting points emerge in the context of this reference. First, the
term "unnatural offence" is an English translation and does
not appear in the original text as such.[24] The term in the original is *maithunaṁ puṁsi*, or copulation with a male. Second, the
preceding verse refers to "an unnatural crime with a female"
(XI.174), and there too the term does not appear as such in the
original. Third, the entire verse regarding the "unnatural offence" reads as follows:

> A twice-born man who commits an unnatural offence with a
> male, or has intercourse with a female in a cart drawn by oxen, in
> water, or in the day-time, shall bathe, dressed in his clothes.[25]

It is clear that only a twice-born, or *dvija*, is involved in the
offense here, not all men. Here the *varṇa* distinctions of Hindu
society come into play. The term *dvija* can refer to either
Brāhmaṇas or to the three upper castes: Brāhmaṇas, Kṣatriyas,
and Vaiśyas. It excludes the Śūdras, the last and lowest order.
We know that the Śūdra is excluded from the stricture; it remains to be determined whether, depending on the meaning of
the word *dvija*, Kṣatriyas and Vaiśyas are included or excluded.
Here one needs to be reminded that "although the code of
Manu has had the effect of law throughout much of Indian history, interpretations of the law have varied."[26] The answer to
the above question is a good illustration of this fact. A *dvija*, or
twice-born, is one who has undergone the sacred investiture

ceremony that was originally undergone by all the male members of the three higher Varṇas—Brāhmaṇa, Kṣatriya, and
Vaiśya (Manu II.42–46)—but gradually was restricted to the
Brahmins. The class of people affected by the ruling will therefore vary through history, but it is bound to apply to the Brahmins, it would appear. Another point worth noting is that
according to a commentator, "the verse refers to an unintentional offence."[27] One could, on this basis, reconcile the lighter
punishment laid down for homosexuality here with the much
heavier ones for other forms of homosexual contact elsewhere.

A key factor to be considered is the fact that the penalty is
mentioned in the context of the higher castes. When this is
compared with the kind of practices associated with the lower
castes on the basis of other evidence,[28] it seems possible to suggest that the prevalence of homosexuality among the lower
classes may have been overlooked[29] and became justiciable only
in the case of the higher castes because they were supposed to
uphold higher moral standards.[30]

The verse under consideration may be usefully compared
with the previous one (XI.174):

A man who has committed a bestial crime, or an unnatural
crime with a female, or has had intercourse in water, or with a
menstruating woman, shall perform a *Sāmtapana Kṛcchra.*[31]

A comparison of the two verses reveals the fact that an
"unnatural offence" with a male involved a lighter penance
than one with a female; for compared with bathing with one's
clothes on, *Sāmpatana Kṛcchra* involves subsistence on the urine
of cows, cow dung, milk, sour milk, clarified butter, and a decoc-
tion of *kuśa* grass, and fasting for twenty-four hours (XI.213).

All these considerations seem to suggest that anal intercourse with men was treated more lightly than anal intercourse
with women.[32] In other words, female virtue and propriety was
a far greater concern of the law-giver than that of the male. Lesbian relationships carry a more severe penalty than homosexual
ones. Thus VIII.369–370:

369. A damsel who pollutes (another) damsel must be fined
two hundred (*paṇas*), pay the double of her (nuptial) fee, and
receive ten (lashes with a) rod.

370. But a woman who pollutes a damsel shall instantly have (her head) shaved or two fingers cut off, and be made to ride (through the town) on a donkey.[33]

Here again there is greater concern with the protection of the virtue of the virgin than of a woman who is no longer one. Prior carnal knowledge seems to attract leniency. This is clear from the facts stated above that "lesbian love between girls is punished with a heavy fine and ten strokes of the whip (śiphā); the married woman who thus stains a maid shall be at once shaved bald, have two fingers cut off, and be led on an ass through the place."[34] There is the further point to be considered that in this case too, according to some commentators, caste distinctions came into play: "The verse prescribes three different punishments, . . . a Brāhmaṇī offender is to be shaved, a Kṣhatriyā to be led through the streets on a donkey, while women of other castes are to lose two fingers." And according to others: "Punishment is to be regulated by the circumstances."[35] Here, however, the higher the caste, the more lenient the punishment, as contrasted with the case of males.

Thus the central concern of Hindu law books was first the protection of virginity and then, in the same spirit, the protection of the proper normal sexual role of women. To these concerns, homosexuality posed little threat, but its main modality, anal intercourse, did and was disapproved all around. It is worth noting here that according to the Mahānirvāṇatantra (XI.44), whosoever had unnatural intercourse with his wife could be punished with death, while according to Vasiṣṭha Dharma-sūtra (XII.22), "his forefathers had to live the month through in his seed."[36] It must be pointed out here that the more severe Tantrika punishment is perhaps not because of the procreational concerns which dominate the Dharma literature and which Tantrika literature does not share, but because of the high honor accorded to women in Tantra.[37]

There is another provision in the Dharmaśāstras that must now be considered. According to Manu XI.68 and Viṣṇu XXXVIII.5, homosexuality led to loss of caste. The text in Manu runs as follows:

68. Giving pain to a Brāhmaṇa (by a blow), smelling at things which ought not to be smelt at, or at spirituous liquor, cheating,

and an unnatural offence with a man, are declared to cause the loss of caste (*Jātibhraṁśa*).[38]

However, this loss of caste is not permanent, for according to Manu XI.72 the offense can be expiated. It is far from clear whether the expiation for the *dvija* mentioned in XI.175 is in addition to that of loss of caste or not. Geoffrey Parrinder simply notes that whereas "one law" laid down bathing dressed in clothes, "another prescribed loss of caste."[39] Meyer simply notes that according to the passages from Manu and Viṣṇu cited above, "By homosexual perversion the man loses his caste; while Manu XI, 175, Vishṇu liii, 4, prescribe bathing in the clothes as an atonement."[40] They seem to overlook the fact that Manu XI.175 applies to *dvijas*, but Manu XI.68 applies to all and sundry. Yet ambiguity still surrounds the reconciliation of these two dicta, especially because according to Manu X.126 a Śūdra "cannot commit an offence causing loss of caste."[41]

Two very important distinctions must be kept in mind here in assessing the provisions regarding homosexual offenses, especially as found in Manu. The first is the distinction between major and minor offenses. Although no such clear distinction is explicitly made in Chapter XI, it is clear from the tenor of the provisions that homosexuality as included in XI.68 seems to be part of a more serious order of offenses from the point of view of hieratic ethics than the reference in XI.175, which in general deals with sexual offenses. As a purely *sexual* offense, homosexuality seems to attract less condemnation than does the *social* offense involving miscegenation. The second distinction to be kept in mind is between intentional and unintentional offenses (Manu XI.45–47). The commentator seeks to explain the lightness of the punishment in XI.175 in terms of its being unintentional. It prescribes only bathing with clothes as an atonement for a twice-born, although the Brāhmaṇa is not to bathe naked in any case (IV.45). He is also not supposed to bathe frequently dressed in all his garments (IV.129). The next verse (XI.176), which uses the expression "unintentionally," lends credence to this view. It is worth noting that "unintentional" homosexuality, if our reading is correct, is less culpable than "unintentional" adultery with a woman of low caste, which resulted in loss of caste. How these acts could be performed "unintentionally" is somewhat puzzling.

On the basis of the ritual purifications laid down by Manu, it has been suggested, as for instance by Vern L. Bullough, that among the Hindus "even when sexual acts are forbidden, it is more because they involve ceremonial impurities than because they are evil in themselves, and the impurities could be removed by undergoing the necessary ablutions."[42] If homosexuality and lesbianism are included in forbidden acts, then this constitutes a rather soft statement of the Hindu position. This becomes clear when other texts dealing with Hindu ethical norms are taken into consideration. Although the Dharmasūtras and Dharmaśāstras are the repository of Brahmanical norms and values, the literature of popular Hindu edification—the Mahābhārata, the Rāmāyaṇa, and the Purāṇas—reflect more widely diffused moral values and ethical standards. These find homosexuality repugnant. For instance, at one point the implication of homosexuality in Karmic terms is spelled out in a dialogue in the Mahābhārata between god Śiva and his spouse Pārvatī. Pārvatī wants to know why some people are born blind, some are chronically ill, and yet others are impotent. Śiva's explanation of the last condition, namely impotence, runs as follows (XIII.145.52):

> Those fools of evil conduct who engage in intercourse in other than the female organ and *among men*—those extremely perverse-minded end up as eunuchs.[43]

It is only fair to point out that the term *viyoni* in the text, which I have rendered as "in other than the female organ," is capable of other implications, such as bestiality, sexual commerce with women of low or even different caste (as perhaps in XII.228.45),[44] and also homosexuality,[45] but the last sense in the context of this verse would be tautological.

Homosexuality is thus certainly a vice.[46] The statement by Vern L. Bullough, cited earlier, that among the Hindus "even when sexual acts are forbidden, it is more because they involve ceremonial impurities than because they are evil in themselves, and the impurities could be removed by undergoing the necessary ablutions"[47] is too ritualistic and mechanistic and fails to recognize the moral dimension. But is it a "dreadful sin"[48] according to the aforementioned Hindu texts, as claimed by Johann Jakob Meyer? Meyer argues that one of the reprehensible characteristics of the Kaliyuga (or the present dark age in which we live and which according to traditional Hindu calculation commenced on Feb. 18, 3102 B.C.) will, according to the scriptures, be the widespread prevalence of homosexuality. Meyer cites Mahābhārata verses in support, after stating that "homosexuality is a dreadful sin":

> "The blind ones, evil-livers, very foolish ones, however, who find their delight in intercourse with a base womb (especially of an animal, but also of a woman of low rank) (*viyonau*), and with men, are born again as men incapable of begetting" (xiii, 145.52). Here, too, seems to belong the passage from the description of the evil state of things at the time when a world age is coming to its end: "Men and women will walk their ways after their own wishes, and not be able to suffer one another, when the end of a yuga has come about. Then, when the end of the world is at hand, the woman will not find content with her husband, nor the man with his wife" (iii, 190.45, 50).[49]

The passage, however, seems to indicate promiscuity rather than homosexuality; and unless we insist on including the latter in the former, the point is inconclusive, at least on the basis of this reference. The frequent references to the *mlecchas* (or unclean foreigners) in the Kaliyuga is again more suggestive than conclusive. As Meyer himself notes, the outstanding evil in the matter of sexual mores in the Mahābhārata, the Rāmāyaṇa, and the Purāṇas is really promiscuity basically understood as violation of chastity.[50] Another factor worth keeping in mind is that, according to the Vāyu Purāṇa, there "will be more women than men"[51] in the Kaliyuga. This would seem to reduce the probability of homosexuality with which the texts seem to be concerned, though it does, by the same token, increase the probability of lesbianism with which the texts also seem to be concerned!

According to some texts, oral-genital contact is extremely reprehensible. It "was classed by some lawgivers as equivalent to the killing of a Brahmin, and the sin involved could not be expiated in less than 100 incarnations."[52] It is difficult to decide how seriously this is to be taken. A person who does not approach his wife when it is the right time of the month for fulfilling one's conjugal duties is also said to be guilty of the sin of killing a cow and a Brahmin! Perhaps such statements are *arthavāda*—exaggerations to make a point. Moreover, according to Manu (V.130), the "mouth of a woman is always pure."[53] One is not quite sure how literally this is to be taken, but it does seem to imply that oral-genital contact in a hetero-sexual marital setting carries no opprobrium. This would, by implication, reserve the strictures to homosexual contact. Therefore, because such contact is associated primarily but not solely with base people in the Kāmasūtra, one must again won-der what proportion of the severity of the indictment reflects sensitivity to class distinctions and what proportion repre-sents moral revulsion at the practice itself.

At this point, one may revive the suggestion that the prevalence of homosexuality may represent not only a case of individual moral corruption but may also indicate societal de-cay and indeed presage its destruction. If the prevalence of ho-mosexuality could be established in the case of the Yādava clan, which perished after the end of the Mahābhārata war, then the suggestion would gain some credence. The destruction of this clan is associated with the notorious deeds of a son of Kṛṣṇa (that incarnation of Viṣṇu) called Sāmba—so called because he was born as a result of a boon conferred by Śiva when he ap-peared in his hermaphrodite, or *ardhanārīśvara*, form to Kṛṣṇa. Sāmba married the sister of Duryodhana and used to live in Dvārkā, where the Yādava clan headed by Kṛṣṇa had moved from Mathurā. "Śāmba became notorious for his drunkenness, venery, gluttony and *homosexuality*. He seduced the wives of others, sported openly with his companions dressed as a fe-male, mocked the devotions of the sages Viśvāmitra, Durvāsas and Nārada. His name, as Śāmbalī, later became a synonym for eunuch."[54] Subsequently, his antics culminate in the self-destruction of the entire tribe. However, despite his generally profligate and otherwise reckless conduct, there is no indica-tion in the original sources, which have been carefully exam-ined by Vettam Mani, that Sāmba was a homosexual in addition to being a transvestite, an incestuous seducer, and a person of generally opprobrious conduct.[55] Unfortunately, the passage from Walker cited above is virtually reproduced by

Vern L. Bullough along with the mention of homosexuality.[56] In the case of Sāmba, however, the fact of his being a homosexual, as distinguished from his Casanovaesque capacities, is far from certain.

Even in the general state of precipitous moral decline in the Kaliyuga, which followed upon the destruction of the Yādavas, it is not so much men but women who, it is said, will "engage in sexual intercourse against the order of nature."[57]

Homosexuality and Artha

The Arthaśāstra is another source of information about Hindu attitudes to homosexuality. This famous work, usually but not universally assigned to the third century B.C., lays down a fine for "a person who copulated with animals 12 *panas*, much less than for anal intercourse among humans."[58] Similarly, it prescribes a fine of 48–94 *panas* for male homosexuality and 12–24 *panas* for lesbianism.[59] The punitive scale provides us with a clue to assess the judicial Indian attitude toward variant sexual practices. Male homosexuality was the most heinous; female was less so, and bestiality even less so. *This is in contrast with the provisions of the Dharmaśāstras.* The punitive index also suggests that the approach of secular law to homosexuality was more lax than that of sacred law. For unnatural offenses, or offenses against the order of nature, Kauṭilya (IV.13), Yājñavalkya (II.289.293), Viṣṇu Dharmaśāstra (V.44), and Nārada (XV.76) provide fines of 12, 24, 100, and 500 *panas,* according to P. V. Kane.[60] A comparison shows that sacred law levied higher fines than did secular law.

It is clear, therefore, that in contrast to the provisions of Dharmaśāstra, the Arthaśāstra (1) took a more indulgent view of homosexuality and (2) regarded male homosexuality as more obnoxious than female homosexuality.

The question might naturally be asked, Which provisions actually prevailed in real life? The question is difficult to answer because of the fluctuating relationship between the sacred and secular wings of society in India. The Arthaśāstra itself may well represent the actual administrative arrangements under a particular dynasty, namely, the Mauryas.[61] But a later

king of the Sātavāhana dynasty boasts of virtually having instituted sacred law,[62] which in general is said to take precedence[63]
over secular law, according to most law books except that of
Nārada. He lays down that the royal decree is the ultimate
source of law, thereby subordinating sacred to secular law.[64] The
actual situation, therefore, must have varied over time.

Homosexuality and Kāma

Kāma is another *puruṣārtha,* or legitimate goal of human endeavor. As noted earlier, it includes not only the category of
sexual pleasure but also more generally the whole realm of aesthetic enjoyment. In fact, Vātsyāyana, the author of Kāmasūtra,
defines kāma as "a state where all our senses and our mind get
satisfaction."[65] The Kāmasūtra as such, however, focuses primarily on the physical aspect of sex. "The *Kāma Sūtra* enjoins
every male member of the three upper castes first to complete
his educational training and then to marry, set up a home, and
follow the ways of a man of taste and culture. Both men and
women are encouraged to study closely and to perfect the
methods of love for the enhancement of the aesthetic quality of
their lives. In addition, a person should augment his expertise
in the sixty-four fine arts. *The experience of physical love between
two people of either the same or opposite sex is to be engaged in and
enjoyed for its own sake as one of these arts.*"[66]

   That homosexuality of the oral-genital variety was accepted as a valid modality of sexual expression finds detailed
support in another section of the Kāmasūtra. This section was
considered too delicate, or indelicate, by Victorian standards
and was often bowdlerized out of earlier editions or retained
only in a Latin translation.[67]

   The presentation hitherto might create the impression that
from the point of view of Kāma virtually no opprobrium attached to homosexuality of the oral-genital variety. This may
be so if the matter is treated from a purely hedonistic point of
view, but the context suggests that such practices were associated with eunuchs and barbers. Devangana Desai observes on
the basis of historical evidence that often the royalty consorted
"with lower caste women who were usually recruited by

Tantrikas. The depiction on the temples of the much criticized oral-genital relations, which had become the favourite pose of sculptors, can possibly be explained in this light. For, this was a pose practiced by lower caste women and eunuchs according to the Kāmasūtra (II.IX.22)."[68] It is remarkable that hardly any scene of oral-genital congress among males has been depicted in the erotic art of India, although Vātsyāyana clearly testifies to the fact that "male servants of some men . . . engage in mouth congress with their masters. Even some citizens who knew each other well performed it on each other. He also recognized that women, particularly those of the harem, also engaged in oral-genital sex with each other. He said that in such cases the act was similar to kissing the mouth, and some women became so addicted to this kind of sexual activity, called the 'congress of the crow' that they sought out those who would do it to them, whether male or female."[69] It has already been pointed out how some authors of the Dharmaśāstras take a rather dim view of oral-genital contact of any kind, heterosexual or homosexual, and compare it to the sin of killing a Brahmin, the most heinous sin in their book, which could be expiated only over several lives. They consider the prevalence of such practices characteristic of the present degenerate age (kaliyuga).

One must also consider here some more general views on sex or what might be called cultural sexual beliefs. The Greeks believed women to be inferior to men, so true love was thought to be possible only among men. This was the philosophical foundation of Greek preference for male homosexuality.[70] Perhaps Sappho returned the compliment. In any case, although the Hindu assessment of females was not always complimentary in the area of social life, it was clearly acknowledged that they enjoy sex more than men.[71] As women were presumed to be able to participate fully in passionate love play, men did not need other outlets. In fact, "in the sexual handbooks—lovemaking is often referred to as a refined form of combat."[72] However, it is possible that male insensitivity could have driven women into each other's arms as much then as now.[73]

The mythical dimension of the sex act could also be seen as at least potentially homosexual. There are several Purāṇic and literary accounts of the prodigiously prolonged copulation of the divine pair Śiva and Pārvatī who had been brought together by the gods so that the son to be produced by their union could lead the gods to victory over the demons. The divine pair started honeymooning,

> but a long thousand years of the gods went by, and the heaven-dwellers grew anxious lest the fruit of so endless a begetting should be far too mighty for the world to tolerate. They went therefore to the tireless pair, and begged Śiva that for the weal of all beings he would put a check on his manly powers. He graciously consented, but asked who should catch up the seed already aroused. The earth was chosen for this, but it filled up altogether with it, and so the god of fire was called in to help; he penetrated this flood, and so there arose the mountain Śveta-parvata, and the heavenly cane-forest, where from the god's procreative fluid the war-god Kārtikeya or Kumāra came into being.[74]

The intervention of Agni (a male deity) contains a hint of homosexuality, but only that; and as J. J. Meyer notes, "neither myths like these, however, nor the sensuality so often blazing up in any way alter the ethical view"[75] of sexuality in Hinduism.

The magical dimension associated with sex, which goes as far back as the Atharvaveda and is also reflected in the Kāmasūtra, provides an example of necrophilic homosexuality. "In the so-called black ritual (*nīlasādhana*) the adept sits astride a male and animates the body by occult means. The corpse twitches and struggles, its tongue protrudes, and the penis erects and ejaculates. The fluid was collected and used."[76]

In general, however, one notices a failure to develop erotic material along homosexual lines in Hindu culture. Two examples, one from Vedic and the other from post-Vedic literature, may be cited to illustrate the point.

Vedic material does not seem to refer to homosexuality, although it is full of sexual symbolism. Thus, for instance, "ritual could be interpreted in a sexual way and even minute details might be explained by this symbolism. Thus if in the course of a recitation the priest separated the first two quarters of a verse and brought the other two close together, this was said to be happening because a woman separates her thighs during copulation and the man presses them together. The inaudible recitation of a text was compared to the emission of semen, and when a priest turned his back and went down on his knees this was explained by the imagery of the copulation of animals"[77]—and not with a homosexual image. In the same context, it is interesting that in later literature we find an account of androgynous creation. It runs as follows:

1. When the worlds had thus been formed by Brahmā their creator, but the creatures, for some reason did not engage in action, (2) Brahmā, enveloped in gloom, and thenceforward dejected, formed a resolution tending to ascertain the fact. 3. He then created in himself (a body) of his own, formed of pure gloom (tamas), having overpowered the passion (rajas) and goodness (sattva) which existed (in him) naturally. 4. The Lord of the world was afflicted with that suffering, and lamented. He then dispelled the gloom, and covered over the passion. 5. The gloom, when scattered, was formed into a pair. Unrighteousness arose from activity (?), and mischief sprang from sorrow. 6. That active (?) pair having been produced, he became glorious (?) and pleasure took possession of him. 7. Brahmā after that cast off that body of his, which was devoid of lustre, and divided his person into two parts; with the half he became a male (purusha) (8) and with the half a female: it was Śatarūpā who was so produced to him. Under the impulse of lust he created her a material supporter of beings. 9. By her magnitude she pervaded both heaven and earth. That former body of Brahmā invests the sky. 10. This divine female Śatarūpā, who was born to him from his half, as he was creating, by incessantly practicing austere fervour of a highly arduous description, acquired for herself as a husband a Male (purusha) of glorious renown.[78]

There is a similar account found in Plato. But there, in contrast, homosexual dispositions are also connected with this etiological myth:

In the ancient times there were three kinds of beings, each with four legs and four arms: male, female, and androgynous. They grew too powerful and conspired against the gods, and so Zeus sliced them in two. The parts derived from the whole males are the ancestors of those men who tend to homosexuality and pederasty; the parts derived from the whole females are the ancestors of women who incline to be lesbians. The androgynes, who are nowadays regarded with scorn, gave rise to men who are women-lovers and adulterers, and to women who are man-lovers and adulteresses (Symposium 189E–191E).[79]

It may also be a matter of some interest that the author of the Kāmasūtra, Vātsyāyana, composed his work on erotics while leading the life of a celibate. Some regard this as highly improbable, whereas others find in it the possible explanation of the acrobatic coital positions that could only fill the empty spaces in an ascetically deprived or even depraved imagination! In any case, it is useful to conclude this section with his views on the relationship of *dharma, artha,* and *kāma* as a pattern for speculating on what his views on homosexuality in relation to life in general might have been:

> "Thus have I written in a few words the 'Science of love,' after reading the text of ancient authors, and following the ways of enjoyment mentioned in them.
>
> "He who is acquainted with the true principles of this science pays regard to Dharma, Artha, Kama and to his own experiences, as well as to the teachings of others, and does not act simply on the dictates of his own desire. As for the errors in the science of love which I have mentioned in this work, on my own authority as an author, I have immediately after mentioning them, carefully censured and prohibited them.
>
> "An act is never looked upon with indulgence for the simple reason that it is authorised by the science, because it ought to be remembered that it is the intention of the science, that the rules which it contains should only be acted upon in particular cases. After reading and considering the work of Babhravya and other ancient authors, and thinking over the meaning of the rules given by them, the Kama Sutra was composed, according to the precepts of Holy Scriptures, for the benefit of the world, by Vatsyayana, while leading the life of a religious student and wholly engaged in the contemplation of the Deity.
>
> "This work is not intended to be used merely as an instrument for satisfying our desires. A person, acquainted with the true principles of this science, and who preserves his Dharma, Artha, and Kama, and has regard for the practices of the people, is sure to obtain the mastery over his senses.
>
> "In short, an intelligent and prudent person attending to Dharma and Artha, and attending to Kama also, without becoming the slave of his passions, obtains success in everything that he may undertake."[80]

The curious biographical detail that the author of the Kāmasūtra wrote his work while leading the life of a celibate—even if untrue—points to the need of not divorcing the sphere of *kāma,* and of homosexuality within it, from that of *dharma* in the context of Hinduism. In the Bhagavadgītā (VII.11), for instance, Lord Kṛṣṇa identifies himself with *kāma,* thereby legitimizing it—but only when it is not opposed to *dharma.* This attitude may have had wider ramifications. Although the Manusmṛti provides for expiation of nocturnal emission (II.181) for a twice-born student, and severe penance (Manu XI.104–107) for a pupil going to bed with the Guru's wife, any reference to homosexuality is conspicuous by its absence, although the context suggests pubescent males living together in close association. Even in the literature on *kāma*, a commentary on the Kāmasūtra recommends an innovative autoerotic technique, but such novelties are not extended to homosexuality. Even in the medieval period, for which greater prevalence of homosexuality is claimed, the penalty of expulsion from caste may have had the practical effect of curtailing it on account of the increased rigidity of the system during this period.

Homosexuality and Mokṣa

The ultimate state of eschatological felicity in Hinduism is described as *mokṣa,* and several possible ways of achieving it, called *yogas,* are spelled out within the tradition. From the point of the present topic, however, they may broadly be classified as sex-negative, sex-neutral, or sex-positive. Most of the Hindu approaches to salvation, with one notable exception, tend to emphasize sexual restraint in the field of spiritual discipline. Some forms of *yoga*—such as the path of devotion (*bhakti*) or the path of action (*karma*)—are not antithetical to leading a normal conjugal life and may be considered sex-neutral. The spiritual path that emphasizes gnosis rather than devotion or action, however, tends to favor suspension of all forms of sexual activity and the adoption of celibacy. It is here that the first point of intersection between homosexuality and Hindu religious practices emerges. This approach, which involves renouncing of all worldly ties and the adoption of the vow of celibacy, is known as *sannyāsa.* Human experience suggests that this is not an easy vow to keep, so is it not likely that a group of male renunciants living under such a vow but unable to keep it may turn to homosexual practices? Somewhat similar doubts were expressed by a French cleric, Abbé J. A. Dubois, in the early years of the nineteenth century as he toured South India. He presents no evidence but does emphasize the probability of the above-mentioned scenario when he refers to the hypocrites among the renunciants as knaves who "in the seclusion of their retreats, give themselves up to the grossest immoralities."[81] Although remaining charitable to the Hindu institution, he nevertheless implies the existence of variant practices that could well include homosexuality:

It must not be supposed, however, that I am accusing all unmarried Hindus without exception of leading dissolute lives. On the contrary, I have been credibly informed by those whose word may be relied on, and who know what they are talking about, that some few may be found who deny themselves all intercourse with women; but, on the other hand, *one is led to believe that they allow themselves other infamous pleasures of such an abominable character that delicacy forbids one to accept the accusation except under strong proof;* so I prefer to think that there are a few unmarried Hindus who are able to resist all sensual pleasures.[82]

The sex-positive approach to liberation in Hinduism is represented by Tantra. In the Tantrika scheme, the spiritual power in human beings in its dormant state is visualized as a coiled serpent (*kuṇḍalinī*) at the base of the spine which, in the course of spiritual awakening, passes through several *cakras*, or centers, located along the spinal column and completes its journey by reaching the cerebrum—a journey that culminates in Enlightenment. The various *cakras*, or centers, through which it passes may now be depicted. In Śākta Tantra and Haṭha Yoga, the "serpent power (*kuṇḍalinī*) is found in its latent form around the sex organ; that is called Mūlādhāra Cakra. The vital energy, instead of getting out of the organ of generation, is transformed into spiritual energy"[83] by turning inside, whereupon it passes through centers that roughly correspond to the five divisions of the vertebral column: coccygeal (*mūlādhāra*), sacral (*svādhiṣṭhāna*), lumbar (*maṇipūraka*), dorsal (*anāhata*), and cervical (*viśuddha*), while *ājñā* is placed between the eyebrows and *sahasrāra* at the top of the brain.[84]

Attention must now be focused on the first of these *cakras*, the *mūlādhāra*, located in the anal region. It has been pointed out that "the anus (*gudā* or *pāyu*) is one of the most important *chakras* ('center of psychic energy') in the human body, its significance repeatedly emphasized in the Tantric texts with what might be called homosexual overtones. In fact,

anal intercourse of *adhorata* (literally, under love), either between males or between males and females, was one of the
main expedients for using the potential of the rectal center,
whose animation was believed to energize the artistic, poetic,
and mystical faculties."[85] The extent of this practice, at least in
Hindu Tantra, is not entirely clear. No evidence is adduced in
support of the above claim. It must be remembered that seminal potency must be interiorized for salvific purposes; otherwise, all that would happen, in terms of the Hindu belief in
the power of semen, is that "the passive partner would
thrive"—but physically, not spiritually, "being enriched by the
other's semen."[86]

Hindu Tantra seems much more inclined toward the de-
ification of the females and the female principle.[87] Vern L. Bullough seems to assess the situation correctly when he writes:

> There is obvious homosexual connotation in some tantric the-
> ory, although little direct evidence supports its widespread exis-
> tence. Nevertheless, it seems clear that each partner in the sex
> act must reorient and refashion his personality, recognizing the
> elements of the opposite sex in himself or herself. There can be
> a profound personal relationship between a man and a woman,
> but there can also be an overpowering recognition of the oppo-
> site sex within an individual. In tantric cults a man can take on
> a feminine role in identifying with his mother or some other
> woman, and since his ego now feels as female, the woman as a
> love object is obliterated. He assumes the interests of a woman,
> is effeminate, and throws out his masculinity. On the whole,
> however, the person who achieves true integration of his male-
> ness and femaleness deepens the awareness of his emotional
> satisfaction, and those who have found enlightenment will live
> in the center of existence rather than be precariously situated
> on the periphery, that is, neither male nor female.[88]

One may now turn to some forms of Bhakti in which one's
devotion may acquire homosexual overtones. In the practice of
bhakti, devotion to one's chosen deity is often modeled on human relationships, as of servant to master, son to father, lover
to beloved. Of these, two seem to verge on homosexuality. One
is the worship of the divine as mother. In "South India, sexual
union is likened to the hand of the mother feeding rice to the
child," and this is "an image that involves the transformation
of a male partner into a woman (the mother who feeds rice/

seed to the 'child'—the womb/mouth of the female partner)."[89] This could be said to be suggestive of homosexuality. But a stronger case of this type appears to be connected with devotion to the deity on the lover-beloved model (*madhura bhāva*). The famous example here is the devotion of Caitanya, the celebrated saint of the 15/16th centuries, to Rādhā, the consort of Kṛṣṇa:

> Caitanya's involuted relationship with Kṛṣṇa, Rādhā, and his own external form may be seen as a kind of *imitatio dei;* for it is said that once, after a quarrel, Kṛṣṇa himself dressed like a woman in order to be close to Rādhā; Rādhā embraced "her" passionately, whereupon Rādhā became Kṛṣṇa (*Vilvamaṅgala* 2.75). The worshiper who imagines himself as female, and dresses like one, in order to be with Kṛṣṇa, is expressing the explicitly heterosexual (and perhaps implicitly homosexual) erotic relationship with god; but that god himself is also imagined as participating in an explicitly homosexual embrace (he, as female, embracing the female Rādhā) with his actually heterosexual consort. This tension is then resolved by yet another transformation: Rādhā becomes Kṛṣṇa. For most Vaiṣṇavas, direct identification with Kṛṣṇa was forbidden; Caitanya was an exception. But any worshiper might identify with Rādhā—and, as she becomes Kṛṣṇa, her own transmutation forms a mediation for the worshiper, her own androgyny linking the male worshiper with the male god.[90]

Examples could be multiplied, but the fact remains that although homosexual models may be identifiable in the kaleidoscopic range of relationships possible between a devotee and a deity in Hindu devotional theism, homosexuality per se is not claimed to lead to *mokṣa*.

Conclusions

Vern L. Bullough concludes his survey of sexual variance on the Indian subcontinent in this way: "In effect, it seems as if the Indian subcontinent turned the ideas of the West almost totally around, and much that was desirable in the West was undesirable in India and what was undesirable in the West was desirable, or at least tolerated in India. This view lends added support to the belief that many of our Western ideas about sex have been based on Greek philosophical assumptions rather than on any moral absolutes indigenous to civilized humanity."[91]

How far does the evidence regarding homosexuality and attitudes to it confirm or challenge such a conclusion? Is Parrinder's comment that in India "some medieval writers regarded 'under-love' or male homosexuality, as quite common and not a perversion"[92] capable of being upheld and perhaps even capable of a wider application? Or is it an exaggeration?

It appears from the foregoing account that, *save for the emphasis on renunciation,* Hinduism is a sex-positive religion in relation to all the three ends of human life—*dharma, artha, kāma*—and even in relation to *mokṣa* in the context of Tantra. This should not be taken to mean, however, that it also views homosexuality within the general field of sex in a positive light. Dharma and Artha literature is somewhat opposed to it; Kāma literature is not opposed to it but is not markedly supportive either. In any case, it is constrained by Dharma values. Mokṣa literature would have no sex at all, heterosexual sex as in some forms of Tantra, or only symbolic homosexualism in some forms of devotional Hinduism. That even symbolically some forms of Hinduism should be latently homosexual is indeed significant.

We should, however, distinguish between Hindu religious attitudes and Hindu cultural attitudes. As a religion, Hinduism is perhaps more tolerant of homosexuality than it is as a culture, and the underlying reason seems to be historical. Among the various non-Hindu cultures with which Hindu culture has undergone significant periods of encounter are the Greek, the Islamic, and the British. It has been suggested that such traces of homosexuality as one finds in ancient India may have been at least in part due to the Greek presence.[93] This point must remain conjectural. The evidence in relation to Islam is easier to document. Albiruni (973–1048), for instance, informs us that "when Kabul was conquered by the Muslims and the Ispahbad of Kabul adopted Islam, he stipulated that he should not be bound to eat cow's meat nor to commit sodomy (which proves that he abhorred the one as much as the other)."[94] Albiruni perhaps found it indelicate to draw the equally obvious conclusion—that the Hindus associated beef eating and sodomy equally with Islam. The autobiography of Bābar[95] further confirms the strong association of homosexuality with later Muslim rulers of the Moghul dynasty, which is regarded as the last major dynasty prior to the establishment of British rule in India.

One of the best-known leaders of the Indian National Movement, J. L. Nehru, observes:

> It is clear from Greek literature that homosexual relations were not looked upon with disfavor. Indeed there was a romantic approval of them. Possibly this was due to the segregation of the sexes in youth. A similar attitude is found in Iran, and Persian literature is full of such references. It appears to have become an established literary form and convention to represent the beloved as a male companion. There is no such thing in Sanskrit literature, and homosexuality was evidently neither approved nor at all common in India.[96]

No invidious comparison seems to be intended by the passage, and it is interesting that Nehru associates homosexuality with Persia as a culture rather than with Islam as a religion. This may reflect the facts of the situation more accurately; nevertheless, it is clear that given the moral ethos of the time when the passage was written, the Hindus come out looking better. As for Christianity, in popular Hindu perception it did not figure prominently. "Even Mr. Gandhi, when a young man, had the impression that Christianity compelled men to eat beef, drink liquor, and wear European clothes, and he was repelled by a religion which appeared to him not to deserve its name."[97] There is, however, no insinuation that Christianity was involved in homosexuality, though Western culture was probably not exempted, and homosexuality may well be part and parcel of the general profligacy prevailing in the West, according to Gandhi.[98] But the West to India then meant Britain. The British presence in India was represented in the main by the British Army[99] and the British Administration. The latter was headed by the I.C.S., usually with Oxbridge and public school connections[100] in which homosexuality seems to have flourished.[101] The racial exclusiveness maintained by the British may have prevented them from practicing homosexuality with Indians, but presumably the British continued their "Greek" tradition in racially exclusive clubs and in the mother country.[102]

Thus, although within classical Hinduism homosexuality was only a matter of marginal concern and disapproval, medieval and modern Hinduism[103] tends to associate the practice with an outgroup with whom its encounter has not always been pleasant or peaceful. It seems that in Neo-Hinduism, with the strong element within it of Hindu nationalism as a cultural reaction to foreign domination, homosexuality has come to be identified increasingly as characteristic of the dominant minorities—the Muslims and the British—and therefore reprehensible by association. The influence of the Gandhian idealism that imparted a puritanical tone to Indian nationalism, of the Independence Movement,[104] of Gandhi himself (who, like Hinduism itself,[105] is better characterized by psychological bisexuality or androgyny than homosexuality), and of the depiction of the struggle for independence as between virtue and vice (with homosexuality included in the category of vice by implication)[106] has injected a stronger moral dimension into the assessment of homosexuality than might have been the case otherwise. It is interesting that Gandhi should have called Western civilization Satanic when there is no Satan per se in Hinduism, and it is further a point of some interest that although Luther sees the desire "contrary to nature" as "undoubtedly from Satan,"[107] Gandhi does not say so but would have agreed inasmuch as for him even desire not "contrary to nature" was not entirely free from Satan's influence.[108]

If traditional Balinese culture is taken as representative of at least a trans-Indian form of Hinduism, the Hindi attitude to homosexuality is one of mild amusement bordering on indifference;[109] but if modern India is taken as representative, Neo-Hinduism is now so hostile to it that "no community admits of homosexual practices, though each accuses the others."[110]

Notes

1. *Webster's Third New International Dictionary*, s.v. "homo."

2. Ibid., s.v. "lesbianism."

3. The word *sodomy* will be avoided as far as possible because of its ambiguity. In the subentry under India for this term given in James Hastings, ed., *Encyclopedia of Religion and Ethics* (New York:

Charles Scribner's Sons, 1921), p. 673, not a single instance of homosexuality has been cited, only cases of immoral sexual intercourse.

4. Benjamin Walker, *The Hindu World* (London: George Allen & Unwin, 1968), vol. 2, p. 199.

5. Monier Monier-Williams, *A Sanskrit-English Dictionary* (Oxford: Clarendon Press, 1964 [1899]), p. 238.

6. K. J. Dover, *Greek Homosexuality* (London: Gerald Duckworth & Co., 1978).

7. Vern L. Bullough, *Homosexuality: A History* (New York: New American Library, 1979).

8. A. L. Basham, *The Wonder That Was India* (New York: Grove Press, 1954), p. 172. See, for instance, Sushil Kumar, *Ancient Indian Erotics and Erotic Literature* (Calcutta: Firma K. L. Mukhopadhyan, 1969), passim.

9. See G. Morris Carstairs, *The Twice-Born* (Bloomington: Indiana University Press, 1967), pp. 72 and 148 for examples; pp. 161, 163, and 167 for repressed homosexuality in modern India. As for earlier times, I do not have the results of some recent research available to me as represented by Leonard Zwilling's paper "Homosexuality in Pre-Muslim India," presented at the Conference on South Asia, Madison, Wisconsin (1978), nor the Buddhist evidence on the point presented by Leonard Zwilling at the 1987 annual meeting of the American Academy of Religion in Boston entitled "Homosexuality as Seen in Indian Buddhist Texts."

10. See Leonard Zwilling, "Sanskrit Terminology of Sexual Variation and Dysfunction with Special Reference to Homosexuality," paper presented at the annual meeting of the American Oriental Society, Boston (1981). The importance of the issue can be gauged from the following passage: "The laws of Manu say (V, 85), 'When he has touched a *Caṇḍāla*, a menstruating woman, an outcaste, a woman who has just given birth, a corpse . . . he purifies himself by bathing.' Here the three occasional impurities are identified with that of the 'outcaste' and the *Caṇḍāla*, who is none other than the old prototype of the Untouchable. There is another list in the same book at III, 239, 'A *Caṇḍāla*, a domestic pig, a cock, a dog, a menstruating woman and a eunuch must not look at Brahmans while they are eating,' and the following verse adds that the same people likewise render certain sorts of ritual ineffective. We shall see that a man who is eating is particularly vulnerable to impurity; moreover the animals mentioned feed on refuse and filth which they find in the village and its outskirts. Here again, functional characteristics are thus equated with individual events as sources of impurity, and different sorts of impurity are confused. *The case of the eunuch remains to be explained*" (Louis Dumont, *Homo Hierarchichus*, trans. Mark Sainsbury [Chicago: University of Chicago Press, 1970], p. 52, emphasis added). If eunuch

is a synonym or even a reincarnatory reference to a homosexual, the mystery is lessened.

11. Dover, p. vii.

12. Vern L. Bullough, *Sexual Variance in Society and History* (Chicago: University of Chicago Press, 1976), p. 263.

13. Ibid.

14. Walker, p. 199.

15. S. Geoffrey Parrinder, *Sex in the World's Religions* (London: Sheldon Press, 1980), p. 21.

16. Johann Jakob Meyer, *Sexual Life in Ancient India* (London: Routledge & Kegan Paul, 1952 [1930]), p. 242.

17. Meyer, p. 243: "Also MBh., xii, 228.73 would belong here, if *kaścic chishyasakho guruḥ* has been rightly translated by Deussen: 'Now and then the teacher was the disciple's lover' (the immorality which spread among the Daityas is being spoken of). But perhaps it only means that the disciple's reverential relation towards the teacher vanished, and too little restraint, or over-familiarity, came in its stead. As an evil habit of the degenerates it may here be further mentioned that the men dressed in women's clothes and the women in men's, and they so associated with one another (śl. 68), which reminds us of other phenomena known. Cp. xiii, 104.85.—The passage in the text (iii, 190.45, 50) could, it is true, also be speaking only of adultery."

18. Wendy Doniger O'Flaherty, *Sexual Metaphors and Animal Symbols in Indian Mythology* (Delhi: Motilal Banarsidass, 1980), pp. 50–51.

19. Henry K. Beauchamp, ed., *Hindu Manners, Customs and Ceremonies by the Abbé J. A. Dubois* (Oxford: Clarendon Press, 1959), p. 288.

20. Evidence on the prevalence or otherwise of homosexuality among Hindu communities outside India would also enlarge the database. A study of twins in traditional Balinese culture contains the interesting information that the "Balinese consider homosexual relations to be a form of play activity (*main-main*) not to be taken seriously" and that although barren women are destined to hell, "no such fate awaits the homosexual" (Jane Belo, ed., *Traditional Balinese Culture* [London: Columbia University Press, 1970], p. 5). Also see *Journal of Homosexuality* 11, no. 3/4 (Summer 1985), the thematic issue on anthropology and homosexual behavior, for more evidence both within and outside India.

21. For a detailed discussion, see Arvind Sharma, *The Puruṣārthas: A Study in Hindu Axiology,* South Asia Series, Occasional Paper No. 32 (East Lansing: Michigan State University Press, 1982).

22. William Theodore de Bary et al., *Sources of Indian Tradition* (Delhi: Motilal Banarsidass, 1963), p. 211.

23. See Heinrich Zimmer, *Philosophies of India,* ed. Joseph Campbell (New York: Pantheon Books, 1951), pp. 34–42.

24. Bullough, *Sexual Variance*, p. 277, n. 5.

25. G. Bühler, trans., *The Laws of Manu* (Delhi: Motilal Banarsidass, 1967 [1886]), p. 466.

26. Bullough, *Sexual Variance*, p. 248.

27. Bühler, p. 466, n. 175.

28. Kāmasūtra II.IX.22.

29. The association of homosexuality with lower classes persists to this day; see Carstairs, p. 321.

30. A recent study of homosexuals in Indian prisons has shown that (1) homosexual acts are highest among illiterate inmates and (2) they are found to be highest among inmates sentenced under dacoity with murder; see S. P. Srivastava, "Social Profile of Homosexuals in an Indian Prison," *Eastern Anthropologist* 26, no. 4 (1973): 313–322.

31. Bühler, p. 466. It is surprising to claim in view of this verse that Manu does not mention "act in the improper parts even with one's wife" (R. S. Betai, *A Reconstruction of the Original Interpretations of the Manusmṛti* [Ahmedabad: Gujerat University Press, 1970], p. 428).

32. This seems to be the basis of the observation that "lesbianism . . . brought fines and beatings to a girl, and head shaved or two fingers severed for a woman who polluted a girl and she had to ride through the town on a donkey. Male homosexuality seemed to receive less punishment, 'a twice-born man who commits an unnatural offence with a male shall bathe, dressed in his clothes' says one law, but another prescribed loss of his caste" (Parrinder, pp. 20–21).

33. Bühler, p. 466.

34. Meyer, p. 242, n. 2.

35. Bühler, p. 318, n. 370.

36. Meyer, p. 242, n. 1.

37. P. V. Kane, *History of Dharmaśāstra* (Poona: Bhandarkar Oriental Research Institute, 1977), vol. 5, pt. 2, p. 1056. It has sometimes been suggested that the ritual elevation of women was not accompanied by improvement in their social position (see Y. Y. Haddad and E. B. Findly, eds., *Women, Religion, and Social Change* [Albany: SUNY Press, 1985], p. 373, n. 28). Although not questioning the need for caution on this score, it is clear that the Tantrikas had a social agenda as well (see Arvind Sharma et al., *Sati: Historical and Phenomenological Essays* [Delhi: Motilal Banarsidass, 1988], pp. 16–17).

38. Bühler, p. 444.

39. Parrinder, p. 21.

40. Meyer, p. 242.

41. Bühler, p. 429.

42. Bullough, *Sexual Variance*, p. 248.

43. The reference here is to the vulgate edition, emphasis added.

44. The reference here is to the vulgate edition as well.

45. Meyer, p. 242. Another possible meaning of *viyoni* may be added: "The importance of self-stimulation is evident by the number of artificial aids, *apadravya*, literally 'bad implements,' or in the West what are known as *olisboi* or dildos. There were *apadravya* designed to take the place of the *yoni*, to take the place of the *liṅga*, and to heighten satisfaction in intercourse itself. The first category is not so numerous but included the *viyoni* ('without *yoni*') employed by men. It was made of wood and cloth and shaped like the female, with a *yoni*-shaped aperture of fruit, vegetables, and leaves. They were probably used more in fertility rites than for other purposes, since as a general rule, a punishment was prescribed for any man who availed himself of an idol of any kind for self-gratification" (Bullough, *Sexual Variance*, p. 264).

46. The fact that "Vātsyāyana also gave an overview of the various parts of India where the inhabitants engaged in different kinds of sexual techniques, and of the type of *olisboi* or dildos used, and of whether they preferred anal, oral, or vaginal intercourse" involves descriptive statements rather than moral judgment.

47. Bullough, p. 248.

48. Meyer, p. 242.

49. Ibid., pp. 242–243.

50. Ibid., pp. 245ff.

51. D. R. Patil, *Cultural History from the Vāyu Purāṇa* (Delhi: Motilal Banarsidass, 1973), p. 75.

52. Bullough, *Sexual Variance*, p. 261.

53. But see M. N. D. Shastri, trans., *The Garuḍa-Purāṇam* (Varanasi: Chowkhamba Sanskrit Series Office, 1968), pp. 300, 303.

54. Walker, p. 343, emphasis added.

55. Vettam Mani, *Purāṇic Encyclopedia* (Delhi: Motilal Banarsidass, 1975), p. 677.

56. Bullough, *Sexual Variance*, p. 267.

57. Kane, vol. 3, p. 893.

58. Bullough, *Sexual Variance*, p. 265.

59. Ibid., p. 263.

60. Kane, vol. 3, p. 534.

61. K. A. Nilakanta Sastri and G. Srinivasachari, *Advanced History of India* (New Delhi: Allied Publishers, 1971), pp. 94, 111ff.

62. Kane, vol. 2, pt. 1, p. 61.

63. Kane, vol. 3, p. 9.

64. Personal communication, Prof. R. W. Lariviere, University of Texas, Austin.

65. D. A. Gangadhar, *Mahatma Gandhi's Philosophy of Brahmacarya* (Bangalore: Christian Institute for the Study of Religion and Society, 1984), p. 38.

66. J. Bruce Long, "Love," in Mircea Eliade, ed., *The Encyclopedia of Religion* (New York: Macmillan, 1987), vol. 9, p. 34, emphasis added.

67. For details, see Bullough, *Sexual Variance*, pp. 261–262.

68. Devangana Desai, *Erotic Sculpture of India: A Socio-Cultural Study* (New Delhi: Tata McGraw-Hill Publishing Co., 1975), p. 176.

69. Bullough, *Sexual Variance*, p. 262.

70. Dover, p. 164.

71. Bullough, *Sexual Variance*, p. 254.

72. Ibid., p. 252.

73. See summary of UN report, Montreal *Gazette*, 10 August 1988, p. A-9.

74. Meyer, p. 240.

75. Ibid.

76. Bullough, *Sexual Variance*, p. 266.

77. Parrinder, p. 19.

78. J. Muir, *Original Sanskrit Text* (Delhi: Oriental Publishers, 1972 reprint), pp. 105–106.

79. Cited by O'Flaherty, p. 295.

80. *Kama Sutra* (New Delhi: R. & K. Publishing House, 1977), pp. 180–181.

81. Beauchamp, p. 206.

82. Ibid., emphasis added.

83. Gangadhar, pp. 37–38.

84. T. M. P. Mahadevan, *Outlines of Hinduism* (Bombay: Chetana Limited, 1960), p. 212.

85. Bullough, *Sexual Variance*, p. 263.

86. Carstairs, p. 72.

87. Kane, vol. 6, pt. 2, pp. 1056, 1092.

88. Bullough, *Sexual Variance*, p. 274.

89. O'Flaherty, p. 106.

90. Ibid., p. 299.

91. Bullough, *Sexual Variance*, p. 276.

92. Parrinder, p. 21.

93. Professor D. P. Singhal expressed this possibility in a discussion of Greek influence on Indian culture. The view gains credence from the fact that alien invasions are associated by historians

with the development of the concept of Kaliyuga (Basham, p. 321), which is characterized by the prevalence of homosexuality (lesbianism) as a symptom of moral decay, and the aliens are often referred to as *Yavanas*, a word used primarily though not exclusively for Greeks in Indian literature.

94. Ainslie T. Embree, ed., *Albiruni's India* (New York: W. W. Norton & Co., 1971), p. 157.

95. See Annette Susannah Beveridge, trans., *The Babur-nama in English* (London: Luzac & Co., 1922), vol. 1, pp. 120–121.

96. Jawaharlal Nehru, *The Discovery of India* (New York: The John Day Company, 1946), p. 146.

97. L. S. S. O'Malley, ed., *Modern India and the West* (London: Oxford University Press, 1941), p. 674.

98. D. G. Tendulkar, *Mahatma* (Government of India: Publications Division, 1951), vol. 1, p. 197.

99. More information on cases of "unnatural offenses" in the British Army will be helpful here.

100. Percival Griffiths, *The British Impact on India* (London: Frank Cass & Co., 1965), p. 203.

101. See, e.g., Louis Crompton, *Byron and Greek Lore: Homophobia in 19th Century England* (Berkeley: University of California Press, 1985); Richard Ellman, *Oscar Wilde* (London: Hamilton, 1987); and Richard Jenkins, *The Victorians and Ancient Greece* (Cambridge: Harvard University Press, 1980).

102. Bullough, *Homosexuality*, pp. 104–108.

103. This should not be taken to mean that modern Hindu scholars are not probing the phenomenon at all. See, e.g., S. N. Rampal, *Indian Women and Sex* (New Delhi: Princtox, 1978), pp. 145–146, 157, 177, 186, for the relevance of the Kinsey report to India. For sexual attitudes in relation to the West in general, see Akhileshwar Jha, *Sexual Designs in Indian Culture* (New Delhi: Vikas Publishing House Pvt. Ltd, 1979), Appendix; Jitendra Tuli, *The Indian Male: Attitude Towards Sex* (New Delhi: Chetana Publications, 1976), p. 17.

104. Tendulkar, vol. 2, pp. 338–340; vol. 5, pp. 194–196.

105. Erik H. Erikson, *Gandhi's Truth* (New York: W. W. Norton & Co., 1969), pp. 44, 157, 402–406. The word *bisexual* has been used here specifically and only in the sense used by Erikson.

106. The influence of prevailing Christian attitudes toward homosexuality on Gandhi cannot be ruled out, ironical as it may be.

107. See Bullough, *Homosexuality*, p. 28. In this context, the fact that Erik Erikson should write a book on Luther and then one on Gandhi is surely a coincidence—but an interesting one.

108. For disapproval of homosexuality among modern Hindus, see Carstairs, pp. 60, 148, 320.

109. Belo, p. 5.

110. Carstairs, p. 320.

A few additional remarks may be in order: (1) References to homosexuality in Hinduism can be traced as far back as the Brāhmaṇa period (circa 1000 B.C.). The *Jaiminīya Brāhmaṇa* refers to "the fruitless coupling of two men or two women" (I.300, I.330; see Brian K. Smith, *Reflections on Resemblance, Ritual and Religion* [Oxford University Press, 1989], p. 52); (2) Homosexuality also appears in the context of sexual metaphors, although sometimes involving "mixed metaphors" as in cases of oral sex (see Wendy Doniger O'Flaherty, *Women, Androgynes and Other Mythical Beasts* [Chicago and London: University of Chicago Press, 1980], pp. 38, 50–51, 88–89, 92–93, esp. pp. 50–51); (3) The adoption of the attitude of a female devotee toward God in Hindu devotionalism is held by some to be latently homosexual (ibid., p. 89); (4) In Tantra, despite its attempt to harness sexuality for spiritual ends, homosexuality does not seem to figure in any significant way in the literature available so far; (5) Some groups "may be closely linked with homosexuality (as in the notorious case of the Hijras, transvestites and homosexual prostitutes)" (ibid., p. 89). This point seems to receive support from the account of the Jesuit Abbé Dubois, "who visited India in the nineteenth century. A Brahmin he asked about the male transvestite prostitutes seen in the streets of all the larger Indian towns replied, 'there was no accounting for tastes'" (David F. Greenberg, *The Construction of Homosexuality* [Chicago and London: University of Chicago Press, 1988], p. 170, n. 267); (6) The Hijras, or eunuchs, are an important group in the context of homosexuality as well. On the Hijras as representing "an institutionalized third gender role in India" with homosexual overtones, see Serena Nanda, "The Hijras in India: Cultural and Individual Dimensions of an Institutionalized Third Gender Role," *Journal of Homosexuality* 11, no. 3/4 (Summer 1985): 42; (7) Current attitudes toward homosexuality in India also tie into the Hindu heritage; for details, see Edward Gargan, "Gays come out in India," Montreal *Gazette,* 16 September 1991, p. B3, in which two accounts from Hindu mythology are alluded to: (a) "In the Mahabharata . . . the tale is told of the God Krishna dressing as a woman and giving himself as the first sexual experience for the first-born son of Arjuna . . . who was heading off to war"; (b) Kerala's most popular God Ayappan "is said to have been born of the homosexual union of Gods Shiva and Vishnu."

Bibliography

Basham, A. L. 1954. *The Wonder That Was India.* New York: Grove Press.

Beauchamp, Henry K., ed. 1959. *Hindu Manners, Customs and Ceremonies by the Abbé J. A. Dubois.* Oxford: Clarendon Press.

Belo, Jane, ed. 1970. *Traditional Balinese Culture.* London: Columbia University Press.

Betai, R. S. 1970. *A Reconstruction of the Original Interpretations of the Manusmṛti.* Ahmedabad: Gujerat University Press.

Beveridge, Annette Susannah, trans. 1922. *The Babur-nama in English.* London: Luzac & Co.

Bühler, G., trans. 1967. *The Laws of Manu.* Delhi: Motilal Banarsidass.

Bullough, Vern L. 1976. *Sexual Variance in Society and History.* Chicago: University of Chicago Press.

———. 1979. *Homosexuality: A History.* New York: New American Library.

Carstairs, Morris G. 1967. *The Twice-Born.* Bloomington: Indiana University Press.

Crompton, Louis. 1985. *Byron and Greek Lore: Homophobia in 19th Century England.* Berkeley: University of California Press.

de Bary, William Theodore, et al. 1963. *Sources of Indian Tradition.* Delhi: Motilal Banarsidass.

Desai, Devangana. 1975. *Erotic Sculpture of India: A Socio-Cultural Study.* New Delhi: Tata McGraw-Hill Publishing Co.

Dover, K. J. 1978. *Greek Homosexuality.* London: Gerald Duckworth & Co.

Dumont, Louis. 1970. *Homo Hierarchichus.* Translated by Mark Sainsbury. Chicago: University of Chicago Press.

Ellman, Richard. 1987. *Oscar Wilde.* London: British Hamilton.

Embree, Ainslie T., ed. 1971. *Albiruni's India.* New York: W. W. Norton & Co.

Erikson, Erik H. 1969. *Gandhi's Truth.* New York: W. W. Norton & Co.

Gangadhar, D. A. 1984. *Mahatma Gandhi's Philosophy of Brahmacarya.* Bangalore: Christian Institute for the Study of Religion and Society.

Greenberg, David F. 1988. *The Construction of Homosexuality.* Chicago and London: University of Chicago Press.

Griffiths, Percival. 1965. *The British Impact on India.* London: Frank Cass & Co.

Haddad, Y. Y., and E. B. Findly, eds. 1985. *Women, Religion, and Social Change.* Albany: SUNY Press.

Hastings, James, ed. 1921. *Encyclopedia of Religion and Ethics.* New York: Charles Scribner's Sons.

Jenkins, Richard. 1980. *The Victorians and Ancient Greece.* Cambridge: Harvard University Press.

Jha, Akhileshwar. 1979. *Sexual Designs in Indian Culture.* New Delhi: Vikas Publishing House Pvt. Ltd.

Kama Sutra. 1977. New Delhi: R. & K. Publishing House.

Kane, P. V. 1977. *History of Dharmaśāstra.* Vols. 2, 3, 5, 6. Poona: Bhandarkar Oriental Research Institute.

Kumar, Sushil. 1969. *Ancient Indian Erotics and Erotic Literature.* Calcutta: Firma K. L. Mukhopadhyay.

Long, Bruce. 1987. "Love." In *The Encyclopedia of Religion,* edited by Mircea Eliade, 9:34. New York: Macmillan.

Mahadevan, T. M. P. 1960. *Outlines of Hinduism.* Bombay: Chetana Limited.

Mani, Vettam. 1975. *Purāṇic Encyclopedia.* Delhi: Motilal Banarsidass.

Meyer, Johann Jakob. 1952. *Sexual Life in Ancient India.* London: Routledge & Kegan Paul.

Monier-Williams, Monier. 1964. *A Sanskrit-English Dictionary.* Oxford: Clarendon Press.

Muir, J. 1972. *Original Sanskrit Text.* Delhi: Oriental Publishers.

Nanda, Serena. 1985. "The Hijras in India: Cultural and Individual Dimensions of an Institutionalized Third Gender Role." *Journal of Homosexuality* 11, 3/4:42.

Nehru, Jawaharlal. 1946. *The Discovery of India.* New York: The John Day Company.

O'Flaherty, Wendy Doniger. 1980. *Sexual Metaphors and Animal Symbols in Indian Mythology.* Delhi: Motilal Banarsidass.

————. 1980. *Women, Androgynes and Other Mythical Beasts.* Chicago and London: University of Chicago Press.

O'Malley, L. S. S., ed. 1941. *Modern India and the West.* London: Oxford University Press.

Parrinder, S. Geoffrey. 1980. *Sex in the World's Religions.* London: Sheldon Press.

Patil, D. R. 1973. *Cultural History from the Vāyu Purāṇa.* Delhi: Motilal Banarsidass.

Rampal, S. N. 1978. *Indian Women and Sex.* New Delhi: Princtox.

Sastri, K. A. Nilakanta, and G. Srinivasachari. 1971. *Advanced History of India.* New Delhi: Allied Publishers.

Sharma, Arvind. 1982. *The Puruṣārthas: A Study in Hindu Axiology.* South Asia Series, Occasional Paper No. 32. East Lansing: Michigan State University Press.

————, et al. 1988. *Sati: Historical and Phenomenological Essays.* Delhi: Motilal Banarsidass.

Shastri, M. N. D., trans. 1968. *The Garuḍa-Purāṇam.* Varanasi: Chowkhamba Sanskrit Series Office.

Smith, Brian K. 1989. *Reflections on Resemblance, Ritual and Religion.* New York and Oxford: Oxford University Press.

Srivastava, S. P. "Social Profile of Homosexuals in an Indian Prison." *Eastern Anthropologist* 26, 4:313–322.

Tendulkar, D. G. 1951. *Mahatma.* Vols. 1, 2, 5. Government of India: Publications Division.

Tuli, Jitendra. 1976. *The Indian Male: Attitude Towards Sex.* New Delhi: Chetana Publications.

Walker, Benjamin. 1968. *The Hindu World.* Vol. 2. London: George Allen & Unwin.

Webster's Third New International Dictionary. Springfield, Mass.: Merriam Webster.

Zimmer, Heinrich. 1951. *Philosophies of India.* Edited by Joseph Campbell. New York: Pantheon Books.

Zwilling, Leonard. 1978. "Homosexuality in Pre-Muslim India." Paper presented at the Conference on South Asia, Madison, Wisconsin.

———. 1981. "Sanskrit Terminology of Sexual Variation and Dysfunction with Special Reference to Homosexuality." Paper presented at the annual meeting of the American Oriental Society, Boston.

———. 1987. "Homosexuality as Seen in Indian Buddhist Texts." Paper presented at the annual meeting of the American Academy of Religion, Boston.

3

*Homosexuality and Buddhism**

José Ignacio Cabezón

Little work of a scholarly nature has been done concerning homosexuality and the religious traditions of Asia in general, but there is a particular scarcity of scholarship in the area of Buddhism and homosexuality. In Gilbert Herdt's recent entry in *The Encyclopedia of Religion,*[1] for example, the Buddhist tradition is never mentioned. Only recently has scholarly attention turned to a discussion of this question.[2] Despite recent advances in the state of scholarship, the present status of research in this area can be considered only preliminary, and conclusions of a general theoretical or comparative nature can, at this stage, be considered only tentative.[3]

As with most of the world's major religious traditions, Buddhism has also enunciated views concerning homosexuality. However, the diversity of the Buddhist tradition (diachronically within a single cultural locus and both diachronically and synchronically from one ethnic and cultural region to another) has, at different places and times, led to divergent opinions regarding homosexuality. We find, for example, that

*An earlier version of this essay was presented at Yale University in 1988 at the Pedagogy and Politics Conference, the second annual meeting sponsored by the Gay and Lesbian Studies Center.

between early and late Japanese Buddhism there exists a distinct difference as regards attitudes toward male love, just as there exist tremendous differences in these attitudes between the Buddhism of India and the Buddhism of Japan. Given this fact, it makes no sense to speak of a single Buddhist position as regards same-sex relations. This makes it necessary to be clear concerning the historical period and geographical location being discussed.[4]

Despite the ambivalence concerning homosexuality in Buddhist history, the evidence seems to suggest that as a whole Buddhism has been for the most part neutral on the question of homosexuality. The principal question for Buddhism has not been one of heterosexuality vs. homosexuality but one of sexuality vs. celibacy. In this sense homosexuality, when condemned, is condemned more for being an instance of sexuality than for being *homos* (involving partners of the same sex).[5] The fact that Buddhism has been essentially neutral in this regard does not imply that the *cultures* in which Buddhism arose and flourished have always been neutral. Some, at certain times, have been tolerant of same-sex relations; others have not. However, because of the essential neutrality of the Buddhist tradition in this regard, it has adapted to particular sociocultural norms, so that throughout its history we find a wide gamut of opinions concerning homosexual activity, ranging from condemnation (never to the point of active persecution) to praise. Were Buddhist doctrine not neutral in this regard, it would be difficult to see how such disparate opinions regarding homosexuality could have emerged throughout Buddhist history.

Where condemnation of homosexuality occurs, it is for the most part ancillary to the general Buddhist critique of sexual desire. Hence, to understand the negative views concerning homosexuality it is first necessary to understand the Buddhist deprecation of sexuality in general. Here a distinction needs to be made between the place of sexuality in the elite/monastic and lay/folk lifestyles. Despite the fact that the Buddha extolled the celibate monastic life as the ideal, it is clear that he was a pragmatist, realizing that such a way of life would be undertaken only by a minority of his followers. Arising as it did from a *kṣatriya* (warrior/ruling caste) social milieu,

Buddhism has always extolled, at least at the lay level, the ideal of the successful and aggressive man in the world. This latter ideal, in obvious tension with the former, is of course that of the sexually active and procreative householder. The tension has been characterized variously by different scholars. Stanley Tambiah, in a sociopolitical context, has described it as the tension between "world conqueror" and "world renouncer."[6] Charles Keyes relies on a similar motif as an interpretive tool in his study of the custom of temporary monastic ordination popular among young men in Thailand, in which he shows how this period in the monastic life acts as an initiatory process that "ripens" the young man sexually, making him fit for marriage.[7] Hence, despite the fact that the celibate life has always been held to be supreme *sub specie aeternitatis,* this monastic ideal has always existed alongside a lay paradigm that extolled, at least for men, sexual, military, and social prowess. What is more, despite the lay precepts that prohibit drinking and adultery, as Leonard Zwilling points out, "it has traditionally been the case that only exceptionally pious or aged laypersons are expected to keep all of the precepts. . . . No Buddhist societies require teetotaling . . . and both the Tibetans and Sinhalese, to take two disparate examples, are far more flexible and nonjudgmental on such matters as pre- and extramarital sexuality than are Hindus, or conservative Christians for that matter."[8] What this means, of course, is that there is a flexibility to Buddhist ethics that takes for granted certain practices that are proscribed at the level of theory. Therefore, despite the ideal of monastic celibacy, the Buddhist tradition as it has manifested itself in various societies and times has been tolerant of diverse forms of sexual expression, especially at the lay level, but at times even in the monasteries, as we will see.

It should also be pointed out that this essay deals almost exclusively with *male* homosexuality, and here particularly in monastic settings. That lesbian relationships existed (and still exist) within Buddhist cultures is something that can hardly be denied. Yet, as in the West, there is a tremendous dearth of information regarding same-sex relations among women.[9] In the end we must conclude that what Judith C. Brown says of medieval European Christian culture rings just as true of the Buddhist case:

For Europeans had long found it difficult to accept that women could actually be attracted to other women. Their view of human sexuality was phallocentric—women might be attracted to men and men might be attracted to men, but there was nothing in a woman that could long sustain the sexual desires of another woman. In law, in medicine, and in the public mind, sexual relations between women were therefore ignored.[10]

Despite the fact that same-sex relations between women have been almost totally ignored, both in the traditional literature of Buddhism and by modern scholars, we do find references to lesbian acts in the *Vinaya,* the portion of the Buddhist canon devoted to monastic rules and discipline.[11] Moreover, both Louis Crompton and Bret Hinsch, in recent essays, have written of a Chinese play by Li Yu (1611–1680) concerning lesbianism, "Pitying the Fragrant Companion" (*Lian xiangban*). In it a young married woman meets and falls in love with a woman two years her junior in a Buddhist convent. They take vows as lovers before the Buddha image, and after several interesting scenes the play culminates with the married woman's convincing her husband to take her lover into the household as a second wife.[12] Hinsch has also written of the practice of lesbian marriages in a woman's organization that flourished in nineteenth-century Guangzhou known as the "Golden Orchid Association."[13] In a different context, Nancy Schuster Barnes writes of the Buddhist influence on this same movement:

Scores of women silk workers refused to marry and lived together as laywomen in groups very like Buddhist nuns' communities. These women were able to choose such a way of life because they were economically independent due to their work, and that was not owed to Buddhism; but the pattern of their lives in the community were. The nun's sangha has always provided an important alternative lifestyle for women in China and wherever else the order was strong; these modern Chinese women simply adapted the institution further to fit their own preferences.[14]

Apart from these few instances, however, there is very little available information concerning lesbianism in traditional Buddhist tradition.

As in various other religious traditions, Buddhist monastic life (or, as above, institutions modeled thereon) has always provided a religious lifestyle for lesbians and gay men who sought a socially acceptable alternative to marriage.[15] This is not to imply that homosexual activity has always been widely practiced in Buddhist monasteries and convents. Although more research needs to be done on the social structures and the interactions of the ordained in Buddhist monastic institutions, preliminary evidence seems to indicate that, apart from cases like that of Japan (see below), the vow of celibacy has traditionally been taken very seriously both by male and female monastics. Nonetheless, in an institution where such a vow has always been of primary importance[16] and in which the path of least resistance to its being broken has, by the unisex composition of the community, been same-sex relations, it is not surprising that we should find such cases discussed in the monastic literature. This, combined with the fact that Buddhist writings are, almost exclusively, the writings of monks, gives the entire discussion a particularly male monastic slant. Until more work is done on the lay aspects of Buddhism, and on those that deal with women, this lack of research will have to be accepted as a limitation of this or any other such study.[17]

One final point is worth commenting upon before turning to the different traditions. It is useful to keep in mind that the notion of "homosexuality" is a nineteenth-century European one, and we should not expect that either it or its modern evolutes will be either applicable or particularly illuminating as conceptual vehicles for explaining same-sex relations in cultural and historical contexts that are radically different from our own. This being the case, especially when dealing with other cultures, it seems to me necessary to unpack the Western notion of homosexuality in terms of its component parts. Therefore, even at the risk of sounding banal, it seems wise to stress at the outset the distinction between homosexual desire, a homosexual act, and a conscious self-identification as a person of homosexual orientation. Homosexual desire, for example, is often never consummated in a sexual act (at times remaining "filial"), and for many cultures a homosexual act implies nothing about the "orientation" of the actor. Indeed, in many cultures where homosexual acts occur, there is simply no notion of "homosexual orientation" with which to self-identify; and even in cultures where the notion is operative,

when a man takes the active role in homosexual anal intercourse (as the "penetrator"), this often never vitiates the man's
status as a normative heterosexual male. Zwilling's studies of
the Indian Buddhist texts, for example, have shown that there
was recognition of the fact that "socially normative males"
could [and did] engage in homosexual acts, without ever being
considered, either by themselves or by society, as homosexual
in their orientation. In addition, he describes the *paṇḍaka*, a category which, though broader than what we might call "persons
of homosexual orientation,"[18] includes within it both some lesbians and some homosexual men. The point is, of course, that
we should not expect that the Western conceptual construct
"homosexuality" will be a perfect fit when we are dealing with
notions operative in other cultures. Indeed, one of the more interesting aspects of comparative and cross-cultural studies of
homosexuality is precisely the exploration of the differences in
the semantic fields of key terms.

Part of exploring Buddhist views on homosexuality is examining homoerotic and filial feelings that were never consummated in a homosexual encounter. That the Buddhist
Order encouraged brotherly feelings among its members can
hardly be denied. We often read accounts of monks who had
unusually strong filial ties. If the Buddhist tradition is, as I
maintain, essentially neutral on the question of homosexuality,
this means that it rarely isolates homosexual activity and homoerotic feelings for special critique. On the contrary, we find
that in certain instances these are not only condoned, but actually praised.

When homosexuality is condemned, it has less to do with
these feelings or actions being *homo*sexual than with their being *sexual*. Of course, because most of our source material on
this subject comes from records related to the institution of
monasticism, and because Buddhist monks have a vow of strict
celibacy, it is not surprising that in these sources homosexuality should be condemned. Because we find in these works a
condemnation of sexuality in general,[19] however, we should not
take a condemnation of homosexual activity or feelings in such
a context as a censure of gay men and women. It is interesting
that, in the lay Buddhist context, we find few instances in

which homosexuality is explicitly condemned.[20] In both the texts that concern the ethical conduct of the layperson[21] and in the oral commentaries, it is noteworthy that the descriptions of the violation of the lay vow prohibiting sexual misconduct (*kāmamithyācarā*) rarely mention homosexuality as a transgression; nor is this due to lack of material on the subject. The tradition is quite specific in describing what constitutes a violation of this vow. It states that engaging in sexual intercourse at the wrong time (during times of special religious focus, such as the new or full moon, for example) or in the wrong place (in front of an image of the Buddha, for example) are all infractions of the vow. However, as noted by Zwilling,

> Buddhist tradition essentially conceives of sexual misconduct in terms of sexual relations with various types of prohibited women (*agamyā*), and the performance of non-procreative sexual acts. Among the commentators only (two) . . . include men among forbidden sexual objects.[22]

Given the fact that the tradition is quite specific about the nature of these violations and that elsewhere (in the monastic context) it does not shy away from explicitly mentioning homosexuality in regard to the vow of celibacy, we might surmise that the relatively infrequent references to such acts in the discussion of the transgressions of the lay vow prohibiting sexual misconduct are an indication of the fact that it was not widely considered to be a violation. We must keep in mind, however, that we are here arguing from silence.[23]

Homosexuality in Four Buddhist Cultures

I have chosen, in the brief survey that follows, to sweep across Asia as Buddhism itself did. Hence, we will examine homosexuality in the culture of classical Buddhist India, in Chinese Buddhist history, in the Buddhism of medieval Japan, and in Buddhist institutions in early twentieth-century Tibet.[24] We end with some reflections on contemporary North American Buddhist views regarding homosexuality.

India

It is primarily Leonard Zwilling's work with the Buddhist *Vinaya* (monastic discipline) and *Abhidharma* (metaphysics and cosmology), and John Garret Jones' work on the *Jataka* (the stories of the Buddha's previous lives) that allows us to glean Indian Buddhist attitudes toward homosexuality. In exhaustive research concerning the concept of *pandaka*, Zwilling shows that the term refers to those who suffer "from a variety of sexual dysfunctions and variations" and that "all share the common quality of being *napumsaka*, 'lacking maleness.'"[25] The term seems to ascribe to the *pandaka* more than the mere quality of being attracted to members of the same sex (which in any case was perceived as a possibility even for a man who fulfilled socially normative gender roles), implying, in addition, a certain effeminacy as well. Therefore, when a *pandaka* is characterized as being exceedingly lustful, incapable of following religious discipline (monastic ordination was denied to them), and vacillating in decision making, qualities that have with some frequency been ascribed to women in Buddhist literature, it is fair to suppose that these qualities in a *pandaka* are perceived as arising more from their effeminacy than from their attraction to members of the same sex.[26] In the end, Zwilling concludes that "when homosexual behavior is not ignored in the Indian Buddhist writings it is derogated much to the same degree as comparable heterosexual acts."[27]

Jones has also shown that the *Jataka* literature, a narrative genre depicting the former lives of the Buddha and his companions, is replete with homoerotic sentiments. Despite the fact that it is condemned in the *Vinaya* literature, he considers it significant that there is no direct reference to male homosexuality in the *Nikāya* literature.[28] He thus considers the silence regarding homosexuality in the *Nikāyas* as an implicit affirmation, though he cautions the reader, as I have done, that "arguments from silence are always hazardous." He concludes, in this regard:

> After all, in loving relationships of this kind, there was no temptation to forsake the Order, since both parties were equally

committed to it; there was no possibility of producing children and, in consequence, becoming saddled with just those cares and responsibilities one had joined the Order to escape; on the other hand, there was the possibility, since both were committed to the same teaching and the same training, of keeping the mutual attachment within reasonable bounds and ensuring that it did not hinder what each considered to be more important objectives.[29]

What is perhaps more significant than the silence of the *Nikāyas* is the eloquence of the *Jatakas.* Here, in explanation of the Buddha's close ties to his disciple and attendant, Ānanda, the texts depict a variety of past-life scenarios that are touching and at times homoerotically suggestive. In one of these the Buddha and Ānanda are depicted as two deer who "always went about together . . . ruminating and cuddling together, very happy, head to head, nozzle to nozzle, horn to horn."[30] In another, they are the two handsome young sons of Brahmin parents who refuse to marry so that they may remain with each other, and in yet another a serpent king falls in love with Ānanda. He "encircled the ascetic with snakes folds, and embraced him, with his great hood upon his head; and there he lay a little, till his affection was satisfied."[31] Jones concludes:

> In what is said about friendship in the Jatakas it is fairly clear that a good deal of homosexual emotion is operating. . . . When one remembers the enormous amount that is said in warning of the dangers of heterosexual relationships . . . it is quite remarkable that there is not one word of warning of the dangers of a homosexual relationship.[32]

What we witness in the Indian context, then, is a certain ambivalence. Where homosexual acts are condemned, they are condemned either for being transgressions of the monastic vow of celibacy or, in the case of the *paṇḍaka*, because it involves men taking on the culturally prescribed role of women through their sexual passivity. At the same time, in the Indian texts there are many "eloquent silences," to use a term of Jones, and in the *Jatakas* even instances of eloquent prose that suggest an acceptance, and occasionally even a eulogy, of homoerotic feelings and, if Jones is right, even of homosexual acts.

China

This same posture—a neutrality that emerges as ambivalence—seems to have characterized the attitude toward homosexuality in China as well.[33] However, very little work has been done on Chinese *Buddhist* attitudes toward homosexuality or on its existence in monastic settings during Imperial times. If, as stated by Louis Crompton, it is the case that the Chinese "perceptions of homosexuality were primarily aesthetic, literary and anecdotal, not moral, social, religious or scientific," then scriptural and other data on which to base our investigation of Chinese Buddhist attitudes toward homosexuality may not be forthcoming. Be that as it may, we know that at the very least both Confucianism and Taoism were neutral on the question of same-sex relations[34] and that, especially during Han times, it became the norm for emperors to have male lovers from all levels of Chinese society.[35] If the basic Buddhist stance toward homosexuality is, as I maintain, a neutral one, then we might expect, given the general cultural acceptance of homosexual love in classical China, that this same attitude would have been equally applicable to Chinese Buddhism, and that those who felt sexual attraction to members of their own sex might very easily have turned to Buddhist monasticism as a religious possibility that was compatible with their sexual preferences, whether or not these were ever physically expressed.

Holmes Welch, in his classic study *The Practice of Chinese Buddhism: 1900–1950,* concludes his section on "Sexual Activity" by stating that "it seems likely that the Monks of China were able to adjust themselves more easily to continence than their counterparts in Europe."[36] Although one of his informants, an ex-monk, claims to have seen homosexual activity in the monastery, when pressed for details what he describes seems to have been, according to Welch, filial relationships (primarily between older and younger monks). Most of Welch's informants, however, characterized homosexual attraction as a "low taste" (*hsia-liu*) and claimed that it was rare. This apparently hostile attitude seems to be a recent phenomenon in Chinese history, however. Hinsch has suggested several factors—influence from the Christian West among them—to explain why in the twentieth century the Chinese attitude toward homosexuality has changed from one of relative tolerance to one of open hostility.[37]

Although we do not know the extent to which homosexual activity existed in Chinese Buddhist monastic institutions, there is a legend that the founder of the Japanese Shingon sect, Kūkai (774–835), brought the practice of homosexuality with him from China. Whether or not the legend has any basis in fact,[38] it is clear from subsequent literature that this was viewed as one of Kūkai's many accomplishments,[39] enhancing his status as a religious figure.[40] This implies, of course, that basic Japanese attitudes toward male love were, by this time, essentially positive.

Japan

Though Buddhist attitudes toward homosexuality can in general be said to be neutral, the exception seems to be Japan, where it was extolled and praised as a secret and mysterious practice that was the greatest source of sexual pleasure available to man. From the fourteenth century on, we find a wide variety of literature devoted to the theme of male love in which the usual pattern is for an older monk to take a young temple acolyte (*chigo*) as a lover.[41] Maggie Childs has written of a short story attributed to the fourteenth century called *Chigo Kannon engi,* in which the bodhisattva of compassion, Kannon, rewards a particularly fervent practitioner with a beautiful young male lover (later revealed to be Kannon herself).[42] This genre of literature, called *chigo monogatari,* describes love affairs between an elder monk and *chigo* and often ends in the tragic death of one of the lovers, whereupon the survivor assiduously pursues a religious life dedicated to praying for the lost lover. Moreover, Paul Schalow has discussed the *Kōbō Daishi ikkan no sho,* a short text said to have been revealed by Kūkai to a monk as a boon for his prayers, in which techniques for seducing a *chigo* and the various positions for anal intercourse are described in detail.[43] The love of the *chigo* eventually gives way to *shudō* (literally, the "way of the young man") as the *samurai* pederastic ideal. Even in this more secular setting, however, we find the ideal of the love of boys still legitimized in Buddhist religious terms. Hence, *Inu tsurezure*, a seventeenth-century text, states:

> If you pray for happiness in future life, you must learn the teaching of the Buddha. If you learn the teaching of the Buddha and expect to achieve Awakening, you will surely practice *shudō*. For this way is truly like that of true Awakening, in that we may give ourselves wholly to it.[44]

In addition to a variety of homoerotic poetry that begins in the seventeenth century with Kitamura Kigin's *Iwatsusuji*, perhaps the most important and extensive work on the subject is the seventeenth-century work by Ihara Saikaku, *The Great Mirror of Male Love* (*Nanshoku ōkagami*). Here the structure of the work is one in which "the norm is the unabashed and enthusiastic enjoyment of male homosexual love, as if it were somehow outside the confines of Buddhist stricture."[45]

Japanese Buddhism (at least in the periods described above) is thus the exception to the rule. Instead of a guarded neutrality, the literature described above uses a variety of techniques to enhance the status of the homosexual love affair. Its origins are made sacred by its association with Kūkai and with the holy land of China. Moreover, the position of the *chigo* is legitimized by his portrayal as a boon for religious devotion, as a cause for his lover's returning to religious practice (after the *chigo*'s death), and by his identification with the figure of various heavenly beings and bodhisattvas. The reasons for this shift to the positive in the Japanese case are difficult to determine. A traditional view, expressed by one leading classical scholar—namely, that "since relations between the sexes are forbidden by Buddha, priests of the law, being made neither of stone nor wood, entered the way of homosexual love as an outlet for their feelings"[46] explains neither why homosexual relations should have attained the status they did only in Japanese Buddhism nor why the literature described above overlaps with the period in which the celibate monastic ideal was being discarded in favor of a married priesthood. Only further historical and literary research will be able to shed light on this question.

Tibet

In Tibet the practice of homosexuality seems to have been confined almost exclusively to the "working monks" of the larger monasteries. The *lDab ldob*, as they were called, were a fraternity of young monks (predominantly under the age of forty) who prided themselves on their abilities as fighters and athletes, participating regularly in inter- as well as intramural competitions. Either unwilling or unable to devote themselves to the rigorous academic curriculum of the monasteries, they took upon themselves the burden of the day-to-day tasks that kept the monastery functioning: "[We *lDab ldobs*] are the outer wall, [the other monks] the inner treasure."[47] Goldstein has written of the homosexual practices of the *lDab ldob*, which apparently included not only the seduction, but, if he is right, even the abduction of boys (and even, in rare cases, of adults) from the community for sexual purposes.[48] Because the monastic discipline defines the type of sexual intercourse that brings expulsion (*pārājika*) as penetration of the mouth or anus (of either sex) or of the vagina, it seems that the *lDab ldob* lived up to the letter, if not the spirit, of the law by engaging in a form of intercourse in which stimulation was achieved by insertion of the penis between the legs of the partner from behind.[49] It should be stated, however, that Goldstein's research was based on information gathered from only five informants, most of them lay persons. Although the fact of homosexual activity among the *lDab ldob* can hardly be denied, the details, especially concerning the abduction of youths, have been challenged.[50] In any case, it is clear that despite the Tibetan perception that the *lDab ldob* had a proclivity for same sex partners, the *lDab ldobs* as a whole were held in very high esteem both by the lay and monastic population.[51] Hence, if the *lDab ldobs'* homosexuality was considered "sinful," as Goldstein suggests, it must have been perceived as only marginally so, for it was something that was overshadowed by other qualities that in the end tipped public opinion in their favor.

Gilbert Herdt has described a morphology for homosexual activity. "It has been demonstrated," he says, "that there are three forms of the cultural structuring of homosexual activities and organization the world over."[52] These he defines as (1) age-structured homosexuality, in which there is a substantial age gap between the partners, (2) gender-reversed homosexuality, in which at least one of the partners adopts the sex roles of the opposite gender, and (3) role-specialized homosexuality, in which a person's "social or religious role" legitimizes his or her homosexual activity. Though the elder monk/*chigo* relationship may be subsumed in the first of Herdt's categories, the work of Schalow, Childs, Watanabe, and Iwata makes it clear that even in the Japanese case not all such relationships involve substantial age differences. These and other examples that fail to fit the pattern suggested by Herdt imply that his categories may not be as universal as he supposes. In any case, it seems far too early to postulate universal morphologies for homosexual behavior, especially when its manifestations throughout Asian societies have yet to be fully explored.[53]

Rita Gross mentions in a recent article that homosexuality is openly practiced in Western Buddhist communities.[54] This is true. To my knowledge, no North American Buddhist institution has ever marginalized its lay homosexual constituency, nor have any ever impeded the full participation of lay homosexual men and women by, for example, requiring their abstinence. To my knowledge, no gay Westerner has ever been denied Buddhist ordination because of his or her sexual orientation. North American Buddhists have, of course, been as susceptible as their non-Buddhist counterparts to homophobia, especially as it has emerged in the wake of the AIDS crisis, but many Buddhists have also been at the forefront of responding to this crisis. In San Francisco, for example, one of the first (and, according to some sources, *the* first) AIDS hospices was started by a Zen Buddhist group.[55]

Conclusions

In our brief survey of Buddhist attitudes toward homosexuality throughout selected regions and distinct periods of Asian history, there emerge the conclusions that (1) Buddhist doctrine is essentially neutral on the question of homosexuality (at least as neutral as it is in regard to heterosexual relations) and that (2) this has made Buddhism flexible in its accommodating to the mores and societal attitudes of the different cultural areas to which it spread. It is possible, given the dearth of scholarship in this area, that a different pattern may emerge in the future: that in Buddhist societies cases of persecution or widespread discrimination against gay or lesbian people may find their way to the surface. I doubt that we will find this to be the case, however. Instead, I suspect that as more research of a scholarly nature is done, this pattern of basic neutrality will be firmly established as the essential Buddhist view toward homosexuality. If so, then Buddhism will join the ranks of other major religions of Asia in its essential tolerance of the variety of human sexual expression.

Notes

1. Gilbert H. Herdt, "Homosexuality," in Mircea Eliade, ed., *The Encyclopedia of Religion* (New York: Macmillan, 1987), vol. 6, pp. 445–453.

2. The work of Leonard Zwilling and John Garret Jones in the context of Indian intellectual/religious history, Paul Schalow, Tsuneo Watanabe, Jun'ichi Iwata, and Maggie Childs in the field of Japanese literature, and Melvyn Goldstein in the field of Himalayan anthropology is particularly noteworthy. My *Buddhism, Sexuality, and Gender* (Albany: SUNY Press, 1992) contains two articles on the subject, one by Zwilling and one by Schalow. See also Randy P. Conner and Stephen Donaldson, "Buddhism" entry in the *Encyclopedia of Homosexuality* (New York and London: Garland Press, 1990), Vol. I, pp. 168–171.

3. Both religion and homosexuality clearly exist in socio-cultural contexts. In approaching the subject, therefore, the socio-anthropological perspective cannot be overlooked. At the same time, it becomes tempting to slip into a methodology in which the overtly religious attitudes regarding homosexual behavior and orientation are disregarded in favor of a more sociological approach that focuses almost exclusively on the cultural setting in which religious traditions and homosexual peoples coexist. The assumption here is that traditional societies are religious creatures and that by analyzing societal attitudes toward the phenomenon of homosexuality, the religious attitudes implicitly emerge. At least one recent general study of this sort exists. Gilbert Herdt's entry, "Homosexuality," in *The Encyclopedia of Religion* (see note 1), despite its tremendous breadth of scholarship, takes such a methodological stance. I opt here for an approach to the problem that considers religious elements (doctrine, ritual, and institutions) overt and explicit foci in the analysis.

4. Even limiting ourselves in this way, it is questionable whether or not it is possible to make generalizations about Buddhism even at specific times and places. In the end, the only valid statements may be very specific ones concerning individual people or individual texts (or even portions thereof). Still, the very general nature of this essay, in which many different cultures and historical periods are discussed, makes the qualification of our findings at every turn impossible. Hence I have opted for not making the types of qualifications that, though perhaps leading to greater accuracy, might confuse the reader and obscure the broader issues.

5. Following John Boswell's distinction between the terms "gay person" and "homosexual person," *Christianity, Social Tolerance, and Homosexuality: Gay People in Western Europe from the Beginning of the Christian Era to the Fourteenth Century* (Chicago: University of Chicago Press, 1980), pp. 41–46, I have for the most part used the latter here, for this essay deals predominantly with the phenomenon of same-sex relations in its broadest sense and is not restricted to a discussion of "persons who are conscious of erotic preference for their own gender," Boswell's characterization of the former.

6. Stanley Jeyaraja Tambiah, *World Conqueror and World Renouncer: A Study of Buddhism and Polity in Thailand Against a Historical Background* (Cambridge: Cambridge University Press, 1976).

7. Charles F. Keyes, "Ambiguous Gender: Male Initiation in a Northern Thai Buddhist Society," in Carolyn Walker Bynum et al., eds., *Gender and Religion: On the Complexity of Symbols* (Boston: Beacon Press, 1986), pp. 66–96.

8. Leonard Zwilling, "Homosexuality as Seen in Indian Buddhist Texts," in J. I. Cabezón, ed., *Buddhism, Sexuality, and Gender* (Albany: SUNY Press, 1992), pp. 203–214.

9. For several instances of this in an early Buddhist text, see Zwilling, p. 207.

10. Judith C. Brown, *Immodest Acts* (New York: Oxford University Press, 1986), p. 6.

11. Zwilling, p. 207, states that "mutual masturbation among nuns is also reckoned with, but is considered a relatively minor offense and there are far fewer references to homosexuality in the *Bhikkhunīvinaya* than in the *Bhikkhuvinaya.*"

12. Louis Crompton, "Homosexuality in Imperial China" (Paper delivered at the Conference on "Homosexuality: Which Homosexuality?" Amsterdam, 1987, pp. 37–38.) See also Bret Hinsch's entry in *The Encyclopedia of Homosexuality*, s.v. "China," vol. I, pp. 215–220.

13. See note 12.

14. Nancy Schuster Barnes, "Buddhism," in Arvind Sharma, ed., *Women in World Religions* (Albany: SUNY Press, 1987), p. 132. See

also M. Topley, "Marriage Resistance in Rural Kwangtung," in *Women in Chinese Society* (Stanford: Stanford University Press, 1975).

15. Regarding the prevalence of homosexual peoples in the Christian clergy in the Early Middle Ages, see Boswell, pp. 187–188.

16. Breaking the vow of celibacy (or any of the other three major vows) is said to bring defeat (*pārājika*), a state of moral downfall that can be corrected in that same lifetime only by the attainment of *nirvāṇa*, i.e., arhatship. Practically speaking, it often brings with it expulsion from the monastic community.

17. Melvyn Goldstein states in his "A Study of the Ldab Ldob," *Central Asiatic Journal* 9 (1964): 134, that "among the Tibetan lay population [homosexuality] carries an extremely derogative stigma and is almost unknown." I believe that Goldstein's conclusions must be accepted cautiously, however.

18. As regards the morphology of the *paṇḍaka*, Zwilling, p. 204, notes that the temporarily and congenitally impotent, voyeurs, and *castrate* are all included in the category along with "that person who satisfies his sexual desires by fellating another to ejaculation."

19. The faults of engaging in sexual activity in general are described in great detail in the *Śikṣāsamuccaya*, P. L. Vaidya, ed. (Darbhanga: Mithila Institute, 1961), pp. 43–45. I discuss this at length in an unpublished paper, "Women and Illusion: Toward an Aesthetic in Buddhism," read at the 1987 annual meeting of the American Academy of Religion, Boston.

20. For a variety of interpretations concerning the meaning of the lay vow concerning sexual misconduct, see Holmes Welch, *The Practice of Chinese Buddhism: 1900–1950* (Cambridge: Harvard University Press, 1967), pp. 365–366.

21. I refer to texts dealing, for example, with the kinds of advice (*śikṣā, bslab bya*) that is to be given to lay people concerning the correct way of keeping the *upāsa(i)ka* vows.

22. Zwilling, p. 207.

23. We are here in the same position as Boswell when he tries to characterize Burchard's view of homosexual behavior. See Boswell, p. 206.

24. I have chosen these four as the focus of this study partly because of the availability of scholarly material concerning homosexual relations and attitudes toward homosexuality, and partly because they show the wide and disparate range of opinions concerning the subject in the Buddhist tradition.

25. Zwilling, p. 205.

26. In this context it is interesting that a Chinese Buddhist text, dated by Beyer to the seventh century but based, no doubt, on an Indian original, the *Ta-ch'eng tsao-hsiang kung-te ching*, lists eight causes

for a woman's being reborn a woman, four causes for a man's being reborn a woman, four causes for a man's being reborn a eunuch (*paṇḍaka?*) [castrating another man, laughing at a monk, transgressing the precepts because of his desire, encouraging others to do the same], four causes for a man's being reborn a hermaphrodite ["uncleanness where there should be reverence," lust for the bodies of other men, self-stimulation, prostitution of himself to other men while in the guise of a woman] and four causes "whereby a man is born with the lusts and desires of a woman, and enjoys being treated as a woman by other men" [despising, slandering, or defaming other men, transvestism, "lewd uncleanness" with his own clanswomen, accepting reverence though unworthy of it]. See S. Beyer, *The Buddhist Experience: Sources and Interpretations* (Belmont, Calif.: Wadsworth Publishing Company, 1974), p. 53.

27. Zwilling, p. 209.

28. Together with the *Vinaya* and *Abhidharma*, the *Nikāya* is the third section of the Buddhist canon, the *tripiṭaka*.

29. John Garret Jones, *Tales and Teachings of the Buddha: The Jataka Stories in Relation to the Pali Canon* (London: George Allen Unwin, 1979), pp. 79–80.

30. Ibid., p. 107.

31. Ibid., p. 114.

32. Ibid., pp. 113, 115.

33. Crompton, p. 28.

34. Giovanni Vitiello suggests in a recent essay that Taoism may have even encouraged male love, because the equal exchange of semen in male homosexual relations preserves the essential life force of both partners. See his essay in M. Stemmeler and J. I. Cabezón, eds., *Religion, Homosexuality, and Literature,* proceedings of the Gay Men's Issues in Religion section of the American Academy of Religion (Las Colinas, TX: Monument Press, 1992), pp. 95–102.

35. Crompton, p. 36.

36. Welch, p. 119. This is similar to the conclusion that Melford E. Spiro comes to in his *Buddhism and Society* (New York: Harper & Row, 1970), pp. 366–368: "By all accounts village monks do in fact comply with the sexual prohibitions, both homosexual and heterosexual, of the Rule," this in the Burmese case. He adds, however: "I was told that homosexuality, too, is not infrequent in the Sinhalese monkhood—between monks and monks, monks and novices, and monks and laymen," though to what extent this is a case of homosexuality as an attribute of the "other" remains to be seen.

37. This point is also made by Tsuneo Watanabe and Jun'ichi Iwata in the context of Japan. See their *The Love of the Samurai: A Thousand Years of Japanese Homosexuality* (London: GMP Publishers, 1989), chap. 5.

38. Iwata, pp. 31–34, finds textual references to homosexual relationships prior to the time of Kūkai, though from the context it seems that the earlier culture seems to have been less tolerant of homosexuality. The truth of the Kūkai legend then may lie not in the fact that he introduced homosexuality into Japan, but in that Kūkai's introduction of pederasty into Japanese monasticism legitimated male love.

39. Contrast this to the case of the Englishman, William Rufus (1087–1100), whose chroniclers "charge him with addiction to sins of the flesh and claim that he introduced into England sins which had not previously been common" (homosexuality predominant among them); see Boswell, p. 209. Here we find a case in which the attribution of the introduction of the practice to a foreigner is used as a means of condemning it.

40. Paul Gordon Schalow, "The Priestly Tradition of Homosexual Love in Japanese Buddhism," in J. I. Cabezón, ed., *Buddhism, Sexuality, and Gender* (Albany: SUNY Press, 1992), pp. 215–230.

41. See Watanabe and Iwata, chap. 2.

42. Maggie C. Childs, "Chigo Monogatari," *Monumenta Nipponica*, vol. 35, no. 2, pp. 127–151 (1978); and also her "Sexuality and Salvation" (Paper delivered at the annual meeting of the Association for Asian Studies, Boston, 1978).

43. Schalow, "The Priestly Tradition," pp. 218–220.

44. Watanabe and Iwata, p. 113.

45. Paul Gordon Schalow, *The Great Mirror of Male Love by Ihara Saikaku* (Stanford: Stanford University Press, 1989).

46. Schalow, "The Priestly Tradition," p. 222.

47. Goldstein, p. 136.

48. If, as Boswell states, "no charge against a minority seems to be more damaging than the claim that they pose a threat of some sort to the children of the majority," (*Christianity*, p. 273), then we must question whether or not such accounts are accurate or are manifestations of intolerance. For other cases of the charge of child stealing as a means of derogating minority groups (e.g., Gypsies, Muslims, and Jews) in Europe, see Boswell, *Christianity*, pp. 273, 283.

49. Goldstein, p. 134.

50. My own sources, who would not deny that homosexual activity existed, not only among the *lDab ldob* but among other monks as well, stated that they were unaware of the abduction scenarios described by Goldstein and his informants.

51. Goldstein, p. 134.

52. Herdt, p. 446.

53. A comment by Boswell in *Christianity*, p. 28, also casts doubt on Herdt's morphology, even as it applies to the clearest case that of the Greeks.

54. Rita Gross, "The Householder and the World Renunciant: Two Modes of Sexual Expression in Buddhism," *Journal of Ecumenical Studies* 22, no. 1 (Winter 1985): 83.

55. See, for example, Tensho David Schneider, "Accidents and Calculations: The Emergence of Three AIDS Hospices," *Tricycle: The Buddhist Review*, vol. 1 (Spring 1992): 78–83.

Bibliography

Barnes, Nancy Schuster. 1987. "Buddhism." In *Women in World Religion*, edited by Arvind Sharma, 132. Albany: SUNY Press.

Beyer, S. 1974. *The Buddhist Experience: Sources and Interpretations.* Belmont, Calif.: Wadsworth Publishing Company.

Boswell, John. 1980. *Christianity, Social Tolerance, and Homosexuality: Gay People in Western Europe from the Beginning of the Christian Era to the Fourteenth Century.* Chicago: University of Chicago Press.

Brown, Judith C. 1986. *Immodest Acts.* New York: Oxford University Press.

Cabezón, José Ignacio. 1987. "Women and Illusion: Toward an Aesthetic in Buddhism." Paper delivered at the annual meeting of the American Academy of Religion, Boston.

———. 1992. *Buddhism, Sexuality, and Gender.* Albany: SUNY Press.

Childs, Maggie C. 1978. "Chigo Monogatari." *Monumenta Hipponica.*

———. 1978. "Sexuality and Salvation." Paper delivered at the annual meeting of the Association for Asian Studies, Boston.

Conner, Randy P. and Stephen Donaldson. 1990. "Buddhism." In *Encyclopedia of Homosexuality.* New York and London: Garland Press.

Crompton, Louis. 1987. "Homosexuality in Imperial China." Paper delivered at the Conference on "Homosexuality: Which Homosexuality?" Amsterdam.

Encyclopedia of Homosexuality. 1990.

Goldstein, Melvyn. 1964. "A Study of the Ldab Ldob." *Central Asiatic Journal* 9:134.

Gross, Rita. 1985. "The Householder and the World Renunciant: Two Modes of Sexual Expression in Buddhism." *Journal of Ecumenical Studies* 22, 1:83.

Herdt, Gilbert H. 1987. "Homosexuality." In *The Encyclopedia of Religion*, edited by Mircea Eliade, 6:445–453. New York: Macmillan.

Jones, John Garret. 1979. *Tales and Teachings of the Buddha: The Jataka Stories in Relation to the Pali Canon.* London: George Allen & Unwin.

Keyes, Charles F. 1986. "Ambiguous Gender: Male Initiation in a Northern Thai Buddhist Society." In *Gender and Religion: On the Complexity of Symbols,* edited by Carolyn Walker Bynum et al., 66–96. Boston: Beacon Press.

Schalow, Paul Gordon. 1989. *The Great Mirror of Male Love by Ihara Saikaku.* Stanford: Stanford University Press.

———. 1992. "The Priestly Tradition of Homosexual Love in Japanese Buddhism." In *Buddhism, Sexuality, and Gender,* edited by J. I. Cabezón, 215–230. Albany: SUNY Press.

Schneider, Tensho David. 1992. "Accidents and Calculations: The Emergence of Three AIDS Hospices." *Tricycle: The Buddhist Review,* 78–83.

Spiro, Melford E. 1970. *Buddhism and Society.* New York: Harper & Row.

Stemmeler, M., and J. I. Cabezón, eds. n.d. 1992. *Religion, Homosexuality, and Literature.* Las Colinas, TX: Monument Press.

Tambiah, Stanley Jeyaraja. 1976. *World Conqueror and World Renouncer: A Study of Buddhism and Polity in Thailand Against a Historical Background.* Cambridge: Cambrdige University Press.

Topley, M. 1975. "Marriage Resistance in Rural Kwangtung." In *Women in Chinese Society.* Stanford: Stanford University Press.

Vaidya, P. L., ed. 1961. *Śikṣāsamuccaya.* Darbhanga: Mithila Institute.

Watanabe, Tsuneo, and Jun'ichi, Iwata. 1989. *The Love of the Samurai: A Thousand Years of Japanese Homosexuality.* London: GMP Publishers.

Welch, Holmes. 1967. *The Practice of Chinese Buddhism: 1900–1950.* Cambridge: Harvard University Press.

Zwilling, Leonard. 1991. "Homosexuality as Seen in Indian Buddhist Texts." In *Buddhism, Sexuality, and Gender,* edited by J. I. Cabezón, 203–214. Albany: SUNY Press.

4

Homosexuality and Judaism

Lewis John Eron

In March of 1988 the Knesset, the Israeli Parliament, as part of a major overhaul of the section of the Israeli Penal Code concerning sex crimes, legalized sexual relationships between adult males. This far-reaching law, whose other provisions include the raising of the penalties for rape and protection of the rights of victims of sex crimes, is the result of the ten-year efforts of MK (Member of the Knesset) Shulamit Aloni of the Citizens' Rights Party.

The report in the *Jerusalem Post* (International Edition, week ending April 2, 1988) described the new law as follows:

> The law's provisions regarding sex between men are covered in three clauses totalling six lines. They treat sexual relations between consenting adult males exactly as they treat relations between consenting males and females: they ignore them.

In addition, the *Jerusalem Post* editorial of Thursday, March 24, 1988, notes:

> MK Aloni has built on the ground laid years ago by Haim Cohn. As attorney-general in the 1950's, he ordered police not to prosecute homosexuals who confined their practices to

consenting adult mates. In 1964, when a member of the
Supreme Court, he issued the ringing declaration that the so-
called law of nature invoked by moralists in their fight against
aberrant sexual conduct could well take care of itself; and that
what was in urgent need of protection was "the dignity, freedom and person of man."

The Knesset, as Israel's Parliament, makes laws for the
State of Israel, the majority of whose citizens are Jews,
although most would not describe themselves as "religious."
The Knesset is not bound by traditional Jewish religious
law (the *halakhah*), nor can its decrees be seen as part of the
development of the *halakhah*. Nevertheless, this new law is a
major turn in the development of Jewish attitudes toward gay
people.

The *halakhah*, traditional Jewish law, prohibits sexual relations between members of the same sex. It takes a harsher position against sexual relationships between men than those
between women because the former are prohibited by biblical
injunctions whereas the latter are prohibited only by later rabbinic legislation.

Although the *halakhah* shows an extensive concern with issues of sexual behavior, the discussions concerning sexual relationships between members of the same sex are limited. This
apparent lack of interest may be explained in three ways: (1) The
prohibitions were clear and required limited additional exposition. (2) Very few Jews were perceived to have had sexual relationships with members of their own sex, so such relationships
were not understood as major social problems. (3) Homosexual
relationships, although prohibited, were not as destructive to
the social fabric as were illicit heterosexual relationships, and,
therefore, the *halakhah* shows a greater concern with the latter
than with the former.

This essay will explore attitudes toward homosexuality
as they appear within the Jewish tradition. Its concentration
will be on halakhic literature, because *halakhah* has been and
remains for many Jews the practical expression of Jewish values in Jewish life. Traditional Jewish attitudes toward homosexuality must be understood in the context of Jewish
attitudes toward sexuality in general. Therefore, the first
part of this essay will describe the theory of sexuality that

provides the foundation for traditional Jewish understandings of homosexuality.

Because the Bible can be seen as the quarry from which
the rabbis took the stones to build rabbinic Judaism, the second
section will first examine the attitudes toward homosexuality
in the Bible that provide the basis for the later rabbinic discussion of the issue. It will then describe the attitudes toward
male homosexuality as they appear in Talmudic and halakhic
sources. Finally, it will describe the attitudes toward female
homosexuality in the same sources.

Although there is very little description of the lives of gay
people in Hebrew literature, several medieval Spanish Hebrew
love poems seem to describe homosexual love. The nature of
this poetry, however, makes it a poor source for the attitudes
toward homosexuality and gay people among the Jews in Islamic Spain. It does, however, provide an insight into their attitudes toward love in general.

The final section will briefly describe some contemporary
Jewish attitudes toward homosexuality and gay people. The essay concludes with some observations as to ways in which the
tradition may be used to develop a more accepting Jewish approach toward the physical aspects of the loving relationship
between gay people.

Jewish Attitudes Toward Sexuality[1]

In 1972, the American Medical Association Committee on
Human Sexuality offered the following definition of human
sexuality:

> Human sexuality is not confined to the bedroom, or to the
> night time or to any single area of the body. It involves what we
> do, but it also involves what we are. It is an identification, an
> activity, a drive, a biological and emotional process, an outlook
> and an expression of the self. It brings great fulfillment, but it
> also engenders problems. It is strongly influenced by social and
> personal beliefs and in turn strongly influences both beliefs
> and behavior. It is an important factor in every personal rela-
> tionship and in every human endeavor from business to poli-
> tics. Human beings see, hear, feel, think, act and react in

masculine and feminine ways and parents, in doing so, influence their children in similar directions.[2]

Such an understanding of sexuality does not appear in traditional Jewish sources. Instead of an attempt to understand human sexual activity by a theory of sexuality, these sources present an understanding that people are both male and female and perform sexual acts, some of which are permitted and others of which are forbidden. Sexual desire is the motivating force for both permitted and prohibited sexual acts. Whereas sexual desire can be a force for good, it is more often seen as a potentially destructive power (the *yetzer hara*, the "evil inclination") that needs to be channeled in order to serve a beneficial purpose (*Gen. Rabba.* 34.14; *m. Berakot* 9.5).

According to the first account of creation in the Book of Genesis, God creates humanity as male and female in the Divine One's image. In the second account, the creation of man and woman forms a narrative frame within which the rest of creation takes place. Creation begins with the molding of man from the earth and concludes with the creation of woman from man as his equivalent partner, *ezer kenegdo* (Gen. 2:18).

One midrashic interpretation of these two accounts attempts to harmonize them by claiming that when God created Adam, the primordial human, he created him bisexual, male and female, back to back. The appearance of Eve is the result of the splitting of the primordial Adam into two separate people. As a result, the union of a man and a woman in the marriage relationship is an attempt to regain our original unity (see *b.Erubim* 18a; *Midrash Tehillim* 139.5).

This *midrash* is similar to Aristophanes' explanation of the origins of heterosexual and homosexual attraction in Plato's *Symposium* 191D–192B. Whereas Aristophanes pictures two-faced beings that are either male-female or male-male, the rabbis use only the image of the male-female two-faced being to show that heterosexual couplings alone are natural.

Sexual acts, not sexuality, provide the foundation for traditional Jewish understandings of the role of sex in human life. People perform sexual acts. Marriage is seen as the proper relationship in which sexual intimacy is to occur. A minority of rabbinic authorities, however, permit men and women to co-habit without marriage under certain conditions.[3]

The sexual relationship plays an important role within a marriage. The Talmud acknowledges the sexual needs of the woman and requires the husband to care for them just as he provides for her food and clothing (Exod. 21:10; Rashi [Rabbi Solomon ben Isaac, France, 11th cent.] on Exod. 21:10; *b. Nedarim* 15b). Even within the marriage bond, however, sexuality is restricted. The laws of family purity, *taharat ha-mishpachah*, prohibit intimate contact during certain periods of the woman's menstrual cycle.

A primary purpose for sexual intimacy is procreation. The first commandment given to humanity is "to be fruitful and multiply" (Gen. 1:28; 9:1). Yet sexual intimacy within marriage is not restricted to procreation. It is considered healthful and, of most importance, it is a legitimate source of pleasure as much for the woman as for the man (*b. Yebamot* 118b). During intercourse, a husband and wife may do as they wish with each other (Rambam [Rabbi Moses ben Maimon or Maimonides, Egypt, 12th cent.], *Yad*, Issurei Biah 21:9).

Even though certain sexual positions and activities may result in the extravaginal ejaculation of semen, several rabbinic authorities permitted these activities.[4] Generally, however, extravaginal ejaculation is considered to be male masturbation, which is strongly prohibited (*Tur Shulchan Arukh* 23; *Arukh HaShulchan* 23). This prohibition against masturbation thus restricts many forms of sexual intimacy between males.

In the twelfth century, Rabbi Abraham ben David of Posquieres (Rabad) identified four proper motivations (*kavanot*, "intentions") for sexual activity within marriage. They are (1) procreation and the prescribed times for *onah*, the conjugal rights due to a wife, (2) improving the health of a fetus, (3) satisfying the sexual desires of the woman beyond the prescribed frequency, and (4) restraining the man's sexual desire (*Ba'alei Ha-Nefesh*, Sha 'ar Ha-Qedusha).[5]

Within Jewish sources one finds an ambivalence toward sexual activity. Freedom of sexual expression may be allowed within the marital relationship, but often the pious individual is encouraged to refrain from sexual excess.

This ambivalence appears clearly in the writings of Maimonides (Rambam), the twelfth-century philosopher and jurist.[6] In the same section in his code of laws in which he permits a husband and wife to do as they wish in their sexual relations, he tempers the remark:

> Nevertheless, it is an attribute of piety that a man should not act in this matter with levity and that he should sanctify himself at the time of intercourse. . . . A man should not turn aside from the normal way of the world and its proper procedure, since the true design of intercourse is fruitfulness and multiplication of progeny (*Yad,* Issurei Biah 21:9).

Although great freedom of sexual expression is permitted, though not always encouraged, within the marital relationship, other sexual acts are seen as a willful breaking of the proper norms of behavior (Lev. 18). These include incest, adultery, masturbation, sexual relations between members of the same sex, and sexual relations between people and animals. With an understanding of Jewish attitudes toward sexual activity in general, one can now look at Jewish attitudes toward sexual activity between members of the same sex.

Biblical Roots of Jewish Attitudes Toward Homosexuality

The English term *sodomy* has a range of meanings that runs from anal copulation of one man with another to anal or oral copulation in general to sexual acts with animals.[7] It derives ultimately from *Sodoma,* the Latin form of the Hebrew word "Sodom," the name of one of the five cities that God destroyed in the time of Abraham (Gen. 19).

In the Genesis account, the utter wickedness of the Sodomites is illustrated by the attempt of the men of Sodom to rape, en masse, the two angelic figures who arrived in the city in human form to warn Abraham's nephew, Lot, of the forthcoming destruction of the city. The meaning of the English term "sodomy" reflects the later tradition in which homosexual activity is the characteristic sin of the Sodomites.[8]

The Hebrew Bible, on the other hand, does not focus on the sexual wickedness of the Sodomites but pictures Sodom as the archetype of the sinful nation. The prophets charge the Sodomites with a variety of crimes, including lack of justice (Isa. 1:10; 3:9), disregard of moral and ethical values (Jer. 23:14), and ignoring the impoverished (Ezek. 16:48–49).

In the Apocrypha and Pseudepigrapha, the Sodomites are accused of a variety of sins, including inhospitality (Wisd. of Sol. 19:13–14) and pride (Ecclus. 16:8). *Jubilees* 16:5–6 and 20:5–6 holds that the Sodomites were guilty of unspecified sexual sins and pollutions, while in the *Testament of Naphtali* the sins of the Sodomites appear to be sexual relations between men (*T. Naphtali* 3:1–4:2).

Only Josephus and Philo describe the sins of the Sodomites explicitly as homosexual relations. Josephus claims that the Sodomites were overcome by desire for the youthful beauty of Lot's visitors (*Antiquities* 1.199–204). Philo employs the story of Sodom to present a strong polemic against homosexuality in general (*On Abraham* 133–134; *Questions and Answers on Genesis* 4.3).

On the whole, the rabbis of the Talmud do not interpret the Sodomites' sin as that of homosexuality. Rather, they describe the Sodomites as mean, inhospitable, uncharitable, and unjust (*b. Sanhedrin* 109a; *b. Ketubot* 103a; *b. Baba Batra* 12b; 59a; 168a; *b. Erubim* 49a). However, Targum Pseudo-Jonathan, one of the ancient translations of the Hebrew Bible into Aramaic, states explicitly that the Sodomites wished to have sexual relations with the visitors. In addition, some midrashic sources also identify the crimes of the Sodomites as sexual in nature (*Lev. Rabba.* 23:9; *Gen. Rabba.* 26.5; 50.5, 7).

The account of the Sodomites' attempted rape of their male visitors has a parallel in the story of the attempt of the men of Gibeah to rape the visiting Levite (Judg. 19:1–21:25). Here, too, the violation of hospitality laws by the attempt to molest guests physically serves to illustrate the general lawlessness of the times. Neither here nor in the case of Sodom are sexual acts between men singled out.

The prohibition against cult prostitution in Deuteronomy 23:18–19 has had little influence in the development of Jewish attitudes concerning homosexual behavior.

No Israelite woman shall be a cult prostitute (*qadeisha*), nor shall any Israelite man be a cult prostitute (*qadeish*). You shall not bring the fee of a whore (*zonah*) or the pay of a dog (*kelev*) into the house of the Lord your God in fulfillment of any vow, for both are abhorrent to the Lord your God. (Translation: Jewish Publication Society, 1962)

Ritualized sexual activity played a role in the religious celebrations of the Canaanite peoples and was not fully eradicated from Israelite worship until the reign of King Josiah (2 Kings 23:7). The *qadeish*, male prostitute, appears to have been one of the religious functionaries in Canaanite-style of worship that some of the Israelites adopted (1 Kings 14:24; 15:12; 22:47). There is no reason to believe that the male cult prostitute, the *qadeish* or "sanctified one," was necessarily or exclusively involved in homosexual intercourse.[9]

The term *kelavim* (plural of *kelev*, "dog") appears in a Phoenician list of the functionaries attached to the Temple of Ashtoreth in Cyprus. Many scholars assumed that in the Phoenician, a language closely related to biblical Hebrew, *kelev* is a synonym for *qadeish*.[10]

Whether or not this be the case, in the Hebrew Scriptures the word "dog" serves as well as a term of opprobrium (1 Sam. 17:43; 1 Kings 8:13; Isa. 56:10–11). Its use, therefore, in conjunction with the generic term for a secular prostitute (*zonah*) in verse 19, seems to indicate that the author of Deuteronomy rejected the sacred status of the cult prostitutes (see also the use of *qadeisha* and *zonah* in the story of Judah and Tamar [Gen. 38]).

The cultic significance of these terms was lost to the Jewish tradition. Deuteronomy 23:18 was often interpreted as prohibiting Jews from engaging in heterosexual intercourse outside of a Jewish marriage (Rambam on Deut. 23:18; Targum Onqelos on Deut. 23:18 prohibits the marriage of Jews to slaves). However, others understood it to prohibit sexual activity between men (Rambam, *Sefer Ha-Mitzvot*, negative precept 350) or to prohibit male prostitutes available for homosexual relations (Rashi on Deut. 23:18; Rambam on Deut. 23:18). The term *kelev*, "dog," in Deuteronomy 23:18 was later understood literally to refer to the animal (*m. Temura* 6).

The Hebrew Scriptures often describe rebellion against God in terms of sexual sinfulness. One of the metaphors used to picture the relationship between Israel and her God is that of a marriage. Thus the appearance of foreign cults within the two Israelite kingdoms of Israel and Judah enabled the prophets to describe Israel as an adulterous wife (Hos. 1–3; Ezek. 16; 23).

The Holiness Code, an ancient body of Israelite legal material embedded in the Book of Leviticus (Lev. 17–26),[11] holds the Canaanites and Egyptians guilty of a wide variety of sexual sins that include incest, adultery, male homosexuality, bestiality, and child sacrifice (Lev. 18, see also 20; for a rabbinic view see, *Sifra*, Acharei Mot 86a, on Lev. 18:3). The Israelites are warned not to follow any of these practices lest the Land of Israel spew them out as it has spewed out the previous inhabitants (Lev. 18:24–30; 20:22–26).

The motivating factor behind the legislation in the Holiness Code is the aspiration that the people of Israel emulate their God in holiness. Its decrees cover both ethical and cultic concerns. It claims that obedience to these decrees will distinguish the Israelites from the other nations (Lev. 20:26). Yet sexual misdeeds are, at the least, emblematic of disobedience in general.

The story of Noah's flood is introduced by a story of the intercourse between the heavenly beings and earthly women (Gen. 6:1–4). This account served as the source for the claim in the Pseudepigrapha and in rabbinic *midrash* that the generation of the flood was marked by sexual irregularities as well as other sins (*Enoch* 6–16; *Jubilees* 5).[12]

One example of such an interpretation comes from *Lev. Rabba.* 23.9; see also *Gen. Rabba.* 26.5).

> R. Hiyyah taught why is 'I am the Lord' written twice (Lev. 18:3 and 4)? It implies: I am He who inflicted punishment upon the Generation of the Flood, upon Sodom, and upon Egypt, and I am the same who will inflict punishment upon any one who will act in accordance with their practices. The Generation of the Flood were blotted out from the world because they were steeped in whoredom (*shetufin be-zenut*). . . . R. Huna says in the name of R. Jose: The Generation of the Flood were only

blotted out of the world on account of their having written hymenean songs for sodomy. (Soncino translation)

Rabbinic interpretation also found references to homosexual activity in the story of Noah's nakedness and in Potifar's desire to purchase Joseph as a slave. These two passages underscore the rabbinic contention based on Leviticus 18:3 that the Canaanites and the Egyptians were steeped in sexual immorality. One *midrash* holds that Ham, the ancestor of the Canaanites, took sexual advantage of his grandfather, Noah, while Noah was lying drunk and naked in his tent (*b. Sanhedrin* 70a, see Rashi on Gen. 9:22). The other claims that Potifar purchased Joseph as a slave for his own sexual pleasure (*b. Sota* 13b).

The Levitical Prohibitions

The prohibitions against male-male sexual intercourse that appear as part of the general legislation concerning forbidden sexual relations in the Holiness Code form the basis for rabbinic attitudes concerning homosexual intercourse.

Do not lie with a male as one lies with a woman; it is an abhorrence (Lev. 18:22).

If a man lies with a male as one lies with a woman, the two of them have done an abhorrent thing; they shall be put to death—their bloodguilt is upon them (Lev. 20:13).
(Translation: Jewish Publication Society, 1962)

These statements prohibiting male homosexual intercourse do not stand out in terms of structure and language from the other laws concerning prohibited sexual relations. Sexual intercourse between men is one of many sexual acts prohibited by the Holiness Code.

The rabbis understood the phrases "if a man lies with a male as one lies with a woman" as referring to male-male sexual intercourse *per anum*. The halakhic expression for male homosexual relations, *mishkav zachur* (literally, "lying with a man"), reflects the language of Leviticus for "lying with a woman," *mishkevei 'isha* (Lev. 18:22).

The Talmud defines the amount of penile insertion to initiate any act of sexual intercourse (*b. Yebamot* 55b, *b. Sota* 4a). The violation of the prohibition against male homosexual relations begins once a man initiates sexual intercourse by the insertion of the corona of the penis (*Sefer Ha-Chinnukh* 209). In less precise language, Rashi describes the amount of insertion required as "just a little" (Rashi on Lev. 20:13).

Unlike the rest of the laws concerning prohibited sexual relations, only male-male sexual intercourse is singled out as a *to ʿeivah*, "an abhorrence." This specific marking loses some of its force because Leviticus 18:26, 27, 29, and 30 describe all the forbidden sexual relations in general as *to ʿeivot*, "abhorrences."

The term *to ʿeivah* is a nominal form of a verbal root that means "to be abhorred." The term appears most frequently in Deuteronomy, Ezekiel, and Proverbs. The term *to ʿeivah* may have originally referred to taboo behavior (Gen. 43:32; 46:34; Exod. 8:22), but in the Hebrew Scriptures it acquires a much broader range of meanings. It is used to describe unclean foods, improper sacrifices, sexual irregularities, moral and ethical failings, and idolatrous practices.[13]

In Leviticus, however, the term *to ʿeivah* appears only in the context of forbidden sexual activity (Lev. 18, 20). The Bible describes these "abhorrent" acts as characteristic of the Egyptians and the Canaanites (Lev. 18:3; 27; 20:23), although there is no historical reason to assume that Israel's neighbors were particularly involved in these activities.[14] With the exception of the prohibition of child sacrifice (Lev. 18:21; 20:2–5), there is no reference to idolatrous practice.

In the Talmud (*b. Nedarim* 51a) in a discussion with Rabbi Judah the Prince, Bar Kappara claims the term *to ʿeivah* (abhorrence) is a contraction of the Hebrew sentence *to ʿeh attah bah,* "something in which you go astray." The Tosafot, a collection of medieval Talmudic commentary from the school of Rashi, says that what is meant by "going astray" is that a man will be led astray from his wife and his home by sexual intercourse with other men (Tosafot on *b. Nedarim* 51a). A modern scholar, Baruch Epstein (1860–1942), explained "going astray" as going astray from the "foundations of creation" (*Torah Temimah* on Lev. 18:22).

Universal Prohibition Against
Male Homosexual Relations

According to the rabbis of the Talmud, the prohibitions against male homosexual relations, incest, adultery, and bestiality are part of the Noachide laws (the laws given to Noah and his descendants after the flood), which they saw as binding on gentiles as well as on Jews (t. Avoda Zara 8.4; Sifra, Acharei Mot, on Lev. 18:6; b. Sanhedrin 58a; Rambam, Yad, Melakim 9:5, 6; Rashi on b. Sanhedrin 58a).[15] These activities are seen as perversions of the natural order.

The belief that sexual relations between men per anum are contrary to the natural order has a long tradition within Jewish sources. In the Testament of Naphtali 3:4, the men of Sodom are accused of changing their natural order. Although it is not entirely clear that this refers to male homosexual intercourse, the use of the Greek word for nature, physis, there and in contemporaneous Jewish and Christian literature supports the assumption (Pseudo-Phocylides 187; Barnabas 10:7; Philo, On Abraham 133–141; see also Wisd. of Sol. 14:26).[16]

Although procreation was not considered the only reason for heterosexual intercourse, the fact that procreation was possible only through vaginal intercourse supported the rabbinic understanding that other forms of sexual activity broke the natural order (see b. Erubim 18a; Midrash Tehillim 139.5 cited above). Rabbi Aqiba interprets Genesis 2:24, "Hence a man leaves his father and mother and clings to his wife, so that they become one flesh," to exclude incest, sexual relations between men, adultery, and bestiality (see Rambam, Yad, Hilkot Melakim 9.6).[17]

> "His father" means "his father's wife"; "his mother" is literally meant. "And he shall cleave," but not to a male; "to his wife," but not to his neighbour's wife; "and they shall be as one flesh," applying to those that can become one flesh, thus excluding cattle and beasts. (b. Sanhedrin 58a—Soncino translation)

Rashi's comment on this passage stresses that the pleasure derived from male homosexual sex is not the same as the pleasure derived from heterosexual intercourse because there is no possibility of procreation.

For there is no cleaving [*dibbuq*], because the passive partner [*ha-nishkab*], not receiving pleasure, does not cleave with him [*'immo*]. It is from the seed which goes forth from the mother and the father that "one flesh" is made.[18]

Nevertheless, the Talmud considers the pleasures both partners experience in male-male sexual intercourse to be significant in its evaluation of homosexual activity. In a discussion concerning whether one can acquire a male slave through sexual intercourse as one can acquire a female slave found in *b. Qiddushin* 22b, we read:

> But here [the acquisition of a female slave through sexual intercourse] both derive pleasure. Then what can be said of unnatural intercourse? Said Rabbi Achaiy ben Adda of Acha: Who is to tell us that both do not derive pleasure? Moreover, it is written [*Thou shalt not lie with mankind*] *with the lyings of a woman:* [it is an abhorrence.] {Lev. 18:22} thus the Writ compared unnatural to natural intercourse. (Soncino translation)[19]

The fact that one can receive pleasure from male homosexual relations explains why the individual who partakes in it was considered to be indulging his desire.

In *Sefer Ha-Chinnukh* 209, male homosexual relations are prohibited for three reasons: (1) through them one cannot fulfill the commandment to procreate, (2) they do not satisfy one's obligation to provide for one's wife's conjugal rights and sexual needs, and (3) their sole purpose is to satisfy one's own desire.

> At the root of this prohibition (against male homosexual relations) lies the reason that the Eternal Lord, blessed is He, desires the settlement of the world He created. Therefore He commanded us that human seed should not be destroyed by carnal relations with males: for this is indeed destruction, since there can be no fruitful benefit of offspring from it, nor the fulfillment of the religious duty of conjugal rights [due one's wife]—this apart from the fact that the nature of this filthy business is very repulsive and loathsome in the eyes of every intelligent human being. It is [simply] not fitting that a man, created to serve his Maker, should become perverted by these ugly deeds. And for this reason, our sages of blessed memory said it is forbidden to marry a woman to a small boy, for it is akin to immorality. So too should a man not marry an old or a sterile woman, who is not fit (able) to bear a child.[20]

The belief that male-male sexual relations are unnatural appears in modern sources as well (see Baruch Epstein, *Torah Temima* on Lev. 18:22 on *to 'eivah* cited above). Recently, Robert Gordis described homosexuality as a "violation of God's will and a perversion of nature."[21]

The biblical belief that sexual irregularities and idolatry are associated also appears in postbiblical Jewish literature (see Wisdom 14; *T. Reuben.* 4:6; *b. Megilla* 25a; Ps-Jonathan on Lev. 18:12; *b. Ketubot* 13b). Male homosexual intercourse was seen as a gentile and not a Jewish vice (Josephus, *Antiquities,* 15:2, 6; Sibylline Oracles 3:573–600; 5:386–397: *b. Shabbat* 17b; 149b). One is neither permitted to leave one's animals in the inns of gentiles, for they are suspected of bestiality, nor is one allowed to send a young Jewish boy to study with a gentile, for they are suspected of homosexuality (*t. Avoda Zara* 3:2; *m. Avoda Zara* 2.1; *Tur,* Even Ha-Ezer 24; Beit Yoseph on *Tur,* Even Ha-Ezer 24).

The rabbis prohibited Jewish boys from studying with gentile tutors because they were aware of the prevalence of pederasty within certain classes in Greco-Roman society. In the Middle Ages this prohibition remained in effect because of the fear that the children might be led to forsake the Jewish faith.

Punishment for Male Homosexual Relations

The Bible prescribes two punishments for Jewish men who engage in male homosexual intercourse: (1) *karet,* "being cut off from the people Israel" (Lev. 18:29), and (2) death (Lev. 20:13).

The Mishnah (*m. Sanhedrin* 7.4) includes male homosexual intercourse among those capital crimes that merit "stoning," one of the four forms of capital punishment allowed by Talmudic legislation. The major legal codes also consider such intercourse a capital crime (Rambam, *Yad,* Issurei Biah, 1:14; Moses ben David of Coucy [France, 13th cent.], *Sefer Mitzvot Ha-Gadol,* negative precept 94; Y. M. Epstein [19th cent.], *Arukh HaShulchan,* Even Ha-Ezer 24).

It is doubtful whether this penalty was ever enforced in postbiblical Judaism. First, the Jewish community rarely had the authority to impose the death penalty.[22] Second, even if it did have such authority, in rabbinic literature there is a clear aversion to capital punishment. The strict requirements for evidence in a capital case—two eyewitnesses who warned the perpetrator(s) of the nature of the crime—made it difficult, if not impossible, to arrive at a death sentence.

An account in the Jerusalem Talmud illustrates this in particular regard to male-male sexual intercourse. In the story, R. Judah b. Pazzi discovered two men having sexual relations in the attic of the schoolhouse. They said to him, "Rabbi, please take note that you are one and we are two," indicating that his testimony would be useless (*j. Sanhedrin* 6.4, 23c). Two witnesses would have been required to convict them, and Jewish law prohibits self-incrimination.

Male homosexual intercourse also appears among those transgressions that merit *karet* (*m. Keritot* 1.1). The rabbis explained *karet* as the divine punishment of an untimely death (*b. Moed Katan* 28a). Because the punishment is at the hands of God, witnesses and previous warning are not required. If the transgression was willful, the transgressor suffers the punishment of *karet*. If the transgression was inadvertent, he is obligated to bring a sin offering to the Temple (*m. Keritot* 1.2). One can avoid *karet* through repentance, *teshuvah*.[23]

Both the active and the passive partner in an act of male-male sexual intercourse *per anum* are liable for the penalty (*b. Sanhedrin* 54a). Whether or not the parties were adults determined the nature of the penalty. If both were adults, they were both liable for the death penalty by Torah law. If one was an adult and the other a child of nine years and a day to thirteen, Torah law held the adult liable for the death penalty and the child for a flogging for disobedience by the decree of the rabbis. If one was an adult and the other a child nine years or younger, both were free from penalty by Torah law, although the adult was liable for a flogging for disobedience by the decree of the rabbis (*Sifra* on Lev. 20:13; *b. Sanhedrin* 54a; Rambam, *Yad*, Hilkot Genevah 1.10; *Sefer Ha-Chinnukh* 209).

The punishment for male homosexual relations was thought to go beyond individual retribution to include a disruption of the natural order. Rabbi Acha, a fourth-century Palestinian sage, for example, claimed that earthquakes were a punishment for the sin of male homosexual intercourse (*j. Berakot* 9.2). In addition, male-male sexual relations were counted among the four causes of solar eclipses.

> Our Rabbis taught: On account of four things is the sun in eclipse: On account of an *Ab Beth Din* who died and was mourned fittingly; on account of a betrothed maiden who cried out aloud in the city and there was none to save her; on account of sodomy (male homosexual relations) and on account of two brothers whose blood was shed at the same time. (*b. Sukkot* 29a) (Soncino translation)

Yichud—Can Two Single Men Be Alone Together?

Jewish law considers it to be inappropriate for a man and a woman who are not married to each other to be alone together. This prohibition generally has not been applied to two men, as can be seen in the Mishnah, *m. Qiddushin* 4:14. There, Rabbi Judah holds that a single man may not be a shepherd nor shall two single men sleep under the same cloak. The sages disagree with him and argue that "Israel is not suspected of this [that men would be tempted to engage in homosexual or bestial relations]."

The *halakhah*, Jewish law, follows the opinion of the sages who hold that two single men can be alone together (see Rambam, *Yad,* Issurei Biah 22:2). Jacob ben Asher (Spain, 14th cent.) permits this as well but states that one who takes the more stringent position and does not remain alone with another man is worthy of praise (*Tur,* Even Ha-Ezer 24). In the *Shulchan Arukh,* however, Joseph Caro (Israel, 16th cent.) advises that men should not be alone together because of the lewdness that has spread "in our times" (*Shulchan Arukh,* Even Ha-Ezer 24).

Caro's contemporary and teacher, Solomon Luria (16th cent.), disagreed and claimed that one who followed Caro's strict proscription was guilty of religious snobbery. One hundred years later, a Polish rabbi, Joel Sirkes (17th cent.), argued that because sexual relations between men were unheard of in his time, one need no longer follow Caro's prohibition, although one could do so for pious reasons (*Bayit Chadash* on *Tur,* Even Ha-Ezer 24).

Overall, there are very few responsa and little discussion on the issue of sexual relations between men. Male homosexual relations were clearly forbidden, and such relations do not appear to have been perceived as a major social problem.

Sexual Relations Between Women

Although some streams of rabbinic interpretation extrapolated the prohibition of sexual relations between women from the prohibition in Leviticus 18:3 against following the practices of the Egyptians (*Sifra* on Lev. 18:3; Maimonides, *Yad*, Issurei Biah 21:8), most authorities understand the prohibition to be a rabbinic injunction rather than biblical law. The discussion in the Talmud focuses on the issue of whether women who have sexual relations with other women are prohibited from marrying *cohanim* (members of the ancient priestly tribe). This discussion is part of a larger discussion concerning which forms of sexual activity would have prohibited a woman from marrying a *cohein*, a "priest."[24]

Biblical law prohibits a *cohein* from marrying a *zonah*, usually translated as "prostitute." Although the rabbis suggest various definitions for a *zonah*—a faithless wife, a single woman who has nonmarital sex with a man, an infertile woman who engages in heterosexual relations, a professional prostitute—for the purpose of this discussion, the legal definition of a *zonah* is "a female proselyte, a freed bondwoman, and one who has been subject to any meretricious intercourse" (*b. Yebamot* 76a).

Women who engage in lesbian intercourse are, therefore, permitted to marry *cohanim*.

> Said Raba: The law is [not] in agreement [with the opinion of] . . . R. Huna [who] said: Women who practice lewdness with one another (*mesolelot*) are disqualified from marrying a priest. And even according to R. Eleazer, who stated that an unmarried man who cohabited with an unmarried woman with no matrimonial intention renders her thereby a harlot, this disqualification ensues only in the case of a man; but when it is that of a woman that action is regarded as mere obscenity (*peritzut*). (*b. Yebamot* 76a; see also *b. Shabbat* 65a–b) (Soncino translation)

The term used for women who engage in sexual relations with other women is *mesolelot*, literally "women who rub." This seems to refer to genital stimulation. *B. Sanhedrin* 69b used the verb to describe a mother fondling her son. According to Rashi, this term describes women who rub their genitalia together in a manner not unlike male-female intercourse (Rashi on *b. Yebamot* 76a). In any case, because there is no penile penetration, it is not considered to be sexual intercourse.

Unlike nonmarital heterosexual intercourse, which can be described as *zenut*, "illicit and improper sexual relations," sexual relations between women are described as *peritzut*, "licentiousness," a much lesser offense that lacks a prescribed penalty or legal significance. However, because it is a prohibited activity, Maimonides holds that the Jewish court can order women who engage in such acts to be flogged for rebelliousness.

> Women are forbidden to engage in lesbian practices with one another, these being "the doings of the land of Egypt" (Lev. 18:3), against which we have been warned, as it is said, "after the doings of the land of Egypt . . . ye shall not do" (Lev. 18:3). Our Sages have said, "What did they do? A man would marry a man, or a woman a woman, or a woman would marry two men." Although such an act is forbidden, the perpetrators are not liable to a flogging, since there is no specific negative commandment prohibiting it, nor is actual intercourse of any kind involved here. Consequently, such women are not forbidden for the priesthood on account of harlotry (*zenut*), nor is a woman prohibited to her husband because of it, since this does not constitute harlotry. It behooves the court, however, to administer the flogging prescribed for disobedience, since they have performed a forbidden act. A man should be particularly strict with his wife in this matter, and should prevent women known to indulge in such practices from visiting her, and her from going to visit them. (Maimonides, *Yad*, Issurei Biah 21.8; see also *Tur Shulchan Arukh*, Even Ha-Ezer 21)[25]

Rachel Biale offers three explanations for the limited amount of material concerning sexual relations between women; there are two passages in the Talmud and one from Maimonides. The first is that "women accepted their role as sexual partners in marriage as so self-evident, so powerfully reinforced by the society and culture, that other sexual practices were not entertained." The second is that legal problems concerning lesbian intercourse did arise, but "they were resolved without written record, suppressed because they were too embarrassing." Her third reason is that "lesbianism existed in the lives of women but remained unknown to the men who made the decisions in matters of Halakhah."[26]

Homosexual Love in Medieval Hebrew Poetry and Other Sources

In general, Jewish sources from the Middle Ages record few incidents of homosexual behavior. Although homosexual behavior was not unknown, medieval halakhic authorities suggest that sexual relations between men were more of a problem for the Jewish communities in Muslim than in Christian lands. For example, the author of *Sefer Ha-Chinnukh* (end of the 13th cent.) wrote:

> Well, I saw that . . . Ramban (Nachmanides) of blessed memory [does not] agree with the interpretation of [Targum] Onqelos [on Deut. 23:18], but rather states that the injunction "neither shall there be a *qadeish*" is given to abjure us that we should not permit a male prostitute to exist among us, the holy people—i.e. a man prepared to be used for carnal relations, such as are known to exist in the lands of the Ishmaelites to this day [see Ramban on Deut. 23:18].[27]

As we saw above, the sixteenth-century jurist from Sefat in the land of Israel, Joseph Caro, prohibited two Jewish bachelors from sharing the same blanket because of the lewdness prevalent in "our times." One hundred years later, however, a Polish rabbi, Joel Sirkes, held that the prohibition was no longer necessary because such practices were unheard of in his country (*Bayit Chadash* on *Tur,* Even Ha-Ezer 24).

The most explicit references to gay love, however, can be found in some of the love poetry produced by Jews in Muslim Spain.[28] Although one cannot deny that there is a homosexual element in this poetry, its significance is harder to determine. Of most importance, the poetry reveals little historical data about homosexual love and lovers, except that they existed within a literary culture along with forbidden heterosexual loves and lovers.

Medieval Hebrew poetry drew its meter and themes from contemporaneous Arabic poetry. Love of boys is one of these themes. Unlike Arabic verse, which at times has explicit descriptions of sexual acts with boys, the most explicit reference to sexual activity found so far in the Hebrew poetry is to kissing.[29]

The poetry deliberately reveals little information about the poets' own lives. Raymond Scheindlin notes that the poets' goal "was to write poetry, not autobiography. . . . [T]he love celebrated in the poetry . . . is not given poetic form for the sake of individual expression but on behalf of a communal ideal." This ideal, he claims, is "the celebration of a life devoted to joy and beauty."[30]

Scheindlin argues that "it is a peculiarity of Arabic and Hebrew love poetry that the beloved is regularly, though not consistently, referred to in the masculine gender. . . . The use of the masculine gender creates an atmosphere not of maleness but of indefinite sexuality."[31] The concern of the poetry was to celebrate the ideal of love. Descriptions of sexual activity, heterosexual or homosexual, would tend to lower the beloved into the world of particulars instead of elevate her or him into the ideal world.

In many ways, the idealization of love and beauty in this poetry is a secularized version of the understanding of sex in Jewish religious literature. Scheindlin concludes his description of medieval Hebrew love poetry by claiming:

> Love, whether consummated or chaste, whether heterosexual or homosexual, is spiritual when it is understood by its practitioners as the ennobling service of beauty itself; when its sensual pleasures point the way upward, rather than toward the earthbound extremes of licentiousness on the one hand, domesticity and procreation on the other. Within this great innovation, the quiet use of the masculine gender in love poetry takes its place as a variation on a truly great theme.[32]

Norman Roth notes that this poetry "appears to be the only evidence we have for the love of boys among the Jews." He claims that the most likely additional source, the surviving responsa—legal opinions written by leading jurists—from medieval Spain, provides scant information. Roth argues that this lack is due to the nature of responsa literature. Not only does he claim that responsa often lack "precise details most of interest to historians"; Roth further states that of all the responsa written, only those opinions that had "continuous relevance as a legal precedent" survived.[33]

Nevertheless, Roth finds some additional evidence for homosexual relations from this period. He cites a responsum, which he attributes to the jurist and poet Joseph ibn Abitur, that describes a cantor who was dismissed from his post for his conduct with Jewish and gentile women. The responsum contains a list of this cantor's sexual indiscretions that includes the claim that he had sexual relations with a youth.[34]

Furthermore, Roth also adduces evidence that the important tenth-century Jewish jurist and philosopher, Sa ʿadyah Gaon, had homosexual love affairs. Roth argues that Sa ʿadyah's failure to refute the charges that he had sexual relations with Jewish youths leveled against him during his controversy with the exilarch, head of the Babylonian Jewish Community, David ben Zakkai, suggests that the accusation may have been correct. Roth notes that this failure or omission stands in contrast with Sa ʿadyah's careful refutation of all other charges against him.[35]

Overall, there are very few responsa on the issue of sexual relations between men. The few that do reinforce the contention that Jewish law deals with sexual acts and not sexuality and sexual orientation. A responsum by Rav Kook, the former chief rabbi of British Mandate Palestine, illustrates this point. In 1912, while he was still chief rabbi of Jaffa, Rav Kook concludes that a *shochet*, a kosher slaughterer, could retain his post after he was accused of homosexual behavior, because he may have repented the act.[36]

Contemporary Jewish Views on Homosexuality[37]

Much of the discussion concerning homosexuality in contemporary Judaism starts from the assumption that heterosexuality is the norm.[38] Homosexuality, therefore, is presented as an aberration from the norm[39] and is discussed as either a willful sin[40] or mental illness.[41]

In addition, many of the arguments against homosexuality express concerns that do not necessarily reflect the reality of gay life. Norman Lamm fears that "were society to give its open and even tacit approval to homosexuality, it would invite more aggressiveness on the part of adult pederasts toward young people."[42] David Novak claims that the rabbis' concern with the Sodomites' attempt at homosexual rape "might very well be the rabbis' reflection about the presence of sadistic elements in many homosexual acts, a view found in the halachah."[43] Finally, David Feldman, who understands "homosexual indulgence as a sin," believes that a greater societal acceptance of homosexuality presents a danger to marriage and the family. "In an age of family dissolution," he argues, "it is all the more urgent to assert the stance of halakhah against an antithetical lifestyle."[44]

These fears seem to be unfounded. Hershel Matt correctly notes that as "there is no basis for assuming that homosexuals as such are guilty of such immoral behavior, we must not ourselves indulge in, nor encourage in others, such stereotyped thinking or prejudiced attitudes."[45]

Norman Lamm uses the understanding of homosexuality as a mental disease to argue for an acceptance of the homosexual while still rejecting homosexuality.[46] Because the homosexual has no choice, he cannot be held responsible for his actions. Such an approach, however, is rejected by Immanuel Jakobovitz, because the traditional sources do not present homosexual behavior as disease.[47]

There has been a growing acceptance and institutional support of gay Jews in non-Orthodox Judaism. In 1977, the Central Conference of American Rabbis (C.C.A.R.—Reform) adopted a resolution supporting civil rights for gay people. Similar resolutions were passed by the congregational branch of the Reform movement, the Union of American Hebrew Congregations (U.A.H.C.) in 1975, 1985, 1987, 1989. Gay Jews have formed congregations, and several are now members of the Union of American Hebrew Congregations (Reform).

In 1984, the Reconstructionist Rabbinical College (R.R.C.) established the policy not to consider an applicant's sexual orientation as a criterion for admission to the school. In recent years, the Hebrew Union College—Jewish Institute of Religion (Reform)—has established guidelines similar to those of the R.R.C. and now considers a candidate's sexual orientation only within the context of his or her overall suitability for the rabbinate.

In 1990, the Reconstructionist Rabbinical Association (R.R.A.) adopted a resolution in support of fuller acceptance of gay and lesbian Jews, including a clause that states that in respect to rabbinic placement the Reconstructionist movement expects all congregations to "refrain from discrimination on the basis of gender, marital status, sexual orientation, birth-religion, age, race, national origin or physical disability." Currently, the Congregational and Rabbinic branches of the Reconstructionist movement are working to produce a joint policy statement that would affirm the movement's commitment to full acceptance of gay and lesbian Jews.

Also in 1990, the C.C.A.R. completed a four-year study on the issue of homosexuality and the rabbinate, and issued a resolution that reaffirmed earlier statements of gay rights and expressed support for gay and lesbian Jews in general and gay and lesbian rabbinic colleagues in particular.[48]

The Conservative movement has adhered to a more traditional approach to the issue than have the Reform and Reconstructionist movements. Similar resolutions on gay and lesbian Jews were adopted by the Rabbinical Assembly (R.A.) in 1990 and by the United Synagogue (U.S.) in 1991, the Conservative movement's rabbinic and congregational branches respectively. Although the resolutions affirmed the Jewish tradition's "prescription for heterosexuality," they expressed the R.A.'s and U.S.'s concern for gay and lesbian Jews as individuals. The resolution called for civil equality for gays and lesbians, and requested the members of the Conservative movement to increase their awareness and concern for fellow Jews who are gay and lesbian. In addition, it asked Conservative synagogues to welcome gay and lesbian Jews into membership as Jews.

The Conservative movement's position was further defined in March 1992 in a policy statement issued by the R.A.'s Committee on Jewish Law and Standards. Although the law committee reaffirmed the previous resolutions that call for the welcoming of homosexuals as individuals in Conservative congregations, camps, youth groups, and schools, it prohibited the admission of avowed homosexuals to the Conservative move-ment's rabbinical and cantorial schools as well as to the Rabbinical Assembly and the Cantors Assembly. The law com-mittee also prohibited commitment ceremonies for homosex-ual Jews. It further mandated individual Conservative rabbis to use the responsa accepted by the committee as well as the sensitivities of his or her particular congregation in determin-ing the roles to be played by homosexual Jews in the profes-sional and lay leadership of local congregations.[49]

In recent years, gay Jews have formed their own local, na-tional, and international religious, social, and political associa-tions. Synagogues serving predominantly gay and lesbian communities can be found in most major metropolitan areas. The World Congress of Gay and Lesbian Jewish Organizations, founded in the early 1980s, serves as a coordinating body for many of these groups.[50]

Yet there is still a long way to go before gay Jews will be fully integrated into Jewish life. Non-Orthodox Jews have the same prejudices against gays as do other groups. There is no formal way of acknowledging the lasting bonds of gay couples. Leadership positions still need to be opened up for gay Jews.

Ira Eisenstein, founder of the Reconstructionist Rabbinical College, argues for tolerance. He sees the problem of homosexu-ality as a problem of heterosexuals. He claims that heterosexuals need "to look upon homosexuals as persons with a sexual pref-erence different from their own."[51]

In writing about her experiences in her congregation, Janet R. Marder, the (Reform) rabbi of the gay and lesbian syna-gogue in Los Angeles, Beth Chayim Chadashim, tells how she overcame her prejudices and has come to "see homosexuality as a sexual orientation offering the same opportunities for love, fulfillment, spiritual growth, and ethical action as hetero-sexuality." She argues that liberal Judaism needs to develop ways to affirm the committed relationships of gay people and to open positions of religious leadership to gay members of the Jewish community.[52]

Hershel Matt uses the contemporary understanding of ho-mosexuality as a sexual orientation and not as a preference to undercut objections to gay rabbis. The choice for constitution-ally gay people, he claims, "is not whether 'to be homosexual,' but whether to live openly and with integrity what they truly are." Because people do not choose to be gay but simply are gay, Matt claims that there is no danger that people will be led into homosexuality by the model of a gay rabbi.

Matt argues for the possibility of change in the halakhic understanding of homosexuality. He notes that radical change has taken place in the development of Jewish law. Thus he asks, "Is it not therefore quite conceivable that recognized halakhic authorities may come to 'find,' concerning homosexual acts forbidden in the Torah, that, though they are generally forbidden, for 'constitutional' homosexuals they are permitted."[53]

Bradley Shavit Artson argues that because the Bible and the rabbis of the Talmud were not aware that people could be by nature gay, their prohibitions against homosexual activity cannot be applied to constitutional homosexuals. The term *to 'eivah* (abhorrence), therefore, cannot be rightly applied to a homosexual act within the context of a loving homosexual relationship. "*To 'eivah* (abhorrence) still applies to sexual relations with minors, bathhouse sex, rape, and sadomasochistic sex. In short, all sexual acts that are coercive, degrading or violent were rightly prohibited by the Torah and the rabbis."[54]

Conclusions

Although the Jewish sources frame the question of homosexuality in terms of sexual acts, the issue today centers not on sexual acts but on people's sexual orientation. For many contemporary Jews who are dissatisfied with the traditional approach to homosexuality, the crucial issue, therefore, is to develop a new Jewish approach that encompasses contemporary understanding of sexuality.

We no longer speak of sex acts but of sexuality. We recognize that just as some people are predominantly heterosexual, other people are predominantly gay. The traditional Jewish approach to homosexual relations—which expressed the belief that sexual acts between members of the same sex, like other forbidden sexual acts, were willful indulgences of one's desire (*b. Yebamot* 86a; Rambam, *Yad*, Issurei Biah 1.9)[55]—provides limited guidance. Furthermore, not only does contemporary theory not view homosexuality as willed behavior; it also rejects understanding it as disease. Therefore, the attempts of certain writers to picture homosexuality as an illness are also unsatisfactory.

Jewish sources reject celibacy. Legitimate sexual activity is encouraged. Sexual expression is not restricted to procreation within Judaism. Sexual relations within a marriage are a legitimate source of pleasure and strengthen the love of the couple for each other. Offering celibacy to gay people as the sole option, therefore, seems to run counter to Jewish understandings of the role of sex in human life.

Jewish sexual ethics have changed over time. Polygamy and concubinage, although allowed by biblical and Talmudic law, have been officially banned and have fallen out of practice. David Novak claims that these developments demonstrate that the goal of Jewish sexual ethics is to obtain a "true mutuality" of the two people involved, although he believes that this can be achieved only in monogamy.[56] Yet there seems to be no reason why gay people should be denied the opportunity to achieve such a goal.

These two factors—the new understanding of sexuality and the importance of sex in developing the bonding between two people—may be an avenue to the development of positive Jewish responses to the sexual aspects of the loving relationship of gay men and gay women. Jews, both gay and straight, are following this and other routes to the full incorporation of gay Jews into the life and traditions of the Jewish people.[57]

N.B.

Notes

1. For a general introduction to Jewish sources on sexual issues, see Louis M. Epstein, *Sex Laws and Customs in Judaism* (New York: Bloch Publishing, 1948).

2. *Human Sexuality,* American Medical Association, 1972, p. 3.

3. Gershon Winkler, "Sex and Religion: Friend or Foe?" *New Menorah,* 2d ser., 7 (1987): 1–3, cites Ramban (Rabbi Moses ben Nachman, Spain, 12th cent.) Responsa 2 and Yaakov Emden (Germany, 18th cent.).

4. Winkler, p. 3, cites Rabbi Isaiah de Trani (11th cent.), Tosefot Rid on *b. Yebamot* 34b.

5. Rachel Biale, *Women in Jewish Law* (New York: Schocken Books, 1984), p. 136.

6. Fred Rosner, *Sex Ethics in the Writings of Moses Maimonides* (New York: Bloch Publishing, 1974).

7. *American Heritage Dictionary,* s.v. "sodomy."

8. John J. McNeill, *The Church and the Homosexual,* 3d ed. (Boston: Beacon Press, 1988), pp. 75, 79–83.

9. Derrick Sherwin Bailey, *Homosexuality and the Western Christian Tradition* (New York: Longmans, Green & Co., 1955), pp. 51–52; see also Marvin H. Pope, "Homosexuality," in *Interpreter's Dictionary of the Bible, Supplementary Volume* (Nashville: Abingdon Press, 1976), pp. 415–417.

10. S. R. Driver, *Deuteronomy* (Edinburgh: T. & T. Clark, 1895), pp. 264–265.

11. Norman K. Gottwald, *The Hebrew Bible: A Socio-Literary Introduction* (Philadelphia: Fortress Press, 1985), pp. 207, 478–479.

12. Louis Ginzberg, *Legends of the Jews* (Philadelphia: Jewish Publication Society, 1909), vol. 1, pp. 150–151.

13. M. H. Lovelace, "Abomination," in *Interpreter's Dictionary of the Bible* (Nashville: Abingdon Press, 1962), vol. 1, p. 13.

14. Bailey, pp. 30–37.

15. David Novak, *The Image of the Non-Jew in Judaism* (New York: Edwin Mellen Press, 1983), pp. 201–202, 212.

16. Samuel H. Dressner, "Homosexuality and the Order of Creation," *Judaism* 40 (1991): 309–321.

17. Novak, *The Image,* pp. 201–202.

18. Translation: Novak, *The Image,* pp. 211–212.

19. Natural intercourse refers to vaginal intercourse. See also *b. Sanhedrin* 78a.

20. Translation: Charles Wengrow, *Sefer HaHinnuch* (New York: Feldheim, 1984), vol. 2, p. 365.

21. Robert Gordis, *Love and Sex: A Modern Jewish Perspective* (New York: Farrar, Straus & Giroux, 1978), p. 151.

22. Haim Hermann Cohn and Louis Isaac Rabinowitz, "Capital Punishment," *Encyclopedia Judaica,* vol. 5, pp. 142–147.

23. Israel Moses Ta-Shma, "Karet," *Encyclopedia Judaica,* vol. 10, pp. 788–789.

24. See Biale, pp. 192–197.

25. Translation: L. I. Rabinowitz and P. Grossman, *The Code of Maimonides,* Book Five: The Book of Holiness (New Haven: Yale University Press, 1965).

26. Biale, p. 196.

27. Translation: Wengrow, p. 365. There is no reason to assume that homosexuality was restricted to the Muslim world in the medieval period; see John Boswell, *Christianity, Social Tolerance, and Homosexuality: Gay People in Western Europe from the Beginning of the Christian Era to the Fourteenth Century* (Chicago: University of Chicago Press, 1980).

28. H. Schirmann, "The Ephebe in Medieval Hebrew Poetry," *Sefarad* 15 (1955): 55–68; Norman Roth, "'Deal Gently with the Young Man': Love of Boys in Medieval Hebrew Poetry of Spain," *Speculum* 57 (1982): 20–51; Raymond P. Scheindlin, *Wine, Women, and Death: Medieval Hebrew Poems on the Good Life* (Philadelphia: Jewish Publication Society, 1986), pp. 77–89.

29. Roth, p. 24.

30. Scheindlin, p. 78.

31. Ibid., p. 82.

32. Ibid., p. 89.

33. Roth, p. 23.

34. Ibid., p. 22.

35. Ibid., p. 23.

36. David M. Feldman, "Homosexuality and Jewish Law," *Judaism* 32, no. 4 (1983): 427.

37. For a variety of views, see (1) "Homosexuals and Homosexuality: Psychiatrists, Religious Leaders and Laymen Compare Notes," *Judaism* 128 (1983): 390–444; (2) "Judaism and Homosexuality," *Reconstructionist* 51 (1985).

For arguments for the acceptance of gay people, see Hershel J. Matt, "Sin, Crime, Sickness or Alternative Life Style?: A Jewish Approach to Homosexuality," *Judaism* 27, no. 1 (1978): 13–24; Hershel J. Matt, "Homosexual Rabbis?" *Conservative Judaism* 39 (1987): 29–33; Bradley Shavit Artson, "Judaism and Homosexuality," *Tikkun* 3 (1988): 52–54, 92–93.

For traditional opinions, see Basil F. Herring, "Homosexuality," in *Jewish Ethics and Halakhah for Our Time: Sources and Commentary* (New York: Ktav and Yeshiva University Press, 1984), pp. 175–195; Immanuel Jakobovits, *Encyclopedia Judaica*, vol. 8, cols. 961–962; Norman Lamm, "Judaism and the Modern Attitude to Homosexuality," in Menachem Marc Kellner, ed., *Contemporary Jewish Ethics* (New York: Sanhedrin Press, 1978), pp. 375–399; David Novak, "Some Aspects of the Relationship of Sex, Society, and God in Judaism," in Frederich E. Greenspahn, ed., *Contemporary Ethical Issues in Jewish and Christian Tradition* (Hoboken, N.J.: Ktav, 1986), pp. 140–166, esp. pp. 147–151.

38. See Ellen M. Umansky, "Jewish Attitudes Towards Homosexuality: A Review of Contemporary Sources," *Reconstructionist* 51 (1985): 9–15.

39. Dressner, pp. 319–321. Dressner argues that a traditional Jewish understanding of the order of creation as well as Hellenistic notions of "natural law" presuppose heterosexuality as the norm of human sexual relationships and that such a presupposition has normative force in the construction of a proper sexual ethic.

40. Feldman, p. 427.

41. Nathaniel S. Lehrman, "Homosexuality and Judaism: Are They Compatible?" *Judaism* 32 (1983): 392–404; Lamm, pp. 392–397.

42. Lamm, p. 395.

43. Novak, p. 148.

44. Feldman, p. 429.

45. Matt, "Homosexual Rabbis?" p. 31.

46. Lamm, p. 393.

47. Jakobovitz, pp. 961–962.

48. See Selig Salkowitz, ed., *Homosexuality, the Rabbinate, and Liberal Judaism: Papers Prepared for the Ad-Hoc Committee on Homosexuality and the Rabbinate* (New York: Central Conference of American Rabbis, 1989).

49. On March 25, 1992, the Committee on Jewish Law and Standards adopted four responsa that provided differing legal and philosophical reasons to support the committee's policy statement. They are Joel Roth, "Homosexuality"; Elliot Dorf, "Jewish Norms for Sexual Behavior: A Responsum Embodying a Proposal"; Reuven Kimelman, "Homosexuality and the Policy Decisions of the CJLS"; and Mayer Rabinowitz, "On Homosexuality." The responsum of Bradley Shavit Artson arguing for the acceptance of homosexuality as a "*Halakhically*-acceptable sexual orientation, provided that this sexuality is expressed within the context of a mutually-exclusive, committed, adult relationship," was rejected.

50. For further information, contact the World Congress of Gay and Lesbian Jewish Organizations, P.O. Box 18961, Washington, D.C. 20036. For a list of organizations, see Susan Weidman Schneider, *Jewish and Female* (New York: Simon & Schuster, 1984), pp. 567–570.

51. Ira Eisenstein, "Discrimination Is Wrong," *Judaism* 32 (1983): 416–417.

52. Janet R. Marder, "The Impact of Beth Chayim Chadashim on My Religious Growth," *Journal of Reform Judaism* 32 (1985): 33–36; "Getting to Know the Gay and Lesbian Shul," *Reconstructionist* 51, no. 2 (1986): 20–25.

53. Matt, "Homosexual Rabbis?" p. 32.

54. Artson, p. 92.

55. Herring, pp. 187–189.

56. Novak, "Some Aspects," pp. 151–152.

57. An exciting attempt to forge a "new theology of sexuality" that would stand behind a sexual ethic supportive of gay and lesbian relationships as well as of heterosexual ones appears in Judith Plaskow's *Standing Again at Sinai: Judaism from a Feminist Perspective* (San Francisco: Harper & Row, 1990), pp. 197–210. Plaskow argues that as part of this rethinking of the meaning of sexuality and sexual norms, the "question of the morality of homosexuality becomes one not of halakhah or the right to privacy or freedom of choice, but the affirmation of the value to the individual and society of each of us being able to find that place within ourselves where sexuality and spirituality come together" (p. 208).

Bibliography

Artson, Bradley Shavit. 1988. "Judaism and Homosexuality." *Tikkun* 3, 2:52–54, 92–93.

Bailey, Derrick Sherwin. 1955. *Homosexuality and the Western Christian Tradition.* New York: Longmans, Green & Co.

Balka, Christie, and Andy Rose, eds. 1989. *Twice Blessed: On Being Lesbian, Gay, and Jewish.* Boston: Beacon Press.

Beck, Evelyn Torton, ed. 1982. *Nice Jewish Girls: A Lesbian Anthology.* Watertown, Mass.: Persephone Books.

Biale, Rachel. 1984. *Women in Jewish Law.* New York: Schocken Books.

Boswell, John. 1980. *Christianity, Social Tolerance, and Homosexuality: Gay People in Western Europe from the Beginning of the Christian Era to the Fourteenth Century.* Chicago: University of Chicago Press.

Cohn, Haim Hermann, and Louis Isaac Rabinowitz. "Capital Punishment." In *Encyclopedia Judaica* 5:142–147.

Dressner, Samuel H. 1991. "Homosexuality and the Order of Creation." *Judaism* 40:309–321.

Driver, S. R. 1895. *Deuteronomy.* Edinburgh: T. & T. Clark.

Eisenstein, Ira. 1983. "Discrimination Is Wrong." *Judaism* 32, 3:415–416.

Epstein, Louis M. 1948. *Sex Laws and Customs in Judaism.* New York: Bloch Publishing.

Feldman, David M. 1983. "Homosexuality and Jewish Law." *Judaism* 32, 4:426–429.

Freehof, Solomon B. 1969. "Homosexuality." In *Current Reform Responsa,* 236–238. Cincinnati: Hebrew Union College Press.

———. 1973. "Judaism and Homosexuality." In *American Reform Responsa,* edited by Walter Jacob, 49–52. New York: Central Conference of American Rabbis. [*CCAR Yearbook* 88 (1973):115–119.]

Ginzberg, Louis. 1909. *Legends of the Jews.* Vol. 1. Philadelphia: Jewish Publication Society.

Gordis, Robert. 1978. *Love and Sex: A Modern Jewish Perspective.* New York: Farrar, Straus & Giroux.

Gottwald, Norman K. 1985. *The Hebrew Bible: A Socio-Literary Introduction.* Philadelphia: Fortress Press.

Herring, Basil F. 1984. "Homosexuality." In *Jewish Ethics and Halakhah for Our Time: Sources and Commentary,* 175–195. New York: Ktav and Yeshiva University Press.

"Homosexuals and Homosexuality: Psychiatrists, Religious Leaders and Laymen Compare Notes." 1983. *Judaism* 128:390–444.

Jacob, Walter. 1981. "Masturbation." In *American Reform Responsa,* edited by Walter Jacob, 479–480. New York: Central Conference of American Rabbis.

Jacob, Walter, et al. 1981. "Homosexuals in Leadership Positions." In *American Reform Responsa,* edited by Walter Jacob, 52–54. New York: Central Conference of American Rabbis. [*CCAR Yearbook* 91 (1981):67–69.]

Jakobovitz, Immanuel. "Homosexuality." In *Encyclopedia Judaica,* vol. 8, cols. 961–962.

"Judaism and Homosexuality." 1985. *Reconstructionist* 51.

Kahn, Joel. 1989. "Judaism and Homosexuality: The Traditional-Progressive Debate." *Journal of Homosexuality.*

Lamm, Norman. 1978. "Judaism and the Modern Attitude to Homosexuality." In *Contemporary Jewish Ethics,* edited by Menachem Marc Kellner, 375–399. New York: Sanhedrin Press. [*Encyclopedia Judaica Yearbook* (1984):194–205. Jerusalem: Keter.]

Lehrman, Nathaniel S. 1983. "Homosexuality and Judaism: Are They Compatible?" *Judaism* 32, 3:392–404.

Leneman, Helen. 1988. "Reclaiming Jewish History: Homo-Erotic Poetry of the Middle Ages." In *A Mensch Among Men: Explorations in Jewish Masculinity,* edited by Harry Brod, 143–149. Freedom, Calif.: Crossing Press.

Lovelace, M. H. 1962. "Abomination." In *Interpreter's Dictionary of the Bible* 1:13. Nashville: Abingdon Press.

McNeill, John J. 1988. *The Church and the Homosexual.* 3d ed. Boston: Beacon Press.

Marder, Janet R. 1985. "Getting to Know the Gay and Lesbian Shul." *Reconstructionist* 51, 2:20–25.

———. 1985. "The Impact of Beth Chayim Chadashim on My Religious Growth." *Journal of Reform Judaism* 32:33–36.

Matt, Hershel J. 1978. "Sin, Crime, Sickness or Alternative Life Style?: A Jewish Approach to Homosexuality." *Judaism* 27, 1:13–24.

———. 1987. "Homosexual Rabbis?" *Conservative Judaism* 39:29–33.

Novak, David. 1983. *The Image of the Non-Jew in Judaism.* New York: Edwin Mellen Press.

———. 1986. "Some Aspects of the Relationship of Sex, Society, and God in Judaism." In *Contemporary Ethical Issues in Jewish and Christian Tradition,* edited by Frederich E. Greenspahn, 141–166. Hoboken, N.J.: Ktav.

Plaskow, Judith. 1990. *Standing Again at Sinai: Judaism from a Feminist Perspective.* San Francisco: Harper & Row.

Pope, Marvin H. 1976. "Homosexuality." In *Interpreter's Dictionary of the Bible, Supplementary Volume,* 415–417. Nashville: Abingdon Press.

Prager, Dennis. 1990. "Judaism, Homosexuality and Civilization." *Ultimate Issues* 6, no. 2.

Rabinowitz, Louis Isaac, and P. Grossman. *The Code of Maimonides. Book Five: The Book of Holiness.* New Haven: Yale University Press.

Rosner, Fred. 1974. *Sex Ethics in the Writings of Moses Maimonides.* New York: Bloch Publishing.

Roth, Norman. 1982. "'Deal Gently with the Young Man': Love of Boys in Medieval Hebrew Poetry of Spain." *Speculum* 57:20–51.

Salkowitz, Selig, ed. 1989. *Homosexuality, the Rabbinate, and Liberal Judaism: Papers Prepared for the Ad-Hoc Committee on Homosexuality and the Rabbinate.* New York: Central Conference of American Rabbis.

Scheindlin, Raymond P. 1986. *Wine, Women, and Death: Medieval Hebrew Poems on the Good Life.* Philadelphia: Jewish Publication Society.

Schirmann, H. 1955. "The Ephebe in Medieval Hebrew Poetry." *Sefarad* 15:55–68.

Schneider, Susan Weidman. 1984. *Jewish and Female.* New York: Simon and Schuster.

Schwartz, Barry Dov. 1988. "The Jewish View of Homosexuality." In *A Mensch Among Men: Explorations in Jewish Masculinity,* edited by Harry Brod, 124–142. Freedom, Calif.: Crossing Press.

Ta-Shma, Israel Moses. "Karet." In *Encyclopedia Judaica* 10:788–789.

Umansky, Ellen M. 1985. "Jewish Attitudes Towards Homosexuality: A Review of Contemporary Sources." *Reconstructionist* 51:9–15.

Wengrow, Charles. 1984. *Sefer Hattinnuch.* Vol. 2. New York: Feldheim.

Winkler, Gershon. 1987. "Sex and Religion: Friend or Foe?" *New Menorah.* 2d ser., 7:1–3.

5

Homosexuality and Roman Catholicism

Denise Carmody and John Carmody

After centuries of disparagement, Roman Catholic homosexuals recently have found reason to hope that their tradition might be on the verge of reassessing its pastoral practice toward gay people. The prudent among them are not expecting the past disparagement to vanish quickly but the rise of Dignity, an organization to channel the aspirations of gay Roman Catholics, along with some more positive notes in Vatican instructions on homosexuality and Pope John Paul II's 1988 Christmas plea for AIDS victims, can be read as encouraging signs. This study, which attempts an overview of Roman Catholic attitudes, has three parts: New Testament foundations, historical perspectives, and recent discussion.

New Testament Foundations

Roman Catholics, like other Christians, have considered the Bible to be sacred scripture—writings revelatory of God's being and will. However, Roman Catholics through the centuries have set biblical authority alongside tradition—the church's understanding of the faith and ethics involved in following

Jesus. Thus, although biblical texts thought to bear on homosexuality have been important foundations of Roman Catholic
teaching, they have been far from the whole story.

The texts usually considered to support if not require the
disapproval that church authorities on the whole have shown are
Genesis 19:1–11, Leviticus 18:22 and 20:13, Romans 1:26–27,
1 Corinthians 6:9, and 1 Timothy 1:10. In recent times both
scriptural scholars and gay liberationists have mounted serious
challenges to taking any of these texts as certainly condemning
all aspects of same-sex love. For example, such pro-gay Roman
Catholics as John McNeill and John Boswell have disputed the
traditional antihomosexual interpretation of Genesis 19, arguing that a failure in hospitality is the greater issue. Nonetheless,
McNeill acknowledges that "the Church taught, and people universally believed on what they took to be excellent authority,
that homosexual practices had brought a terrible divine venge-
ance upon the cities of Sodom and Gomorrah."[1]

Because Rabbi Eron has ably discussed the Old Testament
texts in Chapter 4 of this volume, we will concentrate on Roman Catholic exegesis of the New Testament. First, however, it
bears noting that the three Old Testament texts (Gen. 19:1–11,
Lev. 18:22, Lev. 20:13) most likely to be thought to justify or
even require Roman Catholic authorities to condemn homosexual behavior say nothing about lesbianism (female homosexuality), and that only one of the three New Testament sources
even mentions women. The principles that Roman Catholic authorities used when analyzing homosexuality (mainly, that sex
is primarily for procreation) applied to men and women
equally, but, partly because of the Bible's stress on males, lesbianism usually received less attention than male homosexuality. Romans 1:26 was enough biblical warrant for assuming
that, *mutatis mutandis,* same-sex love between women was as
unacceptable as that between men, whereas Romans 1:26–27
seemed to set the two sexes in tandem: "For this reason [serv-
ing the creature rather than the Creator] God gave them up to
dishonorable passions. Their women exchanged natural relations for unnatural, and the men likewise gave up natural relations with women and were consumed with passion for one
another, men committing shameless acts with men and receiving in their own persons the due penalty for their error."

Commenting on these verses, Joseph A. Fitzmyer, S.J., a leading Roman Catholic scholar, wrote some years ago: "The contrast between 'females' and 'males' (1:27) makes it clear that the sexual perversion of which Paul speaks is homosexuality (specifically Lesbianism). The depravity of the perversion is the merited consequence of pagan impiety; having exchanged the true God for a false one (1:25), pagans inevitably exchanged their true natural functions for perverted ones."[2] From a pro-gay position, one might ask how clear the Pauline view of "nature" was and to what extent Paul's hierarchical thinking made a female eros independent of men unacceptable. As Bernadette J. Brooten recently has put it: "What he [Paul] could not accept was women experiencing their power through the erotic in a way that challenged the hierarchical ladder: God, Christ, man, woman."[3] This may also have been an issue in 1 Corinthians 11:2–16, although that is not usually considered a text bearing on homosexuality.

First Corinthians 6:9–10 may have homosexuals in mind when it makes the following sweeping generalization: "Do you not know that the unrighteous will not inherit the kingdom of God? Do not be deceived; neither the immoral, nor idolaters, nor adulterers, nor sexual perverts, nor thieves, nor the greedy, nor drunkards, nor revilers, nor robbers will inherit the kingdom of God." Roman Catholic commentators note that Corinth, like Greek urban centers generally, had a reputation for sexual looseness: "This warning is probably directed against the laxists who stretched Christian liberty into an antinomianism (6:12) and condoned the vilest depravities. The sexual vices that Paul enumerates were all too frequent in Gk city life. *Sensual perverts:* Lit., 'the soft, those who lie with males,' those addicted to pederasty."[4]

First Timothy 1:10, which present-day scholarship generally denies came from Paul himself, says that the law is laid down for the ungodly and sinners, who include "immoral persons, sodomites, kidnapers, liars, perjurers, and whatever else is contrary to sound doctrine." Commentators note that the Pastorals (1 and 2 Timothy, Titus) provide several other catalogues of vices (1 Tim. 6:4–5, 2 Tim. 3:2–5, Titus 3:3), none of which mentions homosexuality. Thus homosexuality is not singled out.

The scriptural basis for Roman Catholic prohibitions of homosexual behavior might be called significant, slim, or disputed, depending on one's exegesis and worldview. Certainly, the cultural assumptions behind the biblical texts could have been quite different from the assumptions of latter-day authorities who categorically condemned homosexual behavior. A further question, not lost on those opposing the tradition of condemnation, concerns whether the cultural assumptions of the biblical authors are aspects of the biblical revelation normative for all later periods. For example, if Paul subordinated women as a matter of course, is his condemnation of lesbianism flawed or subject to debate? If Christians have let go of biblical traditions such as not mixing kinds of animals, requiring kosher foods, prohibiting sexual intercourse during menstruation, and not requiring celibacy for priestly ministers, might they not let go of traditions that globally equated same-sex love with perversion? Third, and perhaps most telling, what is one to make of the silence of Jesus about homosexuality? Logically, one in fact can make nothing of it: silence neither affirms nor denies. Ethically, however, one might suggest that homosexuality must not have been a high priority on Jesus' agenda, which could lead to the conclusion that an adequate Christian estimate of homosexuality (both behavior and orientation) requires as its context those items that were of high priority on Jesus' agenda (God, faith, love). (We will return to this point in the last section of this essay.) Last, the biblical stories of the love between David and Jonathan (1 Sam. 18–20) and the love between Jesus and the beloved disciple (John 13:23–25) have served some pro-gay interpreters as biblical approval of same-sex love.

Historical Perspectives

Having indicated what both Roman Catholic and general reflection on the biblical texts traditionally thought to bear on homosexuality suggest, we turn to the question of how Roman Catholic Christianity tended to treat homosexuality down through the ages. The first point that commentators tend to make is that biblical thought was only part of the heritage

Christianity built upon. Also influential were Greek and Roman culture, which sometimes are joined under the rubric of "Hellenism." The short summary of Hellenistic attitudes, which shaped both Eastern and Western Christianity from New Testament times until at least the demise of Rome in the midfifth century A.D., is that they tolerated homosexuality as a solid minority option. The longer description would have chapters indicating Hellenistic bases for objecting to homosexuality, tributes to homosexuality as the noblest form of love (often in the context of men's depreciating female humanity), and laissez faire attitudes among the upper and urban classes that tolerated bisexual activities. Such luminaries as Plato and the Roman Emperor Hadrian could be claimed as advocates of homosexual love. Other forces in the background of Christian attitudes through the first millennium include tensions between urban and rural views and influences from Islam. Generally, urban mores were more tolerant of homosexual activities than rural, whereas Islam often was perceived as more tolerant than orthodox Christianity.

The urban culture that predominated until the fall of Rome in 430 was a force for tolerance of gay Christians. The early Middle Ages were more repressive, but during the eleventh and twelfth centuries cities revived and gay subcultures flourished. By the end of the twelfth century, a hardening trend had returned, and through to the Reformation homosexuals lived under a cloud of moral disapproval, if not outright fear of legal punishment. Roman Catholic teaching on sexuality continued to stress the primacy of procreation and so usually dismissed homosexuality as unnatural. In the seventeenth century, some Protestant theologians shifted the theology of marriage away from a primary focus on procreation, stressing the personal union of the spouses, but such thought influenced Roman Catholic sexual ethics significantly only in the twentieth century.

Granted such broad outlines, it remains to be said that Roman Catholic attitudes toward homosexuality varied greatly and often paid gay vices no more heed than heterosexual vices. John Boswell's learned study, *Christianity, Social Tolerance, and Homosexuality,* previously cited, provides many specific texts and names.[5] In Boswell's interpretation, a rigorist stratum of

Roman Catholic spirituality coexisted alongside much clerical and monastic indulgence of same-sex love. Key authorities in the rigorist stratum included the *Epistle of Barnabas,* Clement of Alexandria, Augustine of Hippo, and John Chrysostom. The latter three taught that procreation is the only legitimate use for sexuality and considered all sexual pleasure either ignoble or sinful. The *Epistle of Barnabas,* which may have been written before the end of the first century A.D. and which for some parts of the early church had a quasi-scriptural status, inaugurated a comparison of human behavior with that of animals that had great influence in stigmatizing homosexuality as an abhorrent behavior proper to the hare, hyena, and weasel.

The medieval bestiaries continued this tradition, complicating discussions of what behavior was "natural" to human beings and what was contrary to the way God had made them. Rigorist authors tended to argue both ways, using animals either as models of the upright behavior human beings ought to imitate or as symbols of the depravity into which faithlessness could fall.

Another complication was gender expectations. Sometimes male homosexuals were vilified because it was thought at least one of the partners had to be passive and so disgustingly womanish. To a lesser extent, lesbians could be stigmatized for an offensive mannish sexual initiative. Early legal landmarks included the Spanish Council of Elvira's (305) denying communion at the hour of death to men who had defiled boys, and the Roman Emperor Justinian's (533) categorizing homosexuality with adultery and stipulating the death penalty for both sins. Most such laws were indifferently administered.

The influential ninth-century theologian Hincmar of Reims castigated both male and female homosexuality as sodomy, mainly because he thought both forms of sexual activity involved an illegitimate (nonprocreative) release of seed. In the middle of the eleventh century, Saint Peter Damian published *The Book of Gomorrah,* complaining especially about rampant homosexuality among the clergy. By 1300, the gay literary renaissance of the eleventh and twelfth centuries had all but vanished, homosexuality could render one ineligible for clerical ordination, and in some areas homosexual acts could bring the death penalty. The years 1150–1350 in effect ended the tolerance of the homosexual option and promulgated an official condemnation of it as severely sinful.

Influences supporting gay love throughout the Middle Ages included such classical (pre-Christian) stories as the abduction of Ganymede by Zeus and the valor of Greek lovers such as Harmodius and Aristogiton, both of which influenced the medieval courtly love and romance that spread from Provencal toward the end of the first millennium. Medieval monks and nuns also provided sometimes unwitting support by writing of spiritual friendship in passionate, sometimes apparently homosexual tones.

One argument for the prevalence of homosexual behavior among both Christian laity and clergy is the fulminations of preachers such as Chrysostom and Peter Damian. Another is the provision of such monastic authorities as Basil and Cassian for avoiding homosexual attractions among monks. Other arguments include the mildness of canonical penalties for homosexual behavior and the inability of rigorist theologians in many periods to get church authorities to move against homosexual clergy, some of whom were well-known bishops.

These characterizations apply to the first thirteen centuries or so of Christian history and cut across geographical areas. Southern Europe was influenced toward tolerance by a Muslim presence, whereas Eastern Christianity continued to be shaped by Hellenistic sources. Such Hellenistic sources included the schools of Platonism that looked back to Socrates and Plato for their models of human excellence. They could not fail to note the assumption of Socrates and Plato that homosexual love took men to the heights of what the god Eros could accomplish, fully joining reason and passion. The Greek Orthodox who accounted Plato one of the church fathers did not always specifically exclude his views of homosexual love from their praise. The overall result of these roots of Greek Christianity in the classical and Hellenistic worlds was some softening of tendencies to move against homosexuals in a rabid manner. Even when church morality castigated homosexuality, the background of orthodoxy included a reminder that spiritual giants of the past had not clearly seen the morality revealed by Christ. Thus it seemed obvious that only the deep holiness brought by the Spirit of Christ could persuade those of homosexual inclination to seek an alternative in continence or heterosexuality. People of ordinary virtue might be excused their failings.

On the other hand, such regimes as that of the late sixth-century Visigoths in Spain considered homosexuality an especially abhorrent practice and moved against it vigorously. On the whole, though, Boswell makes a good case that the gravity homosexual activity was accorded after the thirteenth century (the rigorist views of Aquinas were representative and influential) was not present in most prior eras. As well, he shows that many eminent medieval Christian writers (Alcuin, Aelred of Rievaulx) composed lyrics open to homosexual interpretation.

Still, most of this data mitigates rather than removes the disapproval of homosexuality suggested by the writings of the rigorists. Apart from writers flaunting same-sex love or propagandizing for it, little literature promotes homosexual love, male or female, as a desirable expression of Christian faith. Gay people understandably often considered themselves fortunate that the authorities, ecclesiastical and civil, were considering their liaisons no more offensive than the irregular sexual contacts of heterosexuals, and later eras could look back on the overall tolerance of the first Christian millennium as the mark of a golden era.

With Aquinas and later authors came precisions about "nature" and actions befitting human beings that were unknown to earlier ages. Many scholastics, stressing procreation, followed Aquinas in condemning bestiality, homosexuality, and masturbation as unnatural acts. This stance dominated Roman Catholic moral theology until very recently, as the article on homosexuality in the *New Catholic Encyclopedia* (1967) suggests. The author's bottom line is that "the homosexual act by its essence excludes all possibility of transmission of life; such an act cannot fulfill the procreative purpose of the sexual faculty and is, therefore, an inordinate use of that faculty. Since it runs contrary to a very important goal of human nature, it is a grave transgression of the divine will."[6] This article makes important distinctions between subjective and objective guilt, and it urges pastoral understanding. But its view of natural law completely rules out the possibility of approving homosexual acts as morally acceptable. Indeed, the implication is that a homosexual inclination, although usually not deliberately chosen, is untoward and must not be expressed. (Moreover, the author limits all sexual expression to married people, so unmarried heterosexual pleasure also is unacceptable.) The pastoral conclusion drawn by the author gives the flavor of the natural law tradition at its kindest: "It should be stressed that a homosexual is just as pleasing to God as a heterosexual, as long as he makes a sincere effort to control his deviant bent will with the help of grace."[7]

Recent Discussion

In the past two decades, Roman Catholic moral theology has observed the various liberation movements. Although the response to the feminist and gay movements certainly has been less accommodating than adherents of those movements have wished, certain changes have occurred. For example, although the procreative dimension of sexuality continues to be very important, Roman Catholic authorities have come to consider the personal love of the people involved as equally important. Overall, one could say that personalist views, often supported by a reappreciation of biblical attitudes toward faith, have considerably shifted Roman Catholic moral thought.[8]

On the other hand, official statements from the Vatican continue to trouble gay liberationists. For, although Pope John Paul II is praised in some quarters as a personalist philosopher and his allocutions on sexuality have stressed the mutual love of the spouses, Vatican moral theology has given little leeway to homosexual lovers. Two publications of the Congregation for the Doctrine of the Faith, the Vatican agency concerned with proper teaching, illustrate recent official Roman Catholic views of homosexuality. The first, *Persona Humana* (December 29, 1975), mainly updated the natural law arguments, although it did make a distinction, which some readers found progressive, between a homosexual inclination and homosexual acts. Taking the view that a homosexual inclination had been called indifferent or even good, some pro-gay writers argued that it could not be wrong to express a good state, and so people of homosexual character could be sexually active. This reasoning contradicted the Congregation's own position (summarized by critical moral theologians such as Daniel Maguire as "be-but-don't-do"),[9] yet it pointed up the flaws in the official distinction between inclination and action.

On October 1, 1986, the Congregation for the Doctrine of the Faith moved to remove misunderstandings, issuing a letter entitled "On the Pastoral Care of Homosexual Persons."[10] The Congregation's way of clarifying matters itself caused considerable furor, because it described the homosexual orientation as "an objective disorder." The main reason given was a twist on the prior natural law arguments. Following John Paul II's views of the "spousal" (maritally loving, with an openness to procreation) character of human sexuality (obtained in good part from an exegesis of Gen. 1–3), the Letter in effect categorized all nonspousal sexual activity as aberrant.

Sympathetic interpretation of the Letter can limit its intent to the genital expression of homosexuality, and so shrink the application of "objective disorder"; but questions remain about this characterization of the homosexual inclination, all the more so because the Letter in other places urges appreciation of homosexuals as individuals and defends them against hatred and injustice. However, the harshness of the Letter itself suggests that homophobia has a toehold in the Vatican. As Bruce Williams, author of an excellent analysis, puts it: "A global hostile assessment of the gay movement is therefore as invalid as a globally benign one; and the former is arguably more apt to generate insensitivity toward injustice and even acute misery suffered by homosexuals—as witness the Letter's inflammatory allusion to AIDS, its one-sidedly negative approach to the question of civil-rights legislation, and its sinister insinuation (all too familiar from other contexts) that gay people by their provocative excesses are themselves largely blameworthy for the violent and insane hatred directed against them."[11]

For those sympathetic to Roman Catholic teaching and sufficiently persuaded by the overall Roman Catholic worldview to be patient with Roman ways of bringing faith to bear on present-day problems, the Letter may be read as an occasion for a positive and mutual challenge to gays and Roman Catholic thinkers. Difficult as it might be to establish the atmosphere for such a mutual challenge, the chance for gays to speak from their experience and faith, for Roman Catholic thinkers sympathetic to the Vatican position to do the same, and for both sides to listen could be beneficial, even healing. It might also get church officials to back away from the restrictions, if not repressions, they have placed on ministering to gays and supporting Roman Catholic gay organizations such as Dignity. Finally, it could spotlight what is sometimes called the principle of "gradualism," giving gays time to work out how much of the official Roman Catholic position they can accept in good conscience. However, to date, Vatican officials and those constrained by their views have seldom shown themselves willing to tamp down their calls for unquestioning obedience and enter into dialogue with gays (or any other dissidents) as people presumed to be of good will, intelligence, experience, and live faith.

Our own sense is that homosexuality and many other moral issues only stand in a fully Christian context when the love of God exemplified by Jesus and given in the Holy Spirit is the prime authority. That love seems to have directed Jesus' own quite radical ethical attitudes (consider his approach to "sinners") and to have relativized particular forms of behavior. If people loved one another, they were not far from the kingdom of God—regardless of how others considered their behavior. The author of 1 John drew from such love the conclusion that even when our hearts condemn us, God is greater. Augustine drew from it the conclusion that believers could love and do what they would. History certainly shows that such liberty can be abused. Equally, however, it shows that unless such liberty rules the church, the church is just another agency of social control, another support of the unjust status quo.

From her experience of working with people down-and-out, Rosemary Haughton—a theologian with few peers when it comes to appreciating how God's love works in history—has reflected on the gap between what people actually undergo and what theology tends to say about their lives. Perhaps the best way for us to conclude, and to suggest how Roman Catholic moral theology ought to move, is to quote some of her words: "I mentioned that some women, and often men too though less often, decide to share their family lives for mainly practical reasons. It is a matter of economic survival and also a protection. But if the arrangement is to succeed there must be a good relationship between the women. In fact, close friendships often develop; the sharing of responsibility and memories brings intimacy. In some cases the relationship is, or may become, overtly sexual. It is natural for intimacy and friendship to be experienced physically, and some kinds of physical endearment seem acceptable, but at a certain point they don't seem acceptable anymore. What are we really trying to do? Is it really possible, in terms of moral theology, to draw a line? Of course we have always done so, but if we do, why do we? What is behind the thinking that assumes that any kind of genital contact creates a morally totally different situation from other kinds of physical intimacy? (Whether or not we *approve* of certain kinds of intimacy is not the point.) We need to ask these questions, and if not to answer them at least to be willing to look at the quality of the relationships we are trying to reflect on in theological terms. It is in the giving and receiving of life and love that we discern the presence of God. At what point and on what grounds does God suddenly cease to be present?"[12]

Notes

1. See John J. McNeill, S.J., *The Church and the Homosexual* (Kansas City, Mo.: Sheed, Andrews and McMeel, 1976), p. 43; John Boswell, *Christianity, Social Tolerance, and Homosexuality: Gay People in Western Europe from the Beginning of the Christian Era to the Fourteenth Century* (Chicago: University of Chicago Press, 1980), pp. 92–99. Boswell also has useful cautions about translations of materials (both biblical and other) pertaining to homosexuality.

2. Raymond E. Brown, S.S., Joseph A. Fitzmyer, S.J., and Roland E. Murphy, O.Carm., eds., *The Jerome Biblical Commentary* (Englewood Cliffs, N.J.: Prentice-Hall, 1968), vol. 2, p. 297.

3. Bernadette J. Brooten, "Paul's Views on the Nature of Women and Female Homoeroticism," in Clarissa W. Atkinson, Constance H. Buchanan, and Margaret R. Miles, eds., *Immaculate and Powerful: The Female in Sacred Image and Social Reality* (Boston: Beacon Press, 1985), p. 78. Brooten offers interesting perspectives on the work of both Boswell and Robin Scroggs in *The New Testament and Homosexuality: Contextual Background for Contemporary Debate* (Philadelphia: Fortress Press, 1983).

4. Brown et al., p. 261.

5. Although we have learned much from Boswell, we find his work tendentious. Many items put forward as evidence are positioned or interpreted to favor homosexuality. Granted the past prejudices against homosexuality, this provides some welcome balance, but it also leaves the reader wondering how fully to trust the historical characterizations being offered.

6. J. F. Harvey, "Homosexuality," in *The New Catholic Encyclopedia* (New York: McGraw-Hill, 1967), vol. 7, p. 117.

7. Ibid., p. 119.

8. See Anthony Kosnick et al., eds., *Human Sexuality: New Directions in American Catholic Thought* (Garden City, N.Y.: Doubleday & Co., 1979).

9. See Daniel Maguire, "The Morality of Homosexual Marriage," in Robert Nugent, ed., *A Challenge to Love: Gay and Lesbian Catholics in the Church* (New York: Crossroad, 1983), p. 120.

10. Congregation for the Doctrine of the Faith, "On the Pastoral Care of Homosexual Persons" (Rome: Vatican Polyglot Press, 1986).

11. Bruce Williams, O.P., "Homosexuality: The New Vatican Statement," *Theological Studies* 48, no. 2 (June 1987): 270–271. See also Jeannine Gramick and Pat Furey, eds., *The Vatican and Homosexuality* (New York: Crossroad, 1988).

12. Rosemary Haughton, "The Meaning of Marriage in Women's New Consciousness," in William P. Roberts, ed., *Commitment to Partnership: Explorations of the Theology of Marriage* (New York: Paulist Press, 1987), p. 151. Haughton's major work on redemptive love is *The Passionate God* (New York: Paulist Press, 1981). Further reading on Catholic theologies of homosexuality should include Richard Woods, *Another Kind of Love: Homosexuality and Spirituality* (Garden City, N.Y.: Doubleday & Co., 1978); and Mary E. Hunt, *Fierce Tenderness: Toward a Feminist Theology of Friendship* (San Francisco: Harper & Row, 1992). BONDINGS, a tabloid dealing with homosexuality and gay Roman Catholics, is published by New Ways Ministry, 4012 29th Street, Mt. Ranier, MD 20712.

Bibliography

Boswell, John. 1980. *Christianity, Social Tolerance, and Homosexuality: Gay People in Western Europe from the Beginning of the Christian Era to the Fourteenth Century.* Chicago: University of Chicago Press.

Brooten, Bernadette J. 1983. *The New Testament and Homosexuality: Contextual Background for Contemporary Debate.* Philadelphia: Fortress Press.

———. 1985. "Paul's Views on the Nature of Women and Female Homoeroticism." In *Immaculate and Powerful: The Female in Sacred*

Image and Social Reality, edited by Clarissa W. Atkinson, Constance H. Buchanan, and Margaret R. Miles, 78. Boston: Beacon Press.

Brown, Raymond E., S.S., Joseph A. Fitzmyer, S.J., and Roland E. Murphy, O.Carm., eds. 1992. *The New Jerome Biblical Commentary.* vol. 2. Englewood Cliffs, N.J.: Prentice-Hall.

Congregation for the Doctrine of the Faith. 1986. "On the Pastoral Care of Homosexual Persons." Rome: Vatican Polyglot Press.

Gramick, Jeannine, and Pat Furey, eds. 1988. *The Vatican and Homosexuality.* New York: Crossroad.

Harvey, J. F. 1967. "Homosexuality." In *The New Catholic Encyclopedia.* Vol. 7. New York: McGraw-Hill.

Haughton, Rosemary. 1981. *The Passionate God.* New York: Paulist Press.

———. 1987. "The Meaning of Marriage in Women's New Consciousness." In *Commitment to Partnership: Explorations of the Theology of Marriage,* edited by William P. Roberts, 151. New York: Paulist Press.

Hunt, Mary E. 1992. *Fierce Tenderness: Toward a Feminist Theology of Friendship.* San Francisco: Harper & Row.

Kosnick, Anthony, et al., eds. 1979. *Human Sexuality: New Directions in American Catholic Thought.* Garden City, N.Y.: Doubleday & Co.

McNeill, John J., S.J. 1976. *The Church and the Homosexual.* Kansas City, Mo.: Sheed, Andrews and McMeel.

Maguire, Daniel. 1983. "The Morality of Homosexual Marriage." In *A Challenge to Love: Gay and Lesbian Catholics in the Church,* edited by Robert Nugent, 120. New York: Crossroad.

> Williams, Bruce, O.P. 1987. "Homosexuality: The New Vatican Statement." *Theological Studies* 48, 2:270–271.

Woods, Richard. 1978. *Another Kind of Love: Homosexuality and Spirituality.* Garden City, N.Y.: Doubleday & Co.

6

Homosexuality and Protestantism

Marvin M. Ellison

In *The Encyclopedia of Homosexuality* Warren Johansson writes: "For homosexuals the Judeo-Christian tradition has meant nothing but ostracism and punishment, exile and death. . . . To find anything positive in this tradition would be an arduous task."[1] Precisely for this reason, many gay men and lesbians repudiate organized religion or at least maintain a healthy distance in order to survive in a hostile context. The oppression of the homosexual community, Protestant ethicist Karen Lebacqz argues, is a form of sexual injustice, frequently accompanied by ostracism, discrimination, and physical violence. "The result," she notes, "is the ruination of people" and their dehumanization.[2] Because the church is the primary cultural legitimizer of antigay oppression, such injustice often takes place, ironically, in the name of a gospel of love, mercy, and peace.

At the same time, it is also true that Protestant churches include numbers of gay men and lesbians both as members and as clergy. However, many choose not to be public about their sexual identity for reasons of personal safety, acceptance by family and friends, and job security. Chris Glaser, a gay Presbyterian who has unsuccessfully challenged his church's ban against ordaining open, self-affirming homosexuals, observes that "usually, for most gay women and men, coming out *in* the church has meant coming out *of* the church. . . . The church has meant more than just a closet. . . . The church has become for them a giant tomb, smelling of death rather than life."[3] John McNeill speaks similarly of the frequent dilemma faced by gay Christians, whether Catholic, Protestant, or Orthodox—a dilemma between two difficult and undesirable options. On the one hand, some find that in their struggle for self-acceptance, they need to leave the church and perhaps even give up their faith in order to maintain their self-respect. On the other hand, some discover that in order to affirm their faith, they have to "repress and deny their sexuality and lead a life devoid of any sexual intimacy."[4]

With the emergence in the 1970s of a gay liberation movement within the churches, many gay men and lesbians are now asserting another possibility, namely, that there is no contradiction between their sexuality and authentic Christian spirituality. As gay persons and as people of faith, they are insisting on their right to full membership in the church and to the same responsibilities and privileges accorded others. The church, not gay men and lesbians, must change. The Protestant tradition is being called upon to continue its reformation, this time in the area of sexuality and social relations. The church—reformed and always reforming—is being called to move from being an exclusionary church steeped in sexual injustice to becoming an inclusive, hospitable church devoted to sexual justice and respectful of a diversity of human sexualities. As a Presbyterian study commission puts the matter: "As the church moves toward the twenty-first century, its moral credibility and capacity to offer creative guidance about human sexuality depend largely, we believe, upon our own willingness to 'seek sexual justice."[5] A significant challenge to traditional antigay church teaching and practice is, therefore, now underway within Protestantism as within other religious traditions.

Denominational diversity and the absence of a centralized teaching authority make it difficult to identify a single, unified Protestant voice about homosexuality or any other issue. A spectrum of opinion ranges from strong rejection and exclusion of gay persons from the church at one extreme, to a position of full, unconditional acceptance of gay men and lesbians within the church. No doubt, significant numbers of Protestants, especially conservative Evangelicals and biblical fundamentalists, reside most comfortably at the negative end of this spectrum. Traditionalists simply find no serious reason even to debate the moral status of homosexuality, much less to consider changes in church teaching and practice. In their view, biblical sources condemning homosexual practices are unambiguous and offer definitive guidance without any qualification. Homosexuality is best handled by religious taboo. For example, Southern Baptists at their 1976 convention passed a resolution affirming their "commitment to the biblical truth regarding the practice of homosexuality as sin" and urging churches "not to afford the practice of homosexuality any degree of approval."[6] In 1988, the Southern Baptist Convention passed, after only ten minutes of debate, a similar resolution condemning "homosexuality as an abomination in the eyes of God, a perversion of divine standards and a violation of nature."[7]

Such condemnation, especially when combined with a desire to punish and control, represents one extreme among contemporary Protestant responses, but not an uncommon one historically. Antigay persecutions, burnings and stonings, imprisonment and forced hospitalizations, and imposition of the death penalty for sodomy have been frequently justified by appeals to Christian conviction. Even today, this rejecting-punitive stance "may still be by far the most common orientation throughout the length and breadth of the church in our society."[8]

Protestants more moderate than Southern Baptists may also view homosexuality with suspicion and disapproval, but it is fair to say that there is significant moral and political ferment within nonfundamentalist, mainstream Protestantism pushing for a reassessment of homosexuality and the morality of same-sex love. In denomination after denomination, a serious, often heated, and rather inconclusive debate has emerged about homosexuality and, more generally, about human sexuality and sexual ethics. Frequently this debate focuses on ordination of gay men and lesbians as clergy and church leaders, a debate urged on by gay and lesbian Protestants and their allies in order to reshape Christian teaching and practice in more positive directions. Although resistance to such change is strong, what Catholic theologian Margaret Farley observes about her tradition is also true for Protestants: "Nearly every traditional moral rule governing sexual behavior in Western culture is today being challenged . . . [and] no question more intensely probed, more politically volatile, more personally troubling or liberating, than that of the moral status of same-sex relations."[9]

Even as Protestants have proceeded to debate a range of sexuality issues from reproductive technologies to teenage pregnancy, from abortion to sex education, ethicist James B. Nelson acknowledges that they "have not been able to deal creatively and forthrightly with sexuality in virtually any form." He cites homosexuality as the prime case in point.[10] There have been some signs of movement, however, including the appearance of gay-affirming denominational caucuses, such as Integrity (Episcopal), Lutherans Concerned, Presbyterians for Lesbian and Gay Concerns, Affirmation (United Methodist), Brethren/Mennonite Council on Gay Concerns, and the Seventh Day Adventist Kinship. These caucuses provide support networks for gay and lesbian church members, as well as resources to engage in education and political advocacy at a variety of levels. Some congregations have challenged exclusionary and restrictive denominational policies by declaring themselves "More Light Churches," "Reconciling Congregations," and so forth, in order to signal their commitment to the full participation of gays and lesbians in the life and ministry of the church. As recently as 1988, the United Church of Canada, following the lead of the United Church of Christ, the Unitarian Universalist Association, and the Universal Fellowship of Metropolitan Community Churches (MCC), approved the ordination of qualified homosexuals as clergy although the decision generated much controversy and there were threats of congregational secession across the church.

Despite these developments toward inclusivity and justice, most analysts of the Protestant debates share the conclusion that "the tensions in the churches between homosexuality and traditional Christian beliefs and values will not . . . be resolved quickly or effortlessly."[11] One strong factor at play is the institutionalized stigmatizing of homosexuality in this culture, but other factors are also at work. Church debates about homosexuality raise difficulties because the topic is, first and foremost, about sex and sexuality. For this reason, denominational studies have tended to follow the early lead of the 1977 United Church of Christ study *Human Sexuality: A Preliminary Study* by incorporating gay/lesbian issues within a more comprehensive framework dealing with a broad range of sexuality issues. A 1992 United Methodist report acknowledges, for example, that "homosexuality is best considered in the context of a more general Christian understanding of human sexuality."[12]

Although a 1991 Presbyterian Church (U.S.A.) study also acknowledges that "fear of sex and passion is pervasive in our churches," the report goes on to analyze how this fear is fostered by two interlocking dualisms, a body-spirit dualism and a male-female dualism. These dualisms contribute to the difficulties of the church debates about homosexuality. The first, or spiritualistic, dualism elevates the superior spirit over and in control of the inferior body. The Presbyterian study conjectures that "much sex-negativity in this culture displays this spiritualistic distortion, which generates both fear of and, simultaneously, fixation with sex and the body." The second, or patriarchal, dualism generates a gender hierarchy of value, status, and power and promulgates the belief that "good order means that men must be in command" of women.[13]

Homosexual relations clearly deviate from the patriarchal cultural pattern of male-dominant and female-subordinate sexual and social relations. As Presbyterian and feminist ethicist Beverly Wildung Harrison observes, homosexuality in this context "represents a break with the strongest and most familiar control on sexuality—compulsory heterosexuality" and the ideology of male control over women.[14] Sexuality shaped by these twin dualisms is an alienated sexuality, uncomfortable with the body (of self and of others) and distrustful of erotic desire and strong feelings. In Western culture, because gay men and lesbians have been stereotyped as highly sexualized "carriers" of this repressed sexuality, they are both envied and despised as representatives of the deep cultural ambivalence about sex and sensuality and as highly visible nonconformists to the cultural norm of male-dominant heterosexual marriage.

Other factors frustrating constructive debate about sexuality and sexual ethics include, in Nelson's words, "a middle-

class therapeutic mentality [ill at ease with moral argument]";
a fear of conflict and divisiveness, especially of any disruption
that might be costly in terms of church membership or financial contributions; a "tendency to react to sexual problems
rather than taking constructive initiatives"; and finally, "the
very complexity of sexuality itself."[15]

Given these deterrents, the intensity and scope of the
contemporary church debates within Protestantism is particularly noteworthy. As recently as 1964, for example, German
Protestant Helmut Thielicke was complaining that theologians
and church leaders were giving "little or no notice" to homosexuality and "therefore a body of opinion . . . is almost
nonexistent." Whatever attention was being given, Thielicke
lamented, it was too often "handled in a doctrinaire way," not
informed by "any pastoral encounter with these persons," and
tended "simply to reject the whole thing in the name
of . . . dogmatic axioms or in the fundamentalist form of biblical quotations."[16]

Early attempts to rethink homosexuality in a Protestant
context include the pioneering work of D. S. Bailey, an Anglican
canon, whose 1955 study *Homosexuality and the Western Christian Tradition* was cited by the Wolfenden Report (1957) leading
to the dismantling of antisodomy laws in England and Wales
and to the elimination of criminal penalties for consenting
same-sex relations. A similar breakthrough came in 1963 with
the publication in England of the Society of Friends' *Towards a
Quaker View of Sex.* Urging the church to "come of age" about
matters of human sexuality, the report recognized the importance of "taking a fresh look at homosexuality." This reexamination had special urgency precisely because "homosexuality
conjures up more passion and prejudice than possibly any
other subject except that of color. The two attitudes have much
in common; it is fear and ignorance behind them that give
them their venom."[17]

For Protestants, the truly unprecedented outpouring of
denominational studies, reports, pronouncements, and debates
about sexuality, including homosexuality, in the last two and
three decades has been remarkable. Three interrelated facts
have been at the center of these discussions or at least behind
the scenes prodding the reexamination. First, homosexuality is

now more commonly recognized as a fact of life.[18] Second, fear of same-sex eroticism and hostility toward gay men and lesbians are pervasive in Western societies.[19] Third, Christianity, including Protestantism, has a very certain role in the oppression of gay men and lesbians. As one Protestant theologian puts the matter: "The sources of the peculiar horror of homosexuality in our culture are obscure and complex. The Christian tradition, both on the formal and on the popular levels, has had something to do with the case . . . [but] whatever judgment may be made on homosexuality, church and society owe to human beings a concern for justice and a respect for dignity and privacy. Morality is not a valid pretext for cruelty."[20]

This concern for justice and respect, as well as recognition that condemnation and persecution of any person or group is incompatible with the Christian vision of the moral life, has recently precipitated an important shift in the very terms of the debate about homosexuality in Protestant contexts. Many suggest that the problem of homosexuality may be more aptly named a problem of oppression and sexual injustice, namely, the intertwined dynamics of homophobia and heterosexism. Homophobia, a deep-seated fear and intolerance of same-sex love, speaks of an internalized feeling of aversion toward homosexuality. Heterosexism is the systemic, institutionalized enforcement of compulsory heterosexuality upon all men and women in this culture, along with the assignment of sexual normalcy and moral legitimacy to heterosexuality alone. Just as this society's race problem is more accurately named a problem of institutionalized white supremacy and the so-called woman question a matter of male gender privilege and sexism, so the issue of homosexuality can be located in the prevailing belief structures and institutional practices legitimating the oppression of this sexual minority.

In light of this critical renaming, the church's agenda refocuses to examine its own involvement in sexual oppression and to challenge yet another form of institutionalized evil within its common life and in the society. As this shift within the Protestant debates over homosexuality progresses, renewed attention is being given to insights from four resources: scripture, the traditions of church teaching and practice, other disciplines of inquiry and knowledge, and contemporary experience, most especially the witness and contributions of gay and lesbian Christians themselves. For mainstream Protestants, these sources inform but do not determine theological and ethical sensibilities. The weight given to any one source or to the dynamic interplay of several sources together will vary from denomination to denomination and from person to person. As particular responses are shaped and given articulation, however, whatever is communicated about same-sex love and relationships also reveals much about the diversity, as well as the depth of disagreement and conflict, among Protestants. A brief review and assessment of developments in each area will follow.

The Bible and Homosexuality

Contemporary Protestants acknowledge the Bible as a primary, though not exclusive, guide on matters of faith and practice. There is a consensus within the nonfundamentalist mainstream that biblical texts are historically and culturally conditioned and must be critically interpreted for their relevance to current issues. Care is needed to examine the meaning of texts within their own historical contexts and how they apply to contemporary issues. However, on matters of human sexuality, and perhaps especially regarding homosexuality, there is often staunch resistance to reconsidering what the Bible does and does not say about such matters. James B. Nelson has observed that it is a rather "curious but unmistakable phenomenon that a great many Christians treat so literally the references to homosexual practice in the Bible, while at the same time they interpret biblical texts on almost every other topic with considerable flexibility and non-literalness."[21]

In dealing more generally with human sexuality, contemporary Protestants exhibit a shifting away from biblical literalism; an interest in locating authority not in specific texts (proof-texting) but in the broad message of scripture within its historical and social context; a sensitivity to the bias of interpreters; and openness to insights from nonbiblical sources. A 1978 statement from the Reformed Church of America notes, for example, that "the contribution of the human sciences to our understanding of homosexuality is an invaluable aid to biblical and theological reflection" even though "the human sciences may not be used to abrogate the biblical witness."[22] United Methodist scholar Victor Paul Furnish insists even more forcefully that the church must be faithful both to "its gospel and open to all of the knowledge that can be gained from the pertinent fields of human inquiry. . . . Nothing can be credible that is heedless of empirical data and reasoned argument."[23]

Influenced by social scientific data about homosexuality as a distinct sexual orientation, Derrick S. Bailey, an early revisionist in the mid-1950s, argued in *Homosexuality and the Western Tradition* that "strictly speaking, the Bible and Christian tradition know nothing of *homosexuality;* both are concerned solely with the commission of homosexual *acts.*"[24] Moreover, argued Bailey, those acts were condemned either because they were associated with idolatry, cultic prostitution, sexual assault, and violation of the rights of others, or because the biblical authors believed that these acts were being undertaken by persons who were otherwise heterosexually constituted.[25] As Protestant evangelical theologian Virginia Mollenkott notes, "this negative context is often ignored" by Christians who absolutize selected texts in an ahistorical manner. She also concludes that "the Bible does not have a great deal to say about homosexuality."[26]

Bailey also argued that the few biblical references about homosexuality have been either misinterpreted or wrongly used to condemn same-sex relations. The sin of Sodom, he claimed, is not homosexuality, but rather inhospitality to strangers. This argument, that the Bible does not provide a blanket condemnation of homosexuality nor proscribe all forms of same-sex relationships, appears in the United Church of Christ 1977 study in this form:

> The larger question is whether the fate suffered by homosexuals over the centuries is biblically based and fully deserved, or whether it is a case where a questionable exegesis has led the Western church and culture to an equally questionable tradition of persecution and moral censure. The more narrow hermeneutical questions are whether the sin of Sodom is really sodomy and whether this can be demonstrated as such beyond a reasonable doubt."[27]

Presbyterian scholar George Edwards provides a variation on this argument by suggesting that phallic aggression and gang rape is the sin of Sodom. Ironically, Edwards then notes, an unwarranted "homosexualized" interpretation of the Sodom story has only served "the subtle purpose of shifting the horrific guilt in these stories from the account of masculinity run amuck to that of homosexuality."[28] Sexualized male violence, not homosexuality, is the proper subject of condemnation from these texts.

This apologetic approach to the Bible seeks to demonstrate that Christianity is not necessarily antihomosexual and that the Bible, when interpreted and used properly, does not justify anti-gay oppression. This apologetic project is carried forth by other scholars, including John Boswell, whose exegetical work is controversial and much debated. For example, Boswell in *Christianity, Social Tolerance, and Homosexuality* argues that "the New Testament takes no demonstrable position on homosexuality."[29] Although Paul, in Romans 1:26–27, appears to condemn homosexuality as unnatural, Boswell insists that the real issue is idolatry and that Paul also mistakenly assumes that all persons are heterosexual, some of whom are forsaking their natural desires because of confusion and willful debauchery. A 1985 Uniting Church of Australia study incorporates these themes directly: "[Paul] apparently understands the situation as one in which heterosexual people have deliberately adopted homosexual practices." Because knowledge of homosexual orientation is a modern insight, this study concludes that "upon close examination, most of the [biblical] passages offer little help . . . [or] shed any real light on the problem at hand"[30] regarding how to evaluate loving relationships between two adults of the same sex.

Biblical apologists argue that the Bible does not really condemn homosexuality. Others take a different approach, but often reach a similar conclusion. For example, a 1991 Lutheran study argues that "even if we conclude that Paul's judgment on same-sex acts is clearly negative, this does not necessarily determine the significance of this text for us today." Or, again, "the few biblical passages that refer to same-sex activity (with a much different social meaning than today) do not settle the issue." What matters are core gospel values and commitments that apply to all persons, gays and lesbians included: "love for neighbors and concern for right relationship"; "Jesus' affirmation of the dignity of all people, particularly those scored and considered to be 'the least'"; "the compassionate character of community"; and the common Christian calling to "care for one another and to live responsibly."[31] Such values make the way possible for Christians to affirm homosexual persons and to do so on biblical grounds.

In addition to debates about the meaning of texts, there is a second, related matter of how texts are to be applied in the current church debates and how these texts function authoritatively, if at all. This debate continues unresolved among mainstream Protestants, but within the gay and lesbian religious community as well. Gay theologian Robin Gorsline contends that "gay liberation is deeply suspicious of attempts, however well intentioned, to address the issue of homosexuality in the Bible." Even more pointedly, he adds: "The issue is not one of homosexuality and whether the Bible sustains, condemns, or is neutral about it. Neither canonical testament carries any authority for gay liberation on the subject of homosexuality. Gay liberation interprets scripture, not the other way around."[32]

Critical biblical scholarship has influenced the church debates by deepening awareness that the Bible cannot be appealed to in any simplistic way. The diversity of both perspectives and patterns of sexuality within scripture make it impossible to speak of a single, consistent biblical ethic of sexuality. Moreover, the vast differences between ancient social structures and the modern world argue against rigidly applying biblical norms without question. Biblical scholar Walter Brueggemann argues that although "the popular mind of the congregation regards the Bible as a seamless cloth with a unified teaching, . . . the Bible present[s] powerful theological views in deep tension with each other, if not in contradiction to each other." Therefore, he concludes, "responsible use of the Bible requires the effort to notice the differences and to sort them out."[33] Among Protestants, the debate is not whether to accept or reject the past, including biblical traditions, but rather how to discern what from within scripture bears authority for the church, and how—and by whom—those judgments should be made.

Diverse Traditions in the
History of the Western Churches

A diverse and pluriform rather than monolithic tradition characterizes the history of Western Christian responses to homosexuality and same-sex love. Contrary to a presumptive claim often rhetorically asserted, the church has not consistently condemned, much less persecuted, homosexual persons throughout its history. There have been periods of silence, indifference, toleration, and even tacit acceptance of homosexuality. Although it is quite true to say, as D. S. Bailey has observed, that "from time to time councils and synods denounce sodomy," it is also true that "we look in vain for that obsessive concern with this one offense which many have imagined that they have detected in the records of ecclesiastical legislation." Bailey rightly notes that "indeed, it is striking to observe how relatively small a place in conciliar and synodal proceedings is occupied by condemnations of homosexual practices."[34]

Although some theologians of the early church denounced homosexual practices, remarkably little attention was given overall to this issue. It was not until the dissolution of the Roman state, from the third through the sixth centuries, that hostility against homosexual persons became visible in church and civil legislation. It is interesting to note that through the twelfth century Christian moral theology was either silent on the subject or "treated homosexuality as at worst comparable to heterosexual fornication," with the result that, as historian John Boswell has documented, "legal enactments were very rare and of dubious efficacy."[35]

In the eleventh and twelfth centuries, with the reemergence of urban centers and more stable social and economic conditions, there appeared a flourishing and publicly visible homosexual subculture that exercised considerable cultural influence, experienced little animosity, and, in fact, was widely tolerated by both religious and civil leaders. In the latter half of the twelfth century, however, a distinctively virulent hostility toward homosexual persons began to surface and increased during the following two centuries. Boswell has argued that although "the causes of this change cannot be adequately explained, . . . they were probably closely related to the general increase in intolerance of minority groups," especially Jews, to the crusades against non-Christians and heretics, and to the rise of the Inquisition and the persecution of witchcraft.[36]

This generalized hostility toward minority groups, particularly those visibly deviating from majority standards, was reflected in the theological and ethical writings of the late Middle Ages. This negativity was not subsequently challenged during or after the Protestant Reformation of the sixteenth century and has continued to influence European societies well into the modern period. What has also been undoubtedly influential in shaping the dominant Christian ethos about homosexuality has been a more general, quite negative theological and moral legacy about human sexuality. Two motifs are particularly significant. The first, dating from the early church writers, is a pervasive negativity toward the body and deep moral suspicion about sexual passion in particular.[37] A second motif is the strongly procreative ethic shaping attitudes and practices.[38] According to this procreative norm, all homosexual activity was judged as intrinsically wrong and disordered because it served no rational purpose and offended "against nature" and reason.

The Protestant Reformers did not challenge the prevailing negative judgment against homosexuality. Martin Luther rejected same-sex activity as an "idolatrous distortion instilled by the devil."[39] John Calvin modified this judgment only slightly by condemning homosexuality as a sin against nature. The Reformers, in their determination to critique clerical celibacy, not only elevated marriage above celibacy, but also made heterosexual marriage virtually obligatory for clergy and laity. As a Protestant theologian remarks, "Probably the most revolutionary thing about the Reformation is its questioning of the value of virginity. . . . Not only should priests be married, said the Reformers, everyone should." However, the Reformers did not suddenly see "sexual intercourse as an untarnished boon," but rather relied on marriage as the proper place for sex and as a hedge against lust. "Intercourse is never without sin for the Reformers, but God provides sufficient grace in marriage to mitigate its sinfulness."[40]

If anything, the Reformers were more quick in condemning nonmarital sexuality than was the medieval church. Throughout the sixteenth century (and no doubt beyond), Protestants used accusations of sexual license, including sodomy, in their diatribes against the Roman Catholic hierarchy and to discredit the monastic movement. As Vern Bullough observes, "no real changes in official church attitudes took place until the twentieth century" when the Society of Friends (Quakers), progressive Anglicans, and the Unitarian-Universalists began a process of revisioning.[41]

Although the Reformers rejected homosexuality, they prepared the ground for new thinking in other ways. For example, they shifted emphasis away from procreation as the sole purpose of sexual activity toward an appreciation of the goodness of the marriage relationship and the unitive purpose of sex between partners. In the theological writings of John Calvin, in particular, companionship and the mutual care and love between husband and wife are given normative weight. Marriage becomes viewed less and less as a necessary restraint against disordered lust and more appreciatively as an institution blessed by God for the proper ordering of male-female relationships in complementary harmony. Although this emphasis on gender complementarity only reinforces the normative status of heterosexuality and heterosexual coupling, the focus on the unitive and bonding purposes of sexuality opens a door, however slightly, to a more sympathetic appraisal of nonprocreative and, eventually, nonheterosexual relations.

Statements from two Protestant traditions illustrate how this Reformation heritage has been appropriated in recent debates. The Lutheran Church in America issued a 1970 report, "Sex, Marriage, and Family," with this statement on homosexuality: "Homosexuality is viewed biblically as a departure from the heterosexual structure of God's creation." However, gay people are not to be singled out as uniquely sinful, and furthermore, there is recognition of unfair discrimination and prejudice against this minority. For this reason the LCA recommended that "such persons [are] entitled to understanding and justice in church and community."[42] The American Lutheran Church's 1980 "Human Sexuality and Sexual Behavior" has a similar message. Although "homosexual erotic behavior [is] contrary to God's intention," Christians "need to be more understanding and more sensitive to life as experienced by those who are homosexual."[43] A 1991 Evangelical Lutheran Church in America study acknowledges that although Luther himself affirmed the goodness of sexuality within marriage and rejected celibacy for the clergy, "he did not promote radical changes in the structure of 16th century society with regard to sexuality," and for the most part, neither have contemporary Lutherans.[44]

By the end of the sixteenth century, all of Christian Europe had enacted legislation making sodomy a capital offense. Between 1555 and 1680, some thirty sodomites were put to death in Geneva, the epicenter of John Calvin's theocratic experiment of the Reformation.[45] Historically, Calvinists have vehemently condemned clerical homosexuality as a sinful indulgence of the Roman Catholic church and have also declared nonprocreative sex as unnatural and morally wrong. Contemporary Calvinists are struggling with this legacy, but with quite different results. On the one hand, a 1978 United Presbyterian Church statement concluded that "unrepentant homosexual practice does not accord with the requirements for ordination," but examining committees are advised not to question candidates directly about their sexual orientation. The church also reaffirmed its 1970 position to work for the decriminalization of same-sex relations between consenting adults. On the other hand, a 1980 study document from the United Church of Canada takes a quite different stance, arguing that "there is no reason in principle why mature, self-accepting homosexuals, any more than mature, self-accepting heterosexuals, should not be ordained or commissioned."[46] A 1977 United Church of Christ study argues similarly that "the only general difference between heterosexuals and homosexuals is sexual preference," and that there should be a single ethical standard—love intertwined with justice—for both heterosexual and same-sex relations.[47] A 1991 Presbyterian Church (U.S.A.) study document was not approved by the church's General Assembly, in part because of its controversial stance that the church is being called to "repent of the sins of sexism and heterosexism" and is "invited to . . . affirm, with conviction and gratitude, that homosexual love, no less and no more than heterosexual love, is right and good."[48]

Today all the mainline Protestant churches publicly support passage of full civil rights legislation for gay men and lesbians and denounce violence and persecution of the gay community. For the most part, Protestants within these denominations have moved away from the rejecting-punitive stance (illustrated earlier by Southern Baptist statements) and have shifted to more moderate positions. A rejecting, though nonpunitive, response declares homosexuality wrong and unacceptable for Christians, but insists that homosexual persons must be treated fairly. In popular language, one is asked to "hate the sin, not the sinner." Rather than punish, the church should encourage gay men and lesbians to repent and convert to a heterosexual life.

Other Protestants have moved further on to a "qualified acceptance" position. The findings of contemporary medical and psychological research are important data for theological reflection, especially the awareness that a minority of persons are constitutionally homosexual in orientation and are unable to reorient their sexuality toward heterosexual eroticism. Because change in sexual orientation is not likely or feasible for these persons, abstinence is recommended. If that is not possible, gay men and lesbians are encouraged to live in an ethically responsible manner and "make the best of their painful situations without idealizing them or pretending that they are normal."[49]

This position of qualified acceptance, more progressive than either the rejecting-punitive or nonpunitive responses, does not question the basic assumption that heterosexuality alone is normal, natural, and capable of expressing the full meaning and purpose of human sexuality, as divinely created. A theological and moral division between heterosexuality and homosexuality is consistently emphasized. However, it is precisely this moral dividing line and the adequacy of the church's understanding of human sexuality that are being questioned increasingly by feminists, gay liberationists, and their supporters in various Protestant contexts. The nature and significance of this challenge will be considered after a brief review of new insights about homosexuality from the social sciences.

Insights from the Social Sciences

As Protestants continue to debate homosexuality, various denominations typically establish study commissions to assess, among other things, fresh insights from the social sciences about human sexuality. There is a general trend toward a more positive evaluation of human sexuality, broadly speaking, and a more reasoned, even sympathetic reading of homosexuality. For the first half of this century, progressive church views were informed by a medical model labeling homosexuality an illness, but not one for which the person was to be blamed. As in the qualified acceptance stance, cure and at least consistent care were seen as the appropriate pastoral responses. This represented an advance over previous religious convictions categorizing homosexuality a personal moral failure or deliberate sin for which the person was punishable, here or in the hereafter. Through the influence of the pastoral care movement, in particular, there has been a gradual movement from a medical model (homosexuality as illness) to an essentialist model (homosexuality as a nonpathological variation in sexual identity, established at an early stage of human development, and not subject to fundamental change).[50]

After 1974, when the Trustees of the American Psychiatric Association ruled unanimously that homosexuality should no longer be listed as a mental disorder or regarded as a deviant form of human sexual development, a United Church of Christ study in 1977 offered a more neutral judgment of homosexuality. The report argues that "most likely little will be known about what makes one a homosexual until we understand more fully how one becomes heterosexual."[51] The Lutherans also agree that "sexual orientation does not by itself determine a person's psychological adjustment" or mental well-being. Acceptance or rejection by family, friends, and society is much more influential on that score.[52] Among Protestants incorporating similar insights, there is now increased awareness that there are a variety of human sexualities. Sexual diversity, not uniformity, is characteristic of the human landscape.

Another influential insight from contemporary social scientific research is that sexual orientation, whether heterosexual, homosexual, or bisexual, is not consciously chosen by individuals but rather discovered in the process of psychosexual development and maturation. Episcopal Bishop John Shelby Spong, writing in 1988, cites "the evidence [pointing] to the conclusion that homosexual persons do not choose their sexual orientation, cannot change it, and constitute a quite normal but minority expression of human sexuality." He argues that "the difficulty comes when a society evaluates heterosexuality per se as good and homosexuality per se as evil."[53] The focus of moral concern should, therefore, shift to the pervasive societal fear and hatred of gay men and lesbians and the intolerance of sexual difference.

In this culture, sexual orientation matters greatly. Through a process of negative social labeling, along with a variety of public and private sanctions, all persons experience pressure and often coercion to maintain conformity to the heterosexual norm. A study by the United Presbyterian Church, for example, incorporated this knowledge and described the process of social labeling in this way: "Many, if not most, heterosexual persons assume that the label 'homosexual' describes a 'master trait' which governs a person's total personality. . . . [Society] expects 'homosexual' persons to be maladjusted, incompetent, unreliable, irreligious, and promiscuous, and it assumes that they are. To be labelled 'homosexual' is to be placed by many people in an excluded deviant class—a category of misfits who would normally be expected to engage in unacceptable activities and to oppose the rest of the social order."[54] Such social labeling functions to discourage dissent from prevailing norms and to punish heterosexuals, as well as homosexuals, for straying from male-dominant and female-subordinate patterns of social and sexual relating.

The 1991 Presbyterian study *Keeping Body and Soul Together: Sexuality, Spirituality, and Social Justice* is richly informed by these critical insights and reports that "the fundamental moral problem is not gay men and lesbians, but rather heterosexism, the oppression of this sexual minority by the privileged majority." Sexual oppression distorts human loving. Furthermore, "the crisis of sexuality in our culture (and in the churches) is precipitated not by the emergence of 'uppity' women or by the visibility of a gay, lesbian, and bisexual community, but by the very patriarchal structuring of our sexual and social relations."[55] These insights resonate with the experience of gay and lesbian Christians, who insist that it is not their sexuality which they or others should experience as problematic, but rather this society's unbridled prejudice and virulent animosity toward this minority population.

In accord with this perception, some sociologists are shifting their investigations away from an organism-deficiency model of research, which identifies homosexual persons as the problem, to a social-deficiency model that sees the problem "embedded in the attitudes and behavior of the majority who define deviancy from their own vantage point." This shift to a critique of homophobia, defined as "any structured belief which does not equate the value of same-sex life-styles and opposite-sex life-styles," has opened up new questions and concerns for the churches. The "problem" of homosexuality is redefined as a problem of social injustice.[56] On this score, gay men and lesbians are the indispensable authorities calling the church to repentance, renewal, and the moral struggle to dismantle sexual oppression in the churches no less than in society.

Gay/Lesbian Liberation and the Challenge to Heterosexism

Voices in the church calling for the full acceptance of gay men and lesbians affirm the value and integrity of same-sex love as a godly love. Powerful testimonies by gay Christians about their spirituality and their struggles with the churches include Chris Glaser's *Uncommon Calling: A Gay Man's Struggle to Serve the Church*, Rosemary Denman's *Let My People In: A Lesbian Minister Tells of Her Struggles to Live Openly and Maintain Her Ministry*, and Troy Perry's *The Lord Is My Shepherd*.

When the National Council of Churches voted in 1983 not to accept the Universal Fellowship of Metropolitan Community Churches (MCC) into membership, the decisive issue was the predominantly gay membership of the MCC, as well as its refusal as a church to discriminate on the basis of sexual orientation. One analyst argued that admission of the UFMCC as a Council member would have contributed to Christian unity by helping to heal the brokenness of the faith community brought about by the majority's sexual exclusionism; but its rejection, because "a principle of exclusion necessarily suggests what is most important theologically, ethically and politically," signals that "sexuality remains Christianity's 'dirty little secret,' for those who occupy the liberal middle ground no less than for those on the reactionary right."[57] In a similar vein, Warren Johansson concedes that "the Church and Synagogue have never been able to accept homosexual love as on a par with heterosexual," and "yet that is the precondition for any reconciliation with the gay community."[58]

In addition, the churches need to grapple with how homophobia negatively affects the heterosexual majority and diminishes their ability to live gracefully and justly with sexual diversity. Louie Crew, a gay Episcopalian, speaks of gay peoples "as an occasion of grace" for the church and admonishes everyone to "go and sin no more":

> I believe that it is sinful for homosexual persons to think of ourselves as less than the children of God. I think that the time has passed for us to go to the back of the bus. I think that it is sinful for heterosexuals not to love their homosexual neighbors as the heterosexuals love themselves. I think that perfect love casts out sinful fear, yes, even homophobia.[59]

In learning how to transcend homophobia, the churches may well need gay men and lesbians much more than the gay community needs the help of the church.

Gay men and lesbians realize that many homosexual persons, including considerable numbers of homosexual clergy, are tolerated in Protestant churches as long as they visibly conform to the heterosexual norm and observe secrecy about their sexuality. The strong negative feelings and intense debate in the churches surface not about homosexuality per se, but rather about gayness. What is rocking the ecclesiastical boat is the gay liberation movement within its own walls, along with the affirmation by self-respecting gay men and lesbians that homoeroticism is sane, healthy, and good. The time for second-class citizenship is past, for as people of faith they, too, have a right to express and enjoy their love as fundamental to the realization of their full personhood.

In Christian perspective, love is the central meaning and purpose of human life. The right to love, to give and receive deep caring and mutual regard, is a moral good and rich blessing belonging to all persons, irrespective of sexual orientation. The gay liberation movement challenges the church to reorder its ethical thinking and practice about human sexuality toward an ethic of common decency, grounded in a vision of egalitarian inclusiveness. Accepting that moral challenge requires embracing sexual diversity as a gift enriching the church's common life. It also requires welcoming gay men and lesbians as coequals within the Christian community. There is no qualitative moral difference between same-sex love and love experienced by heterosexuals. As Episcopal priest and theologian Carter Heyward notes, "The labels we use do not express, but rather distort, the most important things we can know and say about our own sexuality and human sexuality in general."[60] A heterosexist stance falsely presumes that the moral rightness or wrongness of sexual activity can be judged on the basis of whether it is heterosexual or homosexual, but sexual orientation does not and cannot determine whether any person acts in morally responsible ways or not. "In point of fact," Franklin Kameny has argued, "homosexuality is far more a matter of love and affection than it is commonly considered to be; and heterosexuality is far more a matter of physical lust than our culture, with its over-romanticized approach, admits it to be. Actually, homosexuality and heterosexuality differ but little, if at all, in this respect."[61]

Because of the inadequacy of making moral judgments on the basis of a heterosexual-homosexual dichotomy, a significant reformation of Christian sexual ethics is currently underway in Protestant contexts. A new consensus is emerging that what matters ethically is not the sameness (or difference) of the gender of the persons in relationship, but rather the moral quality and character of their relation. A single moral standard should apply to all sexual relationships, a standard that attends primarily to concerns about the presence or absence of mutual consent, respect, and commitment, as well as to the distribution of power and of relative vulnerabilities.

The Presbyterian 1991 study uses this reformed perspective in this way: "Although heterosexual marriage is rightly valued as a place to secure loving and justice-bearing relations, it is not the exclusive locus for responsible sexuality." Sexually active single persons, including gay men and lesbians, may also lead responsible, loving, and just lives. Therefore, "the church must teach how to identify, honor, and celebrate all sexual relations grounded in mutual respect, genuine care, and justice-love."[62] This statement was exceedingly controversial for the church. The Presbyterian General Assembly refused to adopt the report by a sizable voting majority. In order to reassure congregations that the status quo had been maintained, a pastoral letter was sent stating that although "the issues raised by this report will not go away," the commissioners "strongly reaffirmed the sanctity of the marriage covenant between one man and one woman to be a [and, most assumed, the only] God-given relationship to be honored by marital fidelity."[63] For many Protestants, the battle line is being drawn to reinforce heterosexuality and heterosexual marriage not only as normative, but also exclusively so, although these internal debates demonstrate that the "normative" and conventional criteria for moral judgment are being rigorously questioned.

Inside and outside the churches, the moral contention about sexuality, and about homosexuality in particular, is heated and not likely to dissipate any time soon. Sociologist James Davison Hunter suggests that these church debates are one component of an intensifying struggle he calls culture wars. Western white liberal society is increasingly polarized by conflict between antagonistic forces operating out of not only opposing, but truly irreconcilable, moral visions of the human good and the proper ordering of society. As Hunter observes about the current religious landscape, "The dominant impulse at the present time is toward the polarization of a religiously informed public culture into two relatively distinct moral and ideological camps."[64] Furthermore, a significantly new alignment of religious pluralism is underway, actually a realignment across a barrier Hunter labels as orthodox and progressive. Heretofore, religious differences followed along denominational lines so that the divisions among various faith communities were much more consequential than any differences found within a single church tradition. Today the map of moral conflict is dramatically altered.

Progressive Protestants, Roman Catholics, and Jews now have much more in common with one another—theologically, ethically, and politically—about such contested issues as sexuality than they have in common with any of their more conventional orthodox colleagues from within their particular traditions. Yes, it is true that Southern Baptists, by and large, condemn homosexuality, but not all Southern Baptists line up the same way. In 1992 the Southern Baptist Convention voted to oust two congregations from its membership because one ordained a gay man to preach and the other solemnized a same-sex union. Progressive Southern Baptists clearly share a greater affinity with progressive Presbyterians, Episcopalians, and Lutherans than they do with many of their own Baptist kin.[65]

Church debates over homosexuality divide Methodists from Methodists, Roman Catholics from Roman Catholics, Jews from Jews, and so forth. It may well be that the great divide is not denominational but rather theological-ethical in character. And one of the most contested areas of conflict is over the meaning and place of sexuality, as well as over the connections between sexual justice and spirituality. A 1990 ecumenical report from the World Council of Churches begins by stating that "the fact that the churches are so greatly exercised on the subject [of sex and sexuality] suggests that God is calling us to rethink it."[66]

Although fresh thinking about homosexuality and same-sex love may well be needed, more than new understanding is at stake. As gay liberation theologian Dan Spencer suggests, gay men and lesbians stay in the church for a particular reason, namely, to be "involved in remaking the church." The church entrapped by homophobia and heterosexism is not a church free to embody the gospel with passion. Therefore, as Spencer contends, gay and lesbian people of faith "offer both challenge and invitation to the broader church to experience the Gospel of Jesus free of homophobic trappings, to join us in celebrating, with the early church, 'once you were no people, now you are God's people.' That's the Good News. It's worth staying for and offering to others."[67]

How Protestants, by and large, will receive this invitation—to join their gay brothers and lesbian sisters of faith in a shared commitment to seek sexual justice and spiritual renewal—is not yet determined, but their responses will certainly tell much about the integrity and vitality of Protestantism at the close of the twentieth century.

Notes

1. Warren Johansson, "Judeo-Christian Tradition," in Wayne R. Dynes, ed., *The Encyclopedia of Homosexuality* (New York: Garland Publishing, 1990), vol. 1, pp. 648–649.

2. Karen Lebacqz, *Justice in an Unjust World* (Minneapolis: Augsburg Publishing House, 1987), p. 35.

3. Chris Glaser, "A Newly Revealed Christian Experience," *Church and Society* 57, no. 5 (May–June 1977): 11. For an account of one gay man's struggle to maintain personal integrity and spiritual authenticity while confronting the church's heterosexism and homophobia, see also Chris Glaser, *Uncommon Calling: A Gay Man's Struggle to Serve the Church* (San Francisco: Harper & Row, 1988).

4. John McNeill, S.J., "Homosexuality: Challenging the Church to Grow," in *Sexual Ethics and the Church: After the Revolution* (Chicago: The Christian Century, 1989), p. 10.

5. Presbyterian Church (U.S.A.), *Presbyterians and Human Sexuality 1991* (Louisville: Office of the General Assembly, 1991), p. 10.

6. William A. Percy, "Protestantism," in Wayne R. Dynes, ed., *The Encyclopedia of Homosexuality* (New York: Garland Publishing, 1990), vol. 1, p. 1062.

7. Cited in Robert Nugent and Jeannine Gramick, "Homosexuality: Protestant, Catholic, and Jewish Issues: A Fishbone Tale," in Richard Hasbany, ed., *Homosexuality and Religion* (New York: Harrington Park Press, 1989), p. 25.

8. James B. Nelson, *Embodiment: An Approach to Sexuality and Christian Theology* (Minneapolis: Augsburg Publishing House, 1978), p. 189. See also Nelson's *Between Two Gardens: Reflections on Sexuality and Religious Experience* (New York: The Pilgrim Press, 1983), esp. pp. 93–94. Nelson maps out a useful four-point spectrum of church opinion on homosexuality, a spectrum used in the following discussion and also employed, for example, by Nugent and Gramick, "Homosexuality."

9. Margaret A. Farley, "An Ethic for Same-Sex Relations," in Robert Nugent, ed., *A Challenge to Love: Gay and Lesbian Catholics in the Church* (New York: Crossroad, 1986), p. 93.

10. James B. Nelson, "Needed: A Continuing Sexual Revolution," in *Sexual Ethics and the Church: After the Revolution* (Chicago: The Christian Century, 1989), p. 64.

11. Nugent and Gramick, p. 43.

12. Cited in Nancy C. Yamasaki, "The Committee to Study Homosexuality Offers the Church . . . Its Report, Its Conclusions, Its Recommendations!" *Circuit Rider* 15, no. 10 (December 1991–January 1992): 5.

13. Presbyterian Church (U.S.A.), *Presbyterians and Human Sexuality 1991*, pp. 9, 14.

14. Beverly Wildung Harrison, ed. Carol S. Robb, *Making the Connections: Essays in Feminist Social Ethics* (Boston: Beacon Press, 1985), pp. 136–137.

15. Nelson, "Needed: A Continuing Sexual Revolution," p. 65.

16. Helmut Thielicke, *The Ethics of Sex*, trans. John W. Doberstein (New York: Harper & Row, 1964), p. 269.

17. Friends Home Service Committee, *Towards a Quaker View of Sex* (London: Friends House, 1963), p. 26.

18. Statistics tell part of the story: approximately five of every one hundred persons self-report as exclusively homosexual throughout their lifetime; approximately one adult person in every three has had some kind of homosexual experience. Moreover, various popular assumptions about human sexuality are now being seriously questioned, including the (supposedly) exclusively bipolar nature of sexual attraction and erotic desire. Current research backs up what many persons know from their own erotic histories, namely, that they are neither exclusively heterosexual nor homosexual in their basic orientation, but are able to respond erotically, in varying degree, to both women and men. Human sexuality is much more complex, diverse, and multidimensional than prevailing theories and categories, including theological and ethical ones, often allow us to appreciate.

19. Although homosexuality is known in virtually every society and culture, social codes differ markedly in the evaluation of same-sex liaisons. No universal pattern exists. Some societies discourage but tolerate homosexual behavior; others grant special status and honors to homosexual persons for possessing unique gifts and powers. Cross-cultural studies indicate that "in 49 (64 percent) of the 76 societies other than our own, homosexual activities of one sort or another are considered normal and socially acceptable for certain members of the community." Our society is at one extreme in forbidding and punishing same-sex relationships for persons of any age and of either gender. A 1970 survey, based on in-depth interviews with more than three thousand adults in this country, found that 70.2% believe that sex acts between persons of the same sex who love each other are "always wrong," 65.2% find homosexuality to be "very much" obscene and vulgar, and 59% agree that "there should be a law against sex acts between persons of the same sex." See Eugene E. Levitt and Albert D. Klassen, Jr., "Public Attitudes Toward Homosexuality: Part

of the 1970 National Survey by the Institute for Sex Research," *Journal of Homosexuality* 1 (1974): 31, 40. A 1989 Presbyterian survey showed similar patterns among both church members and clergy. Some 81% of members and 68% of pastors believe that same-sex relations between two adults is "always wrong" or "almost always wrong." When asked about loving, caring same-sex relationships, a strong majority of members and nearly half the ministers disagree that such a relationship could be "all right in some circumstances." Jack Marcum, "Presbyterian Panel Memorandum: November 3, 1989," p. 9.

20. Roger L. Shinn, "Homosexuality: Christian Conviction and Inquiry," in Edward Batchelor, Jr., ed., *Homosexuality and Ethics* (New York: The Pilgrim Press, 1980), pp. 4–5.

21. Nelson, *Embodiment*, p. 181.

22. Cited in Robin Smith, *Living in Covenant with God and One Another* (Geneva: World Council of Churches, 1990), p. 103.

23. Victor Paul Furnish, "Understanding Homosexuality in the Bible's Cultural Particularity," *Circuit Rider* 15, no. 10 (December 1991–January 1992): 11.

24. Derrick Sherwin Bailey, *Homosexuality and the Western Christian Tradition* (Hamden, Conn.: Archon Books, 1975), p. x.

25. Ibid., p. 10 and passim.

26. Letha Scanzoni and Virginia Mollenkott, *Is the Homosexual My Neighbor? Another Christian View* (New York: Harper & Row, 1978), p. 54.

27. United Church of Christ, *Human Sexuality: A Preliminary Study* (New York: United Church Press, 1977), pp. 68–69.

28. George R. Edwards, *Gay/Lesbian Liberation: A Biblical Perspective* (New York: The Pilgrim Press, 1984), p. 78. John McNeill has also noted that if the fundamental theme of the Genesis 19 story is the violation of hospitality toward strangers, then "we are dealing here with one of the supremely ironic paradoxes of history. For thousands of years in the Christian West the homosexual has been the victim of inhospitable treatment. Condemned by the Church, he [sic] has been the victim of persecution, torture, and even death. In the name of a mistaken understanding of the crime of Sodom and Gomorrah, the true crime of Sodom and Gomorrah has been and continues to be repeated every day." John J. McNeill, S.J., *The Church and the Homosexual* (New York: New Year Publications, 1985), p. 50.

29. John Boswell, *Christianity, Social Tolerance, and Homosexuality: Gay People in Western Europe from the Beginning of the Christian Era to the Fourteenth Century* (Chicago: University of Chicago Press, 1980), p. 117. For a critical response to Boswell, see Richard Hays, "Relations Natural or Unnatural: A Response to John Boswell's Exegesis of Romans 1," *Journal of Religious Ethics* 14 (1986): 184–215.

30. Cited in Smith, p. 107.

31. Evangelical Lutheran Church in America, *Human Sexuality and the Christian Faith: A Study for the Church's Reflection and Deliberation* (Minneapolis: Evangelical Lutheran Church in America, 1991), pp. 23, 44, and 26.

32. Robin Gorsline, "Let Us Bless Our Angels: A Feminist-Gay-Male-Liberation View of Sodom," in Susan E. Davies and Eleanor H. Haney, eds., *Redefining Sexual Ethics: A Sourcebook of Essays, Stories, and Poems* (Cleveland: The Pilgrim Press, 1991), p. 51.

33. Walter Brueggemann, "Textuality in the Church," in Nelle G. Slater, ed., *Tensions Between Citizenship and Discipleship* (New York: The Pilgrim Press, 1989), p. 57.

34. Bailey, p. 98.

35. Boswell, p. 333.

36. Ibid., p. 334.

37. Sexual desire was considered dangerous, capable of overwhelming reason altogether and thereby creating chaos and moral disorder. Sexual activity for the sake of pleasure was judged as self-indulgent and lustful, highly susceptible to loss of rational control and direction, and easily corrupted by catering to the baser passions.

38. Although some proposed that celibacy and a disdain of all sexual desire were necessary for genuine Christian witness, others, including Augustine, argued that sexual intercourse could serve the human good but only if it were properly ordered toward a rational end, namely, the procreation of children. As long as sexual activity was guided by this procreative intent, it could be justified as serving a rational purpose outside itself and then appropriately disciplined by its restriction to the marriage relationship.

39. *Luther's Works*, vol. 3, p. 255, cited in ECLA, *Human Sexuality and the Christian Faith*, p. 28.

40. E. Elizabeth Johnson, "Biblical and Historical Perspectives on Human Sexuality," *Church and Society* 80, no. 2 (November–December 1989): 21–22.

41. Vern L. Bullough, "Christianity," in Wayne R. Dynes, ed., *The Encyclopedia of Homosexuality* (New York: Garland Publishing, 1990), vol. 1, pp. 224.

42. Cited in ECLA, *Human Sexuality and the Christian Faith*, p. 9.

43. Ibid.

44. Ibid., p. 28. An exception to this is the Wingspan Ministry in Saint Paul, Minnesota, a ministry of reconciliation and justice for the gay and lesbian community. See Anita C. Hill and Leo Treadway, "Rituals of Healing: Ministry with and on Behalf of Gay and Lesbian People," in Susan Brooks Thistlethwaite and Mary Potter Engel, eds.,

Lift Every Voice: Constructing Christian Theologies from the Underside (San Francisco: Harper & Row, 1990), pp. 231–244.

45. Percy, p. 1064.

46. Cited in G. William Sheek, ed., "A Compilation of Protestant Denominational Statements on Families and Sexuality," 3d ed. (New York: National Council of Churches, 1982), pp. 88, 90, and 87.

47. United Church of Christ, *Human Sexuality,* pp. 137, 103. This intertwining of love with justice means that "love . . . becomes concerned for power, but it is the empowerment of those who are in any way oppressed so that they have rightful access to the means of human fulfillment. Love with its justice dimension becomes our ongoing struggle for love's fullest possible expression in human relationships" (p. 103).

48. Presbyterian Church (U.S.A.), *Presbyterians and Human Sexuality 1991,* p. 18.

49. Nelson, *Embodiment,* p. 196.

50. For an analysis of these developments, see Nugent and Gramick, pp. 7–46.

51. United Church of Christ, *Human Sexuality,* p. 138.

52. ECLA, *Human Sexuality and the Christian Faith,* p. 42.

53. John Shelby Spong, *Living in Sin? A Bishop Rethinks Human Sexuality* (San Francisco: Harper & Row, 1988), p. 79.

54. United Presbyterian Church in the U.S.A., *The Church and Homosexuality* (New York: Office of the General Assembly, 1978), p. D-23.

55. Presbyterian Church (U.S.A.), *Presbyterians and Human Sexuality 1991,* p. 16.

56. On this shift in sociological perspectives, see Jeannine Gramick, "Prejudice, Religion, and Homosexual People," in Robert Nugent, ed., *A Challenge to Love* (New York: Crossroad, 1986), pp. 3–19.

57. Marvin M. Ellison, "The NCC on the Hook," *The Christian Century* 100, no. 32 (November 2, 1983): 982.

58. Johansson, p. 649.

59. Louie Crew, "Gays as an Occasion of Grace," *Christianity and Crisis* 41, no. 7 (November 2, 1981): 303.

60. Carter Heyward, *Our Passion for Justice: Images of Power, Sexuality, and Liberation* (New York: The Pilgrim Press, 1984), p. 74. For a socio-ethical analysis of homophobia and its connections to misogyny, see also Harrison, pp. 135–151.

61. Franklin E. Kameny, "Gay Is Good," in Ralph W. Weltge, ed., *The Same Sex: An Appraisal of Homosexuality* (Philadelphia: The Pilgrim Press, 1969), pp. 131–132.

62. Presbyterian Church (U.S.A.), *Presbyterians and Human Sexuality 1991,* p. 20.

63. *Presbyterians and Human Sexuality.*

64. James Davison Hunter, *Culture Wars: The Struggle to Define America* (New York: Basic Books, 1991), p. 106.

65. For a progressive Southern Baptist voice, see Mahan Siler, "The Blessing of a Gay Union: Reflections of a Pastoral Journey," *Baptists Today* (March 19, 1992), p. 11.

66. Smith, p. 3.

67. Dan Spencer, "Church at the Margins: Distinctive Marks of Emerging Gay and Lesbian Ecclesiology," *Christianity and Crisis* 52, no. 8 (May 25, 1992): 173, 176.

Bibliography

Bailey, Derrick Sherwin. 1975. *Homosexuality and the Western Christian Tradition.* Hamden, Conn.: Archon Books.

Boswell, John. 1980. *Christianity, Social Tolerance, and Homosexuality: Gay People in Western Europe from the Beginning of the Christian Era to the Fourteenth Century.* Chicago: University of Chicago Press.

Brueggemann, Walter. 1989. "Textuality in the Church." In *Tensions Between Citizenship and Discipleship,* edited by Nelle G. Slater. New York: The Pilgrim Press.

Bullough, Vern L. 1990. "Christianity." In Vol. 1 of *The Encyclopedia of Homosexuality,* edited by Wayne R. Dynes, 221–225. New York: Garland Publishing.

Crew, Louie. 1981. "Gays as an Occasion of Grace." *Christianity and Crisis* 41, 17:290, 302–304.

Edwards, George R. 1984. *Gay/Lesbian Liberation: A Biblical Perspective.* New York: The Pilgrim Press.

Ellison, Marvin M. 1983. "The NCC on the Hook." *The Christian Century* 100, 32:981–982.

Evangelical Lutheran Church in America. 1991. *Human Sexuality and the Christian Faith: A Study for the Church's Reflection and Deliberation.* Minneapolis: Evangelical Lutheran Church in America.

Farley, Margaret A. 1986. "An Ethic for Same-Sex Relations." In *A Challenge to Love: Gay and Lesbian Catholics in the Church,* edited by Robert Nugent, 93–106. New York: Crossroad.

Friends Home Service Committee. 1963. *Towards a Quaker View of Sex.* London: Friends House.

Furnish, Victor Paul. 1992. "Understanding Homosexuality in the Bible's Cultural Particularity." *Circuit Rider* 15, 10:10–11.

Glaser, Chris. 1977. "A Newly Revealed Christian Experience." *Church and Society* 67, 5:5–11.

————. 1988. *Uncommon Calling: A Gay Man's Struggle to Serve the Church.* San Francisco: Harper & Row.

Gorsline, Robin. 1991. "Let Us Bless Our Angels: A Feminist-Gay-Male-Liberation View of Sodom." In *Redefining Sexual Ethics: A Sourcebook of Essays, Stories, and Poems,* edited by Susan E. Davies and Eleanor H. Haney, 45–56. Cleveland: The Pilgrim Press.

Gramick, Jeannine. 1986. "Prejudice, Religion, and Homosexual People." In *A Challenge to Love,* edited by Robert Nugent, 3–19. New York: Crossroad.

Harrison, Beverly Wildung. 1985. *Making the Connections: Essays in Feminist Social Ethics,* edited by Carol S. Robb. Boston: Beacon Press.

Hays, Richard. 1986. "Relations Natural or Unnatural: A Response to John Boswell's Exegesis of Romans 1." *Journal of Religious Ethics* 14:184–215.

Heyward, Carter. 1984. *Our Passion for Justice: Images of Power, Sexuality, and Liberation.* New York: The Pilgrim Press.

Hill, Anita C., and Leo Treadway. 1990. "Rituals of Healing: Ministry with and on Behalf of Gay and Lesbian People." In *Lift Every Voice: Constructing Christian Theologies from the Underside,* edited by Susan Brooks Thistlethwaite and Mary Potter Engle, 231–244. San Francisco: Harper & Row.

Hunter, James Davison. 1991. *Culture Wars: The Struggle to Define America.* New York: Basic Books.

Johansson, Warren. 1990. "Judeo-Christian Tradition." In Vol. 1 of *The Encyclopedia of Homosexuality,* edited by Wayne R. Dynes, 648–649. New York: Garland Publishing.

Johnson, E. Elizabeth. 1989. "Biblical and Historical Perspectives on Human Sexuality." *Church and Society* 80, 2:6–25.

Kameny, Franklin E. 1969. "Gay Is Good." In *The Same Sex: An Appraisal of Homosexuality,* edited by Ralph W. Weltge, 129–145. Philadelphia: The Pilgrim Press.

Lebacqz, Karen. 1987. *Justice in an Unjust World.* Minneapolis: Augsburg Publishing House.

Levitt, Eugene E., and Albert D. Klassen, Jr. 1974. "Public Attitudes Toward Homosexuality: Part of the 1970 National Survey by the Institute for Sex Research." *Journal of Homosexuality* 1:29–43.

McNeill, John J., S.J. 1985. *The Church and the Homosexual.* New York: New Year Publications.

————. 1989. "Homosexuality: Challenging the Church to Grow." In *Sexual Ethics and the Church: After the Revolution,* 9–17. Chicago: The Christian Century.

Nelson, James B. 1978. *Embodiment: An Approach to Sexuality and Christian Theology.* Minneapolis: Augsburg Publishing House.

———. 1983. *Between Two Gardens: Reflections on Sexuality and Religious Experience.* New York: The Pilgrim Press.

———. 1989. "Needed: A Continuing Sexual Revolution." In *Sexual Ethics and the Church: After the Revolution,* 63–70. Chicago: The Christian Century.

Nugent, Robert, and Jeannine Gramick. 1989. "Homosexuality: Protestant, Catholic, and Jewish Issues: A Fishbone Tale." In *Homosexuality and Religion,* edited by Richard Hasbany, 7–46. New York: Harrington Park Press.

Percy, William A. 1990. "Protestantism." In Vol. 1 of *The Encyclopedia of Homosexuality,* edited by Wayne R. Dynes, 1058–1069. New York: Garland Publishing.

Presbyterian Church (U.S.A.). 1991. *Presbyterians and Human Sexuality 1991.* Louisville: Office of the General Assembly.

Scanzoni, Letha, and Virginia Ramey Mollenkott. 1978. *Is the Homosexual My Neighbor? Another Christian View.* New York: Harper & Row.

Sheek, G. William, ed. 1982. "A Compilation of Protestant Denominational Statements on Families and Sexuality." 3d ed. New York: National Council of Churches.

Shinn, Roger L. 1980. "Homosexuality: Christian Conviction and Inquiry." In *Homosexuality and Ethics,* edited by Edward Batchelor, Jr., 3–13. New York: The Pilgrim Press.

Siler, Mahan. 1992. "The Blessing of a Gay Union: Reflections of a Pastoral Journey." *Baptists Today,* p. 11.

Smith, Robin. 1990. *Living in Covenant with God and One Another.* Geneva: World Council of Churches.

Spencer, Dan. 1992. "Church at the Margins: Distinctive Marks of Emerging Gay and Lesbian Ecclesiology." *Christianity and Crisis* 52, 8:173–176.

Spong, John Shelby. 1988. *Living in Sin? A Bishop Rethinks Human Sexuality.* San Francisco: Harper & Row.

Thielicke, Helmut. 1964. *The Ethics of Sex.* Translated by John W. Doberstein. New York: Harper & Row.

United Church of Christ. 1977. *Human Sexuality: A Preliminary Study.* New York: United Church Press.

United Presbyterian Church in the U.S.A. 1978. *The Church and Homosexuality.* New York: Office of the General Assembly.

Yamasaki, Nancy C. 1992. "The Committee to Study Homosexuality Offers the Church . . . Its Report, Its Conclusions, Its Recommendations!" *Circuit Rider* 15, 10:4–7.

7

Homosexuality and Islam

Khalid Duran

Theology: The Judeo-Christian Tradition as the Prototype

The primary source of Islam—its revealed scripture, Al-Qur'an —is very explicit in its condemnation of homosexuality, leaving scarcely any loophole for a theological accommodation of homosexuals in Islam. Quite a few individuals hope to find some sort of an acceptance for gays as creatures of God and fellow believers desirous of partaking of divine grace. However, a theological coming to terms with this issue has not even made a start, despite the fact that the issue is scarcely less burning in Muslim societies than in the Christian and Jewish West. At this time we know of no attempt at granting any kind of recognition of equality to homosexual believers, though some Muslim theologians have repeatedly been requested to initiate a discussion of this subject.[1]

Al-Qur'an broaches the issue in the context of Lot, one of the prophets of the Hebrew Bible greatly honored by the Holy Book of Islam as well. In Islamic terminology, homosexuals are called *qaum Lut*, Lot's people, or, briefly, *Luti*. It may seem odd that a homosexual is thus called a *Lotist*, despite the fact that

Lot's high spiritual position is due to his break with his people because of their homosexuality.

How important the issue is can be gauged from the fact that the story of Lot is mentioned five times in Al-Qur'an: "How can you lust for males, of all creatures in the world, and leave those whom God has created for you as your mates. You are really going beyond all limits" (26:165–166). At another place in Al-Qur'an, God relates the story of Lot's people and concludes: "The mighty Blast overtook them before morning. We turned the cities upside down, and rained down upon them brimstones hard as baked clay" (15:73–74). The Prophet Muhammad is reported to have added: "Doomed by God is who does what Lot's people did [i.e., homosexuality]." He went further by saying that "no man should look at the private parts of another man, and no woman should look at the private parts of another woman, and no two men sleep [in bed] under one cover, and no two women sleep under one cover."

The Prophet also addressed himself to this subject in his last speech to the community, known as the "Farewell Sermon": "Whoever has intercourse with a woman and penetrates her rectum, or with a man, or with a boy, will appear on the Last Day stinking worse than a corpse; people will find him unbearable until he enters hell fire, and God will cancel all his good deeds."

Several of the leading traditionalists (Tirmidhi, Nasa'i, Abu Da'ud, Ibn Ma'ja) report the Prophet to have declared: "If you see people do as Lot's tribe did [i.e., commit homosexuality], kill both the one who does and the one who lets it be done to him." Some scholars doubt the authenticity of this report. Others believe that it applies to lesbians as well. Still others think that lesbians should be punished less, because no penetration takes place.

Except for such modalities, the overall argument against homosexuality differs but little from that of Jewish or Christian sources. Although Al-Qur'an expressly permits sex for pleasure's sake, the purpose of sexual activity is procreation.[2] A pious Muslim begins the sex act with the prayer: "In the name of God, the Most Compassionate, the All-Merciful. Oh, Almighty God, grant me a righteous child." Homosexuality is condemned as a transgression against the will of God. It is

seen as threatening the human race with extinction. God created humanity not in a playful mood, but to worship God. Homosexuality goes against this very purpose of creation.

Al-Qur'an repeatedly calls Islam "the religion of nature,"
the natural religion of humanity. Homosexuality is regarded as
an aberration, as a violation of nature. Like Judaism, and unlike
Christianity, Islam encourages sexual activity by making it a
sacred act. Celibacy is abhorred, polygamy permitted (although
severely restricted). In traditional Muslim societies, an unmarried man stood little chance of holding public office and could
scarcely become a judge or a teacher. "Marriage is half the religion," says a famous dictum of the Prophet, whose married life
was minutely recorded as the good exemplar. He pronounced
himself on many intimate details and recommended, among
others, the *coitus interruptus,* to give just one example.

Against the background of this positive affirmation of
heterosexual life, it becomes clear that there is no room for homosexuality. It was made a punishable offense in the *shari'a,*
the traditional law that evolved in early Islam, primarily under
the impact of the Jewish *halacha.* As with other offenses, the
shari'a demands solid evidence and seems little concerned with
what occurs in private. Like fornication, homosexuality has to
assume the character of a public nuisance in order to become
punishable. There are, therefore, no self-proclaimed gays in
Muslim countries. In many Muslim societies, homosexuals are
comparatively free to do what they like, provided they do not
publicly assert their homosexuality.

Scholars of Islamic law, the *shari'a,* generally regard homosexuality as a crime, not merely a sin. The penalty is not
indicated in Al-Qur'an but was left to the discretion of the
authorities. This means that it does not fall under the categor-
ical punishments called *hadd* but under the more flexible rubric of *ta'zir.* Some scholars such as Fathi 'Uthmán, a
prominent author and resident scholar at the Islamic Center
of Southern California, hold the view that there was no
definitive penalty, as the matter seems to have been left to the
discretion of the Prophet Muhammad and later on to the jurists, who were free to exercise their own judgment (*ijtihad*)
according to the circumstances of the time. This is evident
from the commentaries on the various collections of the

Prophet's statements and pronouncements on such issues, the technical term for which is Hadith.

Those commentaries and deliberations of Islam's great scholars establish that the evidence for proving homosexuality is the same as in the case of adultery, and in both cases it is extremely difficult, if not impossible, to provide such evidence. The only practical evidence would be a defendant's confession given without any physical or moral pressure. But the *shari'a* even discourages the defendant from confessing, urging him rather to repent; this position is based on several Hadith of the Prophet. This extremely cautious attitude was clearly reflected in the leading works of jurisprudence, which may explain why the punishment—or even trials and investigations—of sexual transgressions were never reported in historical works. There are scarcely any anecdotes to this effect in popular literature. In a medieval book of humorous folk wisdom, the *maqamat al-hariri* by Abu Zaid As-Saruji, we learn that in the Iranian city of Tabriz a lady applied for divorce with the argument that her husband had intended "to enter the house from behind," an allusion to anal sex, which most Muslim divines regard as aberrant and sinful even among spouses.

Professor Fathi ʿUthmán states that "Islamic law stands for privacy and protects it by all means. Besides, it repeatedly emphasizes that a person is innocent until proven guilty without any doubt, and everyone should have the benefit of the slightest doubt."[3]

Sociology: The Third World Notion of Homosexuality as a Form of Exploitation

Sociologically speaking, there is probably not much difference between the situation of gays in Muslim and in Christian societies. Certain countries seem to have a more pronounced tradition of homosexuality than others, creating the general impression that some nations are more given to homosexuality than the remainder of the human race. The peoples traditionally forming the core of Muslimhood* are the Arabs, Persians,

---

*I use this unusual term in order not to use *Islam*, when speaking of the community as a social phenomenon.

and Turks; a wider circle incorporates Berbers, Black Africans, and Indians. Of these, the Persians are best known for homosexual tendencies, though there is no way of ascertaining which Muslim country really has the highest ratio of gays.

Iran came to be associated with homosexuality primarily because of its enormously rich poetry that never tires of homosexual allusions and similes. By contrast, specialists on Moorish culture have been struck by the comparative scarcity of homosexual references in the equally rich literature of Muslim Spain. Andalusian poets almost outshone their counterparts in terms of irreverence toward hallowed norms. They boasted, *inter alia*, of having eaten pork and drunken wine with the monks in a monastery—all for the sake of getting closer to a certain Catholic girl. The leitmotif invariably is *cherchez la femme*. In Andalusian poetry, homosexuality is comparatively rare. Prose literature, too, scarcely relates any homosexual anecdotes, whereas they abound in Persian writings.

Although it cannot be emphasized enough that Islam is not a single, unanalyzable reality, there is some unity in this diversity of so many races and nations profession Islam. One feature fairly common to many Muslim countries is a kind of "emergency" homosexuality. In most traditional Muslim societies, males and females live separate from one another. There is no question of coeducation, as girls and boys are strictly kept apart. Houses are often divided into one part for males and another for females. The segregation of the sexes is so farreaching that it even affects the language. The Urdu spoken by women, for example, differs considerably from that spoken by men. In some Arab countries, there is opportunity for sexual contacts between cousins, who are in any case potential marriage partners because of the generally endogamic system. Overall, however, opportunities for premarital sex are very rare.

As a result, a fairly large number of adolescents (of both sexes) resort to homosexuality for some time before marriage. In some of those societies, such as Morocco, bestiality (with she-donkeys), is a more common outlet, at least in the rural areas, though Islam condemns bestiality no less than homosexuality. As a rule, this comes to an abrupt end with marriage, which traditionally took place at an early age: 13–16 years for girls, 17–20 years for boys. Among the rural population (usually 70–80%), things have not changed greatly, but among the urban elite things have changed dramatically, and more people are marrying after thirty and close to forty years of age. Today large numbers of educated Muslims, especially women, do not marry at all, for a variety of reasons. This may have led to some increase in the number of gays and lesbians, but any such increase in homosexuality is an effect, not a cause, of the enormous marriage difficulties of societies in transition.

As for the more genuine, or genetic, type of homosexuality, it appears to be generally less common among the peoples of the "Islamic belt" than in Europe, although such observations are difficult to verify. In any event, this may account for the fact that there is much less concern with this issue and scarcely any sense of urgency to come to terms with the problems of gays and lesbians as a suppressed minority. Muslims, and not only Islamist fanatics, generally insist that homosexuality is characteristic of the "decadent West."

Such belief seems to be shored up by the frequency of homosexuality among converts, especially in Britain and Germany. Such converts are drawn to Islam by the erroneous assumption that Muslims are more tolerant. One might call this a peculiar manifestation of colonialist mentality, because some of those converts mistake prostitution born of poverty for indulgence. Morocco has become a favorite playground for European gay men, just as it has been for decades the foremost country for female sex tourism, with tens of thousands of American and European single women pouring in in search of potent men—"noble savages." The same phenomenon can be observed on the Muslim coast of Kenya, where the picturesque township of Malindi has been turned into a German sex colony frequented by single women and male homosexuals. In both places, religious circles are reacting with increasing bitterness to this type of prostitution engendered by tourists from affluent societies. The long-standing indulgence was certainly not rooted in Islam. On the contrary, an Islamic backlash is gaining momentum, despite the abject poverty.

My point here is that a dispassionate discussion of the human rights of homosexuals is particularly hard to initiate in Muslim societies confronted with a kind of Western homosexual aggression. An instance in point is a representative of a European political foundation who was stationed in North Africa for many years. Extremely extroverted, he projects his homosexuality as a mark of distinction above and beyond his redoubtable academic merits. Such Western extravagances make the task of human rights activists among Muslims very difficult indeed. Aggressive homosexuality of the "haves" creates strong resentment among heterosexual "have-nots." Shutting one's eyes to the plight of gays within Muslim society and labeling homosexuality a symptom of Western decadence may be a fallacy, but it must be judged by situations like the above. Moreover, it has to be borne in mind that traditional Muslim societies observe utmost discretion with regard to heterosexual concerns. Within this context, Western gays in Muslim lands are perceived not merely as demanding equality but as actually asking for greater indulgence than is given to the heterosexual majority. Such a tendency can only be counterproductive as far as human rights are concerned.

Crime: The Supreme Mode of Brutalization

The image of the gay in many Muslim countries is not that of the victimized meek, but that of the brutal aggressor. In order to understand this, one must be aware of the role of homosexual assault in traditional societies with frozen codes of honor. Homosexual rape is regarded as a tool of humiliation surpassed only by the rape of the enemy's female relatives: wife, daughter, sister, mother. In the Afghan Frontier Province of Pakistan, for instance, a man might have an opponent beaten. If that does not suffice, the recalcitrant might be abducted to the tribal areas and held there as a prisoner for a number of days or weeks during which he would be frequently beaten and made to suffer all kinds of indignities. The next step would be to assault him homosexually or let this be done to him by others—and then to let it be known publicly that this is what has happened to him. As a favorite form of intimidation and punishment, this is practiced in much of North Africa also.

Homosexual assault is frequently used by the police of repressive regimes, such as the SAVAK during the reign of the Shah of Iran, or its successor, SAVAMA, the dreaded security organ of the Khomeini government. In Pakistan, the otherwise enlightened government of the "Islamic Socialdemocrat" Z. A.

Bhutto discredited itself by using such tactics against political opponents. Thus Mian Tufail Muhammad, head of the fundamentalist party *jamá'at-e islámi,* is said to have been homosexually assaulted in jail by members of the feared FSF (Federal Security Force). Even if this news was concocted, it is significant that such a rumor was spread in order to demonstrate the utmost humiliation of the aged politician with his pretensions of religious leadership. His party not only did nothing to refute the news; it confirmed it and used it as a weapon to topple a Prime Minister. The *jamá'at-e islámi* rules out political compromise in any case, but it has difficulties selling its policies. The homosexual assault on its leader provided it with a welcome pretext. This was the strongest argument to declare the government "infidel." And yet it was not something unique, but a practice with a tradition, a tradition little known elsewhere and completely foreign to a number of other cultures.

All this should not lead to the wrong conclusion that Muslim countries are replete with frustrated gays who find no other outlet but the sadistic treatment of political opponents. In rural areas, illiterate and undisciplined policemen occasionally gang-rape female offenders at police stations. For this, however, they may be punished. Homosexual assault on political opponents, on the other hand, is a matter of a conscious policy of political repression, one step less than execution and sometimes considered more effective than outright physical elimination.

Such practices may start early and at a lower level. Thus, among high-school boys in the Maghreb it happens that someone goes around bragging that he did "this" to so-and-so among the classmates, or he might actually do "this" in front of other classmates, though he may well have no other homosexual inclinations. The main purpose is the humiliation of a perceived opponent, not sexual gratification. Arabic terms such as *maf'ul* ("the passive partner") or *zamil,* used in most languages spoken in the Muslim world, are common abuses. Whereas the Spanish *marica* or *maricon* simply denotes a gay as effeminate, the Arabic *maf'ul* has the much stronger connotation of "characterless," "depraved," "opportunistic."

A relatively short narrative, *The Jealous Lover,* by Larbi Layachi of Tangier, contains two episodes, actually short stories, dealing with the homosexual rape of minors. In the first story, two culprits are taken to jail, where other prisoners gang-rape them as a form of punishment. Petty criminals are proud of their various trades as pickpocket, some other kind of thief, or smuggler. They consider it a disgrace to have sodomists amongst them in prison. And they feel that these two rapists have not been sufficiently punished by merely being thrown into jail. It is telling that the other prisoners do not beat the rapists; that again would not be a sufficient punishment. The supreme form of chastisement, in their eyes, is to sodomize them, not for the pleasure of the act, but as the worst type of humiliation.

The second episode involves the finding of the corpse of a little boy who had been sodomized, presumably by a government minister. The city of Tangier erupts into violent demonstrations, and the minister is taken to the capital, Rabat, and held in preventive custody. There he is murdered in a kind of suicide operation. Significantly, Larbi Layachi does not propagate a personal opinion. He simply narrates, with stark realism, experiences from his milieu, focusing on the plight of the common people to whom he belongs and whose attitudes he describes in a masterly fashion. Among all the social evils they complain of, nothing enrages them as much as sodomy committed on minors.[4]

Gays seeking active partners in North African countries usually do not realize that their local lovers are often motivated by a hostile attitude toward them as citizens of nations that had once been colonial masters. To sodomize a Westerner provides a kind of psychological relief for some people from among the former "subject races" who now have a chance to take it out on their oppressors. This also holds true of some other African regions; to do it to a white man is like taking revenge, along with having a source of income.[5]

Customs: A Flexible Modus Vivendi

As a result, there seems to be, as yet, no gay movement anywhere in the Muslim world. Some prominent people do not seem particularly worried about their image. No one, however, has openly declared himself a gay. An instance in point is one former Prime Minister, whose unabashed homosexuality was indicative of a fair amount of tolerance. Unabashed is, however, not synonymous with openly professed. No matter his self-assurance, the bisexual Prime Minister always maintained the facade of an ideal family father, as do most of his partners. As a gay, the former Prime Minister was sexually active, but he did abide by the rules of the *shari‘a* and avoided causing public offense.

Deplorable, from a human rights point of view, is the situation of those many women who are married merely for the sake of camouflaging the homosexuality of men. For example, a German convert and Islamist activist married a woman from Malaysia. When she availed herself of the freedom provided by the German environment and broke away, the gay husband was supplied with a substitute, this time a more pliable one. Another convert joined the Ahmadi sect and was appointed Imam of a mosque in the United States. The Pakistan-based sect had him marry a Pakistani girl, convinced that this would automatically put an end to his homosexuality. He fathered five children but remained an active gay. As Imam of a mosque in Europe, he set up a community of gay converts to Islam, but his wife separated from him and the sect finally expelled him. The Imam concerned may be called a self-proclaimed gay, though the fact that he spends the rest of his life in Germany, and as an outcast from the Muslim community, does not render invalid what was said earlier about the death of self-proclaimed gays in traditional Muslim societies. In several conversations with the author, the former Imam made it plain that he had no objection to being cited as a "Muslim gay." The currently most prominent example of such practice is the controversial head of a fundamentalist party of the Afghan resistance. His checkered political career has essentially been determined by homosexual affiliations, but he maintains two wives.

The same holds true of two important historical figures known to have been gay, Sultan Mehmet Fatih, the Ottoman conqueror of Constantinople (Istanbul), and Sultan Mahmud Ghaznawi, who invaded India from Afghanistan. Each had several wives and fathered a number of children. Westerners would regard this as bisexuality. Muslims see the phenomenon in the context of the *shari‘a* that stipulates outward conformity and shows scant concern for what goes on behind closed doors.

In 1986, Isma'il Al Faruqi, a Palestinian professor of Islamics in Philadelphia, and his wife Lois, also an Islamic scholar, were murdered by an American convert to Islam. The assassin claimed that he had killed his former mentor because he believed that the Faruqis had forced Muslim students to perform homosexual acts in return for scholarships at Temple University (Philadelphia *Inquirer*, 30 March 1990). Western colleagues of the slain professors considered this an absurdity, because the two were known as harmonious family people, parents of four children. Muslims familiar with the phenomenon of married gays were less skeptical. Still, in his country of origin Al Faruqi would not have been murdered for being gay, especially because he caused no public offense, being rather an ardent advocate of the *shari'a*. In this sense the murderer, although a convert to Islam, acted more like a Westerner than a Muslim. As a recent convert outside the Islamic environment, he had learned about the condemnation of homosexuality in Al-Qur'an without understanding how Muslim society handles the issue. Besides this, he was most probably mistaken. Al Faruqi had been supplied by foreign governments with student recipients of scholarships. Some of them were reputed to be homosexual. The professor might not even have been aware that those students were gay; if he was, he might not have been concerned as long as he was not confronted with a public offense. It would have been a different matter had those students openly declared their homosexuality. In that case, he would have been constrained to discipline them, including possibly taking some punitive action, such as the discontinuation of their scholarships.

American observers showed incomprehension: "What was wrong if Al Faruqi was gay?" Supposing that this had been established, the position of the Muslim community would have been roughly similar to that of the Roman Catholic church. In view of the controversy over gay rights in the Roman Catholic church, it should not have come as a surprise that another traditional religion should face similar difficulties in coming to terms with the issue. The exceptional thing about the case is that a member of the community arrogated to himself the right to pass an individual judgment and, moreover, resort to murder. Both steps are un-Islamic, though not the *objection* to homosexuality. As mentioned earlier, within the Muslim community there has been no serious attempt at broaching the issue in a human rights perspective. Once a prominent member takes his homosexuality so far as openly to flout the *shari'a* by not camouflaging, he certainly runs the danger of being ostracized by the community.

Another concrete example may serve to illustrate this point. X, a member of a fundamentalist Muslim Community in Europe, was for many years a well-respected activist in community affairs. He has the distinction, rare among converts, of having studied at the famous Azhar theological seminary in Cairo. The tolerance shown toward him as a "nonproselytizing gay" confirms what has been said earlier about the attraction Islam holds for some Western gays. However, X eventually lived his homosexuality too openly, ending up in a kind of marriagelike relationship with another gay. It was too open partly because his partner was a non-Muslim with little understanding of the susceptibility of the Muslim religious community. X was tormented by all kinds of pressures, but not really expelled. Then, in a self-defensive mood, he made reference to a prominent gay convert and his Muslim wives. This made his case even more illustrative of the special nuances in the Muslim attitude toward gays. The community did not accept his argument. When others maintained a facade of heterosexuality, he had no right to point out their homosexuality, even though this was, more or less, common knowledge.

For Western gays with their new self-assertiveness, such prospects must look bleak. It is not likely that the situation will change soon. The heterosexual majority of Muslims presently faces enormous problems due to the migration of laborers. Some ten million men from countries such as Morocco, Algeria, Tunisia, Egypt, Sudan, Afghanistan, Pakistan, India, Turkey, and Jordan are forced to make a living far away from their families. A still larger number are unable to live a proper family life because of housing shortages in poverty-stricken Third World countries. This greatly contributes to the marriage problems alluded to earlier. As a result, the malaise of the heterosexual majority is so acute that few Muslims are in a mood to

attend to the difficulties of the homosexual minority. This statement may sound harsh, but it would be unrealistic to predict a
change until and unless profound and far-reaching developmen-
tal changes in Muslim countries are brought about. Attention
will have to focus on the few Muslim societies that have risen
out of the misery besetting the vast majority. In all likelihood,
changed attitudes and a new way of thinking will first emerge
in the freer climate of diaspora communities sharing the common concerns of developed and affluent societies.

Politics: Islamist Demonization of a Gay West

Islam, not excluding Shi'ism, prides itself on being a churchless
polity, a religion without a priesthood. This is perhaps an ideal
often disproved by reality. In actual fact, most Muslim countries do have some kind of a quasi-clergy, especially Shi'ite
Iran. Religious authorities and preachers are known by many
titles, such as *imam, khatib, faqih, mufti, 'alim, mujtahid, maulawi,
maulana, alfa.* The word *mulla* is a kind of generic term for all of
these. But a *mulla* is not ordained. His role is akin to that of a
rabbi in Judaism. In fact, there is at least one sect that calls its
religious leaders *murabbi* ("educator"), the Arabic equivalent of
the Hebrew *rabbi.* Thus a *mulla* is primarily a teacher and a
community leader. Ideally, every Muslim ought to be able to act
as an *imam,* as a prayer leader.

The Christian problem of ordaining gays or lesbians,
therefore, does not arise. Apart from this formal aspect, however, having a teacher who is gay would be considered intolera-
ble. Traditional Muslim society may tolerate homosexuals in
public offices, but certainly not in the role of teacher or religious role model.

This is one of the reasons why tradition attaches so much
importance to marriage. As mentioned earlier, an unmarried
person was usually not accepted as a teacher or judge, or in
similar public offices. Appointment to such positions is still
sometimes subject to the condition that the candidate be married, partly in order to assure that he is not gay.

It is difficult to imagine that gay rights will be won by a
gay movement analogous to what we witness in the United

States and other Western countries. There is no serious gay movement in Latin America either. The handling of the issue in most of the Muslim world and in Latin America is fairly similar: officially, there is nothing but condemnation, whereas unofficially there may be more toleration than was customary in Europe before postmodernity.

In any event, the situation will probably continue to remain conflictive in the Muslim world more than elsewhere, because a movement for gay rights will not be viewed as indigenous. Rather, it would be considered objectionable as yet another symptom of "Westernization," or what Khomeinists have come to label as "Westoxication" (*gharbzadegi*, literally, "to be smitten by admiration for things Western"). Muslim fundamentalists in particular are fond of rejecting all "imported ideologies" and "foreign isms." They have devised a modern ideology of "Islamism" as an alternative to capitalism and communism, secularism and socialism. They regard Islamism as an alternative to lesbianism as much as to liberalism (if indeed they are prepared to make a distinction.).

A prominent Egyptian educationist and radical Islamist, Dr. Muhammad Al-Bahiy, defined secularism "among young people" as "sexual lust" (*shahwat al-badan wa l-farj*). Fortunately or unfortunately, nobody seems to have dared to ask the prolific propagandist for his opinion on homosexuality. Under Khomeini, hundreds of people were executed as homosexuals. Most of these were not gay at all, just as the hundreds of alleged drug dealers executed in Iran since 1979 were mostly political opponents. Important in the present context is the fact that the accusation of homosexuality is used for the purpose of physically eliminating people not of the party line, as it was in Nazi Germany. Then and now, some of the executioners were gay, whereas the accused were not.

Any improvement in the position of gays can occur, if at all, only if some nongays find the courage to fight for them, just as a man such as Qasim Amin in Egypt fought for women with his epoch-making books *tahrir al-mar'a* (The Emancipation of Women) and *al-mar'a al-jadida* (The New Woman) at the turn of the century.

Such attempts would have to struggle hard with the *shari'a*. This is needed in any case because of the many other burning issues waiting to be resolved theologically, as for example the question of left-handers. (Because the left hand is used for dirty tasks such as cleaning genitals and the nose, Muslims are supposed to be right-handers, and many parents still try to make left-handers point in the opposite direction, as Islamists everywhere seek to implement a stagnated *shari'a* of the seventh and eighth centuries as an unchangeable holy norm in its most rigid form, as if it were a God-given code, not a man-made law.)

In non-Islamist Muslim countries, where public life is still dominated by a liberal elite (as in Indonesia and Morocco), human rights activists are fully absorbed by other, more immediate issues of a political nature. To take up the cudgels in behalf of gays would almost certainly jeopardize their position as fledgling advocates of political and religious pluralism. In the near future, it can scarcely be expected that homosexuals will be allowed to raise their concerns in public anywhere in the Muslim world. If a secularist government were to support their cause or merely grant them protection, the Islamists would use this as a welcome weapon to stigmatize such a government as aberrant and abominable.

Prospects: Radical Humanism Banned, but Not Exterminated

Theologically speaking, there might be some hope for gays in the reformation of Islamic thought brought about by Ustadh Mahmud M. Taha (d. 1985) in Sudan, which allows for the development of a new *shari'a* comparatively detached from the social climate of seventh-century Arabia. Ustadh Mahmud emphasized the ethical principles of freedom and justice enunciated by the Prophet Muhammad in Mecca, that is, before the revelation turned into law at Medina.

Lest there be any misunderstanding, Ustadh Mahmud M. Taha was no advocate of gay rights. We have no statement from him to this effect. His own Gandhian lifestyle seemed to recommend general abstinence rather than indulgence in physical passions. As a typical Muslim reformist, he was very much concerned with the marital problems of an agonizing heterosexual majority. He was an idealist with a lofty vision of human relations in an "ultimate" Islam ethically very distant from the somber realities of today.

Ustadh Mahmud might also be called a Sufi (mystic) humanist. As such, he might have been able to accommodate believers whose love for others has a homosexual focus. An example of this would be the romantic relationship between Jalal-ad-din Rumi, Islam's greatest mystic poet, and his beloved teacher, Shams-ad-din Tabrizi (twelfth century). But from there, it is still a great distance to the right demanded by present-day gays in Western societies to display publicly homosexuality of a corporeal nature.

Ustadh Mahmud M. Taha's reformation of the *shari'a* might be regarded as the most radical attempt in all Muslim history. It is surely the boldest endeavor of this type, because it is honest and not inimical to the concept of a religious law as such. Quite the contrary: the Sudanese theologian, whom a military dictatorship executed as a heretic, could not conceive of true progress except through a new *shari'a* to be developed on the basis of the Islamic sources.

Religious gays in the realm of Islam, then, would have to take recourse in the antinomian sufism (mysticism) that puts *tariqa* in place of *shari'a*. Literally, both words mean "way to salvation," but the *tariqa* followers of the heterodox type seek to pull down the protective walls set up by the followers of the *shari'a*. For them, all that counts is union with the divine through mystic exaltation. On that level, it becomes immaterial whether a believer is hetero- or homosexual. In other words, a homosexual Muslim would have to be heterodox, and only heterosexual Muslims can afford to be orthodox, if consequences are fully drawn. Possibly this is one of the reasons why mystic poetry of the heterodox type made so much of homosexual allusions and similes.

This is not to say that the world of Islam does not know the phenomenon of revolt by gays and lesbians against an antihomosexual tradition. Great figures of literature are surprisingly often forgiven such trespasses. The Pakistani author 'Ismat Chughtai treated lesbians with candor and sympathy, and yet she is highly respected by lovers of modern Urdu literature, except, of course, by the Islamists who curse her as a subversive apostate. She was typical of a large segment of liberal opinion that concedes to every Muslim the right to live the faith his or her own way and does not ostracize heterodox attitudes. The same holds true of Josh Malihabadi, whom many acclaim as the greatest twentieth-century writer of Urdu in either India or Pakistan. Josh, as he is lovingly referred to, was not gay himself, but he was an advocate of individual freedom that extended to homosexuals. Despite his immense popularity, the Islamist military dictatorship under General Zia-ul-Haq (1976–88) had his works banned—because of their "obscenity."

Notes

1. Personal communications have been corroborated by my own experiences as former director of an Islamic Academy in West Germany. I was several times requested by nongays to "work out something"—Islamically—for the recognition of gay rights, and in two cases gays confided their problems directly, without the intercession of nongays. I believe, though, that this was typical of the diaspora situation. Heterosexual Muslims in Europe sometimes feel a kind of public pressure to espouse the cause of homosexuals as an oppressed minority. Wishing to be up-to-date, some go along with the trend. I was also several times approached by Jewish and Christian leaders asking me to contribute to the discussion from a Muslim perspective.

2. S. Geoffrey Parrinder, *Sex in the World's Religions* (London: Sheldon Press, 1980), chap. 8, "Islamic Customs." Cf. Abdelwahab Boudhiba, *La Sexualité en Islam* (Paris: P. U. F., 1975).

3. Professor Fathi 'Uthmán in a reply letter (Aug. 12, 1988) to a questionnaire by Professor Riffat Hassan of the University of Louisville, Louisville, Ky.

4. Larbi Layachi, *The Jealous Lover* (Bolinas, Calif.: Tombouctou Books, 1986).

5. S. Malek Chebel, "Perversions et marginalités au Maghreb," in *L'Esprit de Sérail* (Paris: Lieu Commun/Terre des autres, 1987).

Bibliography

Boudhiba, Abdelwahab. 1975. *La Sexualité en Islam.* Paris: P. U. F.

Chebel, Malek. 1987. "Perversions et marginalités au Maghreb." In *L'Esprit de Sérail."* Paris: Lieu Commun/Terre des autres.

Layachi, Larbi. 1986. *The Jealous Lover.* Bolinas, Calif.: Tombouctou Books.

Parrinder, S. Geoffrey. 1980. *Sex in the World's Religions.* Chap. 8, "Islamic Customs." London: Sheldon Press.

8

Homosexuality and Chinese and Japanese Religions

Sandra A. Wawrytko

The issue of homosexuality in Chinese and Japanese religions is largely a terra incognita. A point common to both cultural traditions is the paucity of direct references to homosexuality in the religious canons. This necessitates a creative extrapolation from various texts and doctrines to arrive at a sense of prevailing attitudes. Moreover, the strict division between religious and philosophical views within Western cultures—often responsible for a tension between the two disciplines—is absent in Asian thought as a whole. Hence a wide range of literary sources can and must be surveyed to uncover relevant data.

Furthermore, the overall cultural context and traditional principles of social organization must be taken into consideration when evaluating homosexuality in China and Japan. The traditional emphasis in both cultures on same-sex relationships evolved from social segregation based on gender. In practical terms, this led to intense, but not necessarily erotic, relationships between men as well as between women. Such relationships were not only tolerated but to a great extent actively encouraged by social mores. Western observers often mistook this culturally specific species of friendship, typified by hand holding in public and other forms of physical contact among individuals of the same sex, as a sign of rampant homosexual practices.

Despite geographical proximity and a history of cultural exchange, China and Japan hold considerably different views of homosexuality in their theories and, most especially, their practices. The following discussions address each of these cultures in turn, beginning with a broad historical overview of attitudes toward sexuality and homosexuality in each. We then will consider more specific religious contexts and literature: Confucianism and Neo-Confucianism as well as Taoism and Neo-Taoism in China; Shintoism and Neo-Shintoism in Japan.

China

A General Overview

The meticulously kept histories of successive Chinese dynasties reveal intimate details of sexual behavior among the aristocracy. Some emperors displayed a fondness for male companionship and openly practiced pederasty. These erotic indulgences were most often supplemented by heterosexual activities for purposes of continuing the royal lineage. Records of the Han dynasty (206 B.C.–220 A.D.) mention a class of ministers, *pi* or "favorites," who rendered sexual services to the emperor, as did young boys (*lüan-tung*). Emperor Wu (140–87 B.C.) is noteworthy for his love of the actor Li Yen-nien as well as Li's sister. Emperor Ai-ti (reigned 6–1 B.C.) was so attached to his companion, Tung Hsien, that he cut off his sleeve, on which the youth was sleeping, rather than disturb him when official duty called. Thereafter homosexuality was poetically alluded to as "the cut sleeve" (*tuan hsiu*).[1] Such lovers also were referred to as *lung-yang*, namesakes of the fourth century B.C. minister Lung-yang-chün, beloved by the Prince of Wei.

An impressive opus of Chinese poetry is dedicated to male friendships, which may well have gone beyond the platonic. The Three Kingdoms and Six Dynasties period (A.D. 221–590) saw the rise of close relationships among literary men. The catalyst was a newfound interest in metaphysics, "pure conversation" (*ch'ing-t'an*), as an escape from the prevailing social

and political upheaval. Such friendships frequently are depicted in landscape scrolls, where we see scholars enjoying
each other's company in secluded scenic spots. Hsi K'ang (A.D.
223–262) and Jüan Chi (A.D. 210–263), two outspoken eccentrics
counted among the "Seven Worthies of the Bamboo Grove,"
were fast friends and very probably lovers.[2] They "met in bamboo groves to drink, write poems, and talk and behave with
utter disregard for social conventions or worldly values."[3] This
antisocial behavior could easily have included homosexual activity. Hsi K'ang eventually was arrested and executed by the
Confucian authorities on charges of corrupting public morals.
His friend Jüan Chi was not charged, but died a year later.

The ensuing T'ang period (618–906) is noteworthy for the
lushness of its sexual expressiveness. One erotic text, the *Poetical
Essay on the Supreme Joy (Ta-lo-fu)* attributed to Po Hsing-chien
(d. 826), devotes a section (xiv) to male homosexuality, providing a history of its occurrence.[4] Despite government attempts at
control, homosexuality flourished during the Northern and
Southern Sung dynasties (960–1279), spawning a proliferation of
male prostitutes and transvestism.[5] Many consider this the peak
period of homosexual activity in Chinese history, after which it
gradually declined to levels commensurate with those in other
societies.[6] Sporadic waves of sexual repression within China
tended to correspond with the incursions of foreign (non-Han)
elements, notably the Mongols in the Yüan dynasty (1279–1367)
and the Manchus in the Ch'ing dynasty (1644–1912).

The generally tolerant attitude toward homosexual activity
is attested to by the reports of Jesuit missionaries to China. Legal
prohibitions of such activity notwithstanding, Matteo Ricci, who
spent nearly thirty years in China during the Ming dynasty
(1368–1644), was shocked by what he encountered in Peking:

> That which most shows the misery of these people is that no less
> than the natural lusts they practice unnatural ones that reverse
> the order of things; and this is neither forbidden by law [an er-
> roneous view], nor thought to be illicit, nor even a cause for
> shame. It is spoken of in public, and practiced everywhere, with-
> out there being anyone to prevent it.[7]

Such activities are documented in the premiere erotic novel
of the Ming period, *The Golden Lotus (Chin-p'ing-mei)*, which

recounts the heterosexual and homosexual adventures of protagonist Hsi-men Ch'ing. Similar bisexual escapades are recounted in Li Yü's *The Flesh Prayer Mat (Jou-pu-t'uan)*, which implies that enlightenment may be the end result, hence its alternate title, *The Chan (Meditational Practice) Beyond (Ordinary) Enlightenment (Chüeh-hou-ch'an)*. The acting profession, which was restricted to men and young boys, was particularly prone to spawn homosexual activities, a circumstance corroborated by Ricci. Ch'en Sen-shou's novel *Precious Mirror for Gazing (P'in-hua-pao-chien)*, published in 1856, is a detailed portrayal of the lives and loves of these artists in the Ch'ing dynasty (1644–1912).

Ricci's report of a lack of moral outrage attached to homosexuality is confirmed by other Western observers, including Friar Gaspar de Cruz. When the Friar berated his Chinese acquaintances for their homoerotic behavior, they were surprised to have such activity called into question and claimed "that they had never had anyone who told them that it was a sin, nor an evil thing done."[8] This state of affairs motivated Ricci to translate the Sixth Commandment against adultery into Chinese as "Thou shalt not do depraved, unnatural, or filthy things."

In view of these vituperous fulminations, it is ironic that the Jesuits, including Ricci, repeatedly found themselves accused of both heterosexual and homosexual acts.[9] This was no doubt due in part to the Chinese devaluation of the celibate lifestyle (that also was challenged in the case of Buddhism).[10] Catholic priests found it repeatedly necessary to defend the theological significance of celibacy.[11] The Chinese populace found it difficult to believe that anyone would choose such an unnatural lifestyle. Given the fact that the priests were unmarried, it was assumed they sought and shepherded boy converts to provide themselves with sexual partners.

Although the men were isolated in their own same-sex groups by professional concerns, women were no less isolated within the domestic arena. This included the imperial harem, where multiple concubines satisfied each other's sexual needs while on a "waiting list" to meet with the emperor. Within the polygnous households of the wealthy, wives also initiated intimate alliances among themselves. Erotic manuals demonstrate that intercourse was often a group endeavor, known as "the Heavenly and Earthly Net." Women, whether wives or servants, thus were likely to come into sexual contact with each other, a contact readily resumed in the absence of the sole male partner. The manuals include depictions of male and female homosexual practices.[12]

Lesbianism also was fostered by the contrary contexts of the nunnery and the "Flower Courts" (brothels). Their point of commonality was that women lived in close physical contact with one another, without establishing (permanent) relationships with men. As Buddhism gained in popularity among women in the Ming dynasty, nuns increasingly were suspected of covert lesbianism. This became a prevalent theme in the literature of the period, following the assumption that nuns used the religious vocation as a means of circumventing their procreative obligations.[13] The most common reaction to these liaisons on the part of males ranged from indifference to delight. Thus Pao Yü, the hero of Ts'ao Hsüeh-ch'in's famous Ch'ing dynasty novel *Dream of the Red Chamber (Hung Lo Meng)*, is quite charmed when he walks in on an intimate exchange between two embarrassed young women, one of whom is a nun. The husband in Shen-fu's *Memoirs of a Poor Scholar* is similarly delighted at his wife's insistence that he take her female lover as a concubine. In the lesbian classic, *Love for the Perfumed Companion (Lien-Hsiang-pan)* by Li Yü, the two heroines vow to seek rebirth as husband and wife, invoking the Buddha as witness to their "marriage": "We could share the same bed and afterwards the same tomb and we would be joined, like two butterflies, flitting hither and thither."[14]

This tolerance, if not outright encouragement, of female homosexuality can be explained in part by the principles of Chinese cosmology. Within the *Yin-Yang* system of primal correspondences that forms the root of Chinese culture, women enjoyed a distinct advantage over men with regard to erotic activities. Male semen, as the repository of *yang* energy, was considered to be limited by its nature, while a woman's *yin* was inexhaustible, particularly given proper stimulation. For purposes of procreation, it was necessary for men to conserve the sexual energy that women could expend as lavishly as they liked. When these liaisons took place within the same household, the overall amount of *yin* was not diminished but merely recirculated among the various women involved.

In view of such a tolerant cultural climate, an explanation for the repressive movements to counter homosexual activity is needed. The primary reservations/objections to homosexual activity as stated by religious sources have fallen primarily into two categories: (1) social and political, as posing a threat to family or government stability and continuity; and (2) physical and metaphysical health, as detrimental to cultivation of one's fullest biological and spiritual potentials. The first set is most often voiced by the Confucianists, whereas the second tends to prevail among Taoists. The respective doctrines supporting these positions are detailed below.

Confucianism and Neo-Confucianism

Emphasis on family and society is evident in Confucian literature beginning with its founder Confucius (K'ung Tzu, 551–479 B.C.). Eight Threads underlying social organization are set forth in the *Great Learning (Ta Hsüeh)*; they stretch from the individual's "the investigation of things" (1) through the "root" of self-cultivation (5), and thence into family regulation (6), ordering of the state (7), and world peace (8). "When the roots are entangled it is impossible for the offshoots to be orderly; it is impossible to have what deserves priority slighted while what is slight is treated as deserving of priority."[15]

Confucian doctrine gave primary importance to the production of progeny to propagate the family line as well as to provide the means for ritual remembrances after death. Filial piety (*hsiao*) was ranked as the highest virtue, and the obligations incurred in its practice were given highest priority. Within this context, homosexuality could well be thought to lack any redeeming social value. Nonetheless, such practices were rarely condemned outright, as long as the fulfillment of one's family and social obligations was not compromised. In a satiric touch, the hero of the erotic Ming dynasty novel *The Flesh Prayer Mat* invokes Confucian doctrine to persuade his prudish wife to indulge his desire for sexual experimentation:

Learning how to conceive and become pregnant and give birth to sons and daughters, this certainly is the Right Way! Your father's only worry is that our union will not produce results. You would certainly not wish to cause him sorrow?[16]

Throughout Chinese history, Confucian morality tended toward austerity, representing the conservative forces of society. Yet in the various Confucian-tinged moral codes that developed throughout the centuries, homosexual activity is not singled out for special rebuke. The vast majority of sexual misdeeds mentioned concern heterosexual relationships. In one such listing of demerits, intercourse with either a prostitute or a young boy incurs fifty demerits per orgasm. This is far lower than the five hundred demerits associated with recruiting a nun or a widow as a concubine, or the thousand demerits assigned to those responsible for producing pornographic literature or art. In fact, pederasty is ranked as equal to the offense of "having more wives and concubines than one can satisfy."[17]

The later doctrines of Neo-Confucianism represented a hybrid philosophy intertwining standard Confucian values with Taoist and Buddhist undertones. A tone of puritanical denial pervades the school's view of "selfish desire," and its texts are largely silent on sexual matters. Although at odds on many points, Chu Hsi (1130–1200) and Wang Yang-ming (1472–1529), proponents of the rationalist and idealist sects of Neo-Confucian thought respectively, agree on the importance of self-discipline (*k'o-chi*). Chu Hsi cautions against extreme behavior and recommends abiding in the natural Mean: "Heaven teaches us to behave this way. When hungry we eat and when thirsty we drink. We follow our natural desires. But it is wrong to let these desires go to extremes."[18] Wang Yang-ming approaches the issue in a more forthright manner, responding directly to a student's question about "the love of sex": "If you eliminate all thoughts of sex, wealth, fame, and so forth, just as you have no thought of becoming a thief, there will be nothing but the original substance of mind. What idle thoughts can there be?"[19]

Chinese legal codes, products of the Confucian state ideology, reflect the primacy given to family. Of the Ten Abominations, considered the most serious of crimes for which no amnesty was possible, the only explicit reference to a sex crime is incest.[20] Because this sexual act is the one most likely to destabilize the family structure, it seems to be a logical concern for Chinese society and Confucianism in particular. Consistent with this family orientation, Shen Te-fu reports that male homosexual couples in Fukien province formed their own household, with the approval and financial support of their parents.[21]

However, for men homosexuality posed a greater risk to family unity by expending their erotic energies in nonproductive ways. Women did not labor under the same social disadvantage. Moreover, lesbianism seemed a more acceptable option for love-starved females than adultery, which was dealt with severely by both the law and social custom. The social condemnation of lesbian nuns, noted above, was probably more a function of the Confucian rejection of Buddhism as disruptive of family bonds than a form of disapproval aimed at "sexual deviance."[22] An additional threat inherent in homosexuality surfaced in the broader social arena, where male lovers were liable to exploit their position to corrupt those in power.[23] Thus the proverbial beautiful face able to topple an empire could be either male or female. Chinese history contained sufficient examples of both kinds of cases to warrant vigilance.

Turning to the new "religion" of modern China, Sinified Communist ideology, distinctly homophobic tendencies can be found. Despite official denunciations of Confucian doctrine, the Maoist regime was heavily influenced by the strict moral code of the supposedly corrupt tradition (as well as the lingering residue of Ch'ing dynasty sexual repression). Intolerance toward homosexual activity escalated. Bao Ruo-Wang reports that homosexuals were summarily executed in the thought-reform prison camps in operation at the height of the Cultural Revolution.[24] This practice was common until quite recently. It is noteworthy that the legal code of the Peoples' Republic of China reserves the death penalty for "criminal elements who commit the most heinous crimes."[25] In present-day China, homosexuals still pursue their proclivities at the risk of their lives, although discretion is more likely to be rewarded by official blindness.[26]

Taoism and Neo-Taoism

It is significant that homosexuality in China was said to have originated in the southeastern region, a stronghold of Taoism, as opposed to the northern provinces that had given rise to Confucian thought. Although Confucianism came to dominate the political arena from the Han dynasty onward, Taoism accommodated the loyal opposition, with occasional forays into the inner sanctums of power through the conversion of rulers. Overall the Taoists advocated a natural, spontaneous lifestyle in emulation of Tao (the Way), contrasting starkly with the rigid, formalized patterns of Confucianism. This included a more free-wheeling, liberated attitude among Taoists toward human sexual behavior.

Two contradictory views of sexuality can be discerned within Taoism: as the means to the end of promoting longevity/immortality or as an obstacle to that same end. The first trend resembled Indian and Tibetan Tantra: "Both seek to reconcile the opposing dualities of life as symbolized by male and female and both accept any moment or experience as a starting point for spiritual growth and as an end point for insight into truth."[27] Certain Taoist sects claimed to be able to teach the sexual path to health and even immortality. Others, less ambitious, vouchsafed only a physical efficacy to sexual intercourse properly pursued.[28] The opposing trend conceived of all sexual activity as a squandering of vital force and concentrated on internalizing the cycling of erotic energy.

The Taoist case against homosexuality can be traced to the assumption of the need to balance *yin* and *yang* energies. Because these energies were stimulated and exchanged during sexual intercourse, homosexuality was liable to be hazardous to one's health/harmony. Moreover, weakened *yang* was believed to result in unhealthy offspring (bringing us back to Confucian family priorities, there being a mixing of the two philosophies throughout Chinese history). Sexologist R. H. Van Gulik summarized the two seminal points of Chinese erotic philosophy:

First, a man's semen is his most precious possession, the source not only of his health but of his very life; every emission of semen will diminish this vital force, unless compensated by the acquiring of an equivalent amount of *yin* from the woman. Second, the man should give the woman complete satisfaction every time he cohabitates with her, but he should allow himself to reach orgasm only on certain specified occasions.[29]

Only veiled references to sexuality can be found in the earliest text of philosophical Taoism, the *Tao Te Ching* attributed to the semimythical sage Lao Tzu (580–480 B.C.?).[30] From these we can surmise a view of sexuality that presupposes the interchange of *yin* and *yang*, following the pattern of heterosexual intercourse, with emphasis on the efficacy of *yin*. Thus, in the sixth chapter Lao Tzu identifies the forces of *yin* with "the profoundly dark female" (*hsüan p'in*):

> The valley spirit never dies—
> This is called "the profoundly dark female."
> The gateway of the profoundly dark female—
> This is called the root of Heaven and Earth.
> Continuous and ceaseless,
> It looks as if it were ever-present;
> Its usefulness never wears out.

Some commentators read this passage as a Taoist prescription for sexual relations in which the male draws upon the woman's "continuous and ceaseless" *yin* energy to supplement his limited *yang*, thereby increasing his vital force and his life.

The indispensability of *yin*, and therefore of women, is repeated in chapter 28:

> Whoever knows the male,
> Yet holds fast to the female,
> Becomes the ravine of the world.
> Whoever becomes the ravine of the world,
> Without departing from the enduring virtue,
> Returns to infancy.

The return to infancy, a primary ideal for the Taoist, represents a return to the apex of one's vitality. This is further depicted in chapter 55 in terms of the male experience:

> One whose virtue is deep can be compared to an infant.
> Poisonous insects will not sting it;
> Fierce beasts will not pounce upon it;

Birds of prey will not feed upon it;
Its bones are soft, its sinews supple,
And yet its grip is firm;
It does not know the union of male and female,
And yet its member is erect—
Its vital essence remains at its peak.

The fact that the ideal infant is innocent of sexual intercourse led some later Taoists to proscribe such activity (at least for men) as an inadvisable drain of primal energy. The warning of doom for the male participant in intercourse resurfaces in chapter 61:

The female always subdues the male by tranquillity,
Tranquilly taking the lowly position.

In his commentary to this passage, the Neo-Taoist Wang Pi (A.D. 226–249) writes: "Because of her tranquillity [the female] can take the lowly position. 'The female' (*p'in*) refers to the female gender (*tz'u*). The male is impulsive, restive, and full of desire; the female always remains tranquil and therefore can overcome the male. Because of her tranquillity as well as her ability to stay beneath, things return to her."[31] Obviously following this line of thought to its logical conclusion, the twelfth Patriarch of the Shang Ch'ing school of Taoism (b. 647) argued that the goal of immortality was incompatible with sexual activity of any kind:

Immortals recognize sensuality as defilement and impurity, wise men compare it to knives and axes of punishment. In life on earth, not eating for seven days will cause death, but a hundred years without sensuality will avert untimely departure. Realize thus that sensuality is not essential or appropriate for the personal body or the mind, but an enemy and thief to inner nature and life.[32]

The *Chuang Tzu*, the second major text of philosophical Taoism by Lao Tzu's heir of the same name (369–286 B.C.), contains no references or even allusions to sexual intercourse, homosexual or otherwise. However, the repeated theme of naturalness (*tzu-jan*) supports the same need to balance *yin* and *yang* forces evident in the passages from Lao Tzu cited above: "The two mingle, penetrate, come together, harmonize, and all things are born therefrom."[33] This interpretation is borne out by modern-day Taoist practitioners. One writer draws upon Western scientific resources to support his view of the unnaturalness of homosexuality for all species, including humans, and therefore its disharmony with Tao.[34] Sexologists Masters and Johnson are invoked to vindicate Taoist theory: "They feel that human happiness and well-being are almost unattainable without feeling regular loving touching between adult men and women. This of course is very similar to the Yin-Yang harmony." It is further argued that lesbianism is a response to the failure of men to provide sufficient physical contact in the form of caressing apart from actual sexual intercourse.[35]

However, the damage is not irreparable. When asked whether homosexuality can "block spiritual development," Master Mantak replied:

> The Taoists are too wise to condemn anything outright, as everything leads back to the Tao. So the question really is how can it be against nature, or the Tao, if the Tao created it? Homosexuality is not against the Tao, but it is also not the highest experience of the Tao possible. It's impossible to experience the full balance of male-female polarity with homosexual love. . . . The problem is greater for two men than for two women, because their double yang energy is too expansive and more easily leads to conflict. A double yin energy can be harmonious, as yin is yielding. . . . Both cases can lead to subtle organ imbalances that require attention if best health is to be maintained.[36]

This corroborates Van Gulik's observation that homosexual relations, seen as acceptable for women, were not entirely condemned for men, because "intimate contact between two *yang* elements can not result in a total loss of vital force for either of them."[37] Mantak Chia does provide advice for gay and lesbian couples on how to forestall the energy balance by having one member of the couple increase their inner resources of *yin* or *yang* energy through environmental and nutritional adjustments.[38]

Japan

A General Overview

Compared with Chinese culture, with its recalcitrant tinges of Confucianism, Japanese attitudes toward sexuality can be characterized as liberal in the extreme. Westerners in particular are often shocked by their initial exposure to the Japanese sex scene—from the cosmology of "Coital Genesis" presented in the earliest texts to the modern proliferation of its conspicuous "love hotels."[39] One observer cautioned, "Be prepared for the fact that in Japan there is no sin, original or otherwise."[40] As we will see, the culture focused on pollution rather than sin from early times. More pointedly, Japan expert Edwin O. Reischauer observes:

> The Japanese do not share Western views about the sinfulness of sexual relations. To them they have always seemed a natural phenomenon, like eating, which is to be enjoyed in the proper place. Promiscuity is in itself no more of a problem than homosexuality. Their attitudes have thus in a sense been permissive. But at the same time, they have a stronger awareness than contemporary Westerners of the necessity for bending the desires of the individual to the surrounding environment.[41]

Chinese influence is evident in the tenth-century medical text *The Quintessence of Medicine (Ishinpo)*, by Tamba no Yasuyori (912–995). Tamba, reputedly a descendent of Chinese immigrants, drew heavily upon Chinese sources in compiling his text. The Chinese theory of the interchange of *yin* and *yang* through sexual intercourse is echoed in the fourth chapter devoted to "Spiritual Harmony Between the Sexes." The correspondence between Nature as a whole and human beings is emphasized: "It is essential to know this natural principle for sexual relationships, so that heavenly and earthly things can be in their rightful places." The text goes on to quote Hsiang-nu from the Chinese text of the same name: "There is no pleasure for *Yang* without *Yin*, and the *Yin* cannot be aroused without the *Yang*."[42] This may be construed as posing problems for homosexual relationships.

Two apparent references to homosexual activity appear in the most famous Japanese novel of the Heian period (794–1192), Lady Murasaki's *Tale of Genji (Genji Monogatori)*.[43] The hero, Prince Genji, spends the night with the younger brother of his latest romantic target as solace for having been rejected by the sister, Utsusemi (chapter 3). The other involves Genji's supposed son, Kaoru, who similarly settles for the younger brother of his lady-love, Ukifune, when she rebuffs his advances. However, because the pervasive sexual climate of this era was one of promiscuous heterosexuality, such behavior may merely be examples of a repeated pattern of surrogacy (*katami*)—seeking available substitutes when obstacles prevent attainment of the intended object of desire.

Beginning in the Kamakura period (1192–1336), with the rise of the shogun system of military hegemony, a high incidence of homosexual activity occurred within the samurai class (which constituted about 10% of the overall population). Homosexuality was known as "Love in the Satsuma way," referring to an area in Kyushu where military training went hand in hand with these sexual practices.[44] The erotic vocabulary also includes the term *Wakashu-do*, or simply *shu-do*, "the way of young men" (that is, those under the age of fifteen), denoting the practice of sodomy. Homosexual activities among ambitious young men also represented a well-accepted avenue for advancement. In 1596, Father Francis Cabral wrote that these activities were "regarded in Japan as quite honorable; men of standing entrust their sons to the bonzes to be instructed in such things, and at the same time to serve their lust."[45] Combining patronage of the arts with pederasty, the powerful shogun Ashikaga Yoshimitsu (1358–1408) advanced the evolution of Nōh drama through his love and support for actor and playwright Zeami (d. 1443).

Numerous works in the Muromachi period (1338–1573) dealt with homosexual love, especially between Buddhist priests and their novice monks. A later piece, *The Story of a Boor (Dembu Monogatori)*, undertook a comparative study of homosexual and heterosexual experiences. However, *The Mirror of Manly Love (Nanshoku Ōkagami)* by Ihara Saikaku (b. 1642), also known as *A Tale of Love Between Samurai*, is noteworthy for its explicit glorification of homosexuality. Saikaku declares:

> Pederasty should be entirely different from mere love between men and women. That is why princes cannot forget their pages even after they marry princesses. A woman is a completely unimportant creature whereas a sincere relationship between two males is true love with both of them detesting women as if they were wretched worms.[46]

The same phenomenon is common in militaristic societies around the world that tend toward a machismo ethic, such as ancient Greece. In contrast, women suffer from a devalued, demeaning status, becoming a necessary evil for the end of procreation. Accordingly, heterosexual intercourse was contemptuously spoken of as "borrowing their wombs." In part, this attitude also reflected contempt for the deposed aristocracy, despised for their effeminate weakness and overindulgence in a species of courtly love.

Jesuit founder Francis Xavier was shocked to find a high incidence of "abominations" (especially among Buddhist monks) during his sixteenth-century sojourn in Japan as a missionary. He was even more mortified by the lack of social opposition to this state of affairs: "This evil, furthermore, is so public, so clear to all, men and women, young and old, and they are so used to seeing it that they are neither depressed nor horrified."[47] Even students studying in the Jesuit houses engaged in homosexual practices, leading to the imposition of strict rules for communal sleeping quarters, including the separation of sleeping mats by wooden benches in rooms kept constantly lit.[48]

During the Tokugawa period (1603–1850), the government sought stricter controls on social activities and thus instituted licensed pleasure quarters that came to be known as the Floating World. These included brothels dedicated to homosexual practices, *hage mazaya*. Being based on monetary profit, such relationships lacked the veneer of honor found among samurai practitioners. These were also subjects of the *ukiyo-e* prints that brought art to the growing merchant audience: "Masanobu and Harunobu catered to the persuasion with prints featuring the merry sodomization of young *chigo* [novice Buddhist monks]." One rather unique scenario of two men engaged in sexual intercourse with a woman, known as *mara-kyodai* (penis brothers), has been described as "homosexuality by proxy" and continues to remain popular.

Women similarly were drawn together by the alienating social climate as well as by prevailing misogyny. During the Tokugawa period, professional "entertainers" constituted a public-access harem, whose inmates sought similar modes of release among themselves, as did those relegated to the shogun's harem. As in Chinese society, neglected wives were wont to engage in lesbian affairs to avoid the considerable risks of adultery. In each case, a wide variety of erotic aids emulating the penis were employed, many borrowed from a centuries-old Chinese tradition. One device, known as a "dual plover" (*ryochi-dori*), allowed two women to bestow mutual pleasure upon each other.

Lesbianism occasionally is a subject in the *ukiyo-e* prints. Nineteenth-century wood block prints for sex manuals include among other explicit illustrations a pair of lesbian nuns practicing oral sex and guidelines for preparing a man for anal intercourse.[49] Following the Chinese social pattern, such practices were and are generally approached by men with indifference or else serve to arouse their curiosity. Nonetheless, these women are even more circumspect about their sexual preferences than their male counterparts. American feminist Kittredge Cherry observes that this is "a state so expected that there is no Japanese phrase for hiding one's homosexuality."[50]

Entertainers play an especially prominent role in Japanese sexuality, past and present. To curb the wantonness occasioned by all-female Kabuki troupes (*Onna Kabuki,* banned in 1629), the government mandated the use of young boys (*Wakashū Kabuki*), only to find heterosexual liaisons replaced by homosexual ones. Accordingly, boy actors were banned from the stage in 1652 and replaced by adult males. This, however, served only to invite both homosexual and heterosexual relationships with male and female members of their audiences respectively.[51] Female impersonators, *onnagata,* traditionally continued their performances offstage, leading a thoroughly female lifestyle in dress and daily habits.

The psychiatrist Takeo Doi has argued that "homosexual feelings," defined as "emotional links between members of the same sex" in preference to those with the opposite sex, are intrinsic to the Japanese character.[52] The situation is eased by the traditional Japanese wife's maternal role vis-à-vis her husband. Given this relationship, she is less likely to experience jealousy over his sexual involvement with another person, either male or female. The core of their relationship is not the mutual support and interdependence of the ideal Western marriage, but the dependency of the husband on the wife (or of a young man on an older man) modeled upon that of the child to the mother (*amae*).[53]

Homoeroticism also has been detected in the seemingly innocuous world of the Japanese comic book (*manga*). The pages of these books, designed to appeal to a wide range of tastes and ages, are inhabited by hundreds of androgynous characters. Notable among these legions are the "beautiful boys and men" (*bishonen* and *binan*) intended for female audiences. Bornoff attributes this convention and repeated literary themes of cross-dressing to "a persistent tendency to confuse gender in the no man's land of pleasure." Freed from the rigid conventions of gender roles imposed by society, a multitude of options can be explored only in this context.[54] Unabashedly lesbian comics are similarly interpreted as imaginative means of liberation for female readers oppressed by a chauvinistic system.[55]

A change in the previously open acceptance of homosexuality is evident in *Confessions of a Mask,* the autobiographical novel of Yukio Mishima (1970), who has been described as "violently Westernized":

> This tale of torture by frustrated and half-conscious [homosexual] desire could have been set anywhere during the first half of the twentieth century, or, of course, earlier. The almost paranoid need to be "normal," the obsession with social disgrace (of which the ethnologist Ruth Benedict has said so aptly that they replace in our cultures the obsession with sin, without any advantage to our freedom), are illustrated on almost every page as they would never have been in ancient Japan, which was more relaxed on the subject of one man's love for another, or conformed to other norms.[56]

Mishima himself has been quoted as stating: "Homosexuality forms part of the Japanese tradition. It was the American missionaries who upset this tradition in the nineteenth century."[57] A survey undertaken in 1987 found 4.5 percent of male college students to be actively homosexual.[58] Practitioners tend to hide their sexual preferences not out of fear of moral condemnation, but rather to avoid shaming their family (as in Mishima's *Forbidden Colors*). Like Mishima, they usually go through the pretence of a "normal" heterosexual marriage both to ensure offspring and forestall public suspicions.

Even in death, Mishima continues to be plagued by the fear of publicly acknowledging his homosexuality, as reflected

in Paul Schrader's experiences in the 1984 filming of his biographical film *Mishima* in Japan:

> Hampered by the widow's contractual proscription of any men-
> tion of her late husband's homosexuality, he [Schrader] was
> shunned by the entire Japanese film community and received a
> sufficient number of threatening calls from rightist extremists
> to finish shooting the film in a bulletproof vest. Despite its ob-
> vious literary merits, Mishima's work is avoided in school cur-
> ricula and the author lives on as an embarrassment in Japan,
> where he is swept under the rug by the literary community and
> exalted by rightist extremists.[59]

The film was never released in Japan. Mishima's case stands as
a poignant metaphor of the confused status of homosexuality
in Japan today.

Shintoism

The primeval roots of Shinto are sunk deep into the soil of ancient Japan and its culture. Shinto literally means "the way of
the *kami.*" Contrary to many Western renderings of the key
term "*kami,*" it does not refer to a restricted category of divine
beings but rather represents an amorphous concept of power,
mystery, superiority, and so forth, that defies translation:
"Everything and everybody being Kami-born therefore has a
Kami-nature and is a potential full-fledged Kami, which may
come to be acknowledged as such."[60] As a religion, Shinto is
based not on doctrines and creeds, but on rituals and feeling. It
is an intensely life-affirming worldview that emphasizes the
existential over the theoretical.

The only texts associated with Shinto fall far short of pro-
pounding clearly delineated set of dogmas and are regarded as
the cultural heritage of the Japanese people: the *Record of Ancient Things (Kojiki-den)* and the *Chronicles of Japan (Nihongi* or
Nihon-shoki). Like the Hebrew Bible, these texts recount the
origin of the world as well as the history of its people, including frequent mention of sexual behavior. What is conspicu-
ously avoided throughout most of the Japanese accounts are
moral condemnations from either a divine force or its human
representatives.

The absence of a detailed moral code, so often associated with religion, has led some to deny Shinto this status. However, by the principles inherent in Shinto, it is the very lack of such a code that signals its superiority. Moral behavior, it is argued, is natural to humans as the descendents of kami, whereas the need to rely on moral laws is a sure sign of degeneration.[61] Guided by these assumptions, many observers have noted the naturalist core of Japanese attitudes toward sexuality:

> The Japanese, whose emotions tend toward "gentle pathos" and soft feelings, find the Western guilt associated with desire of the flesh unnatural, inhuman, or tiresome. Nature is nature, Japanese would say, and whatever exists in nature, including sexual desire, cannot be denied. The Japanese themselves have labeled this attitude toward nature and desire *yukubō shizen-shugi* ("desire-naturalism").[62]

Because of the obvious influence of Korean and Chinese culture in these texts, understanding of the "purely" Shinto values demands a careful reading. We must be alert to any deviations from the Chinese model that may be indicative of more primal views. At this point, the values of Shinto seem to run parallel to, while originating independently of, their Chinese counterparts. For example, an indigenous Japanese version of the Chinese *yin-yang* complements exists in the traditional symbolism of red (as the female) and white (as the male). This color combination suffuses Japanese culture, including its flag.[63]

Another possible parallel to *yin-yang* priorities occurs in a passage that recounts the cosmic disharmony, represented by a solar eclipse, evoked by the burial of two priests together. The text seems to imply some "unnatural" relationship between these two men known for their fast friendship in life. In fact, when one died, the other was unable to go on alone and died of his own accord. After investigating the case as the source of the problem, the ruling empress seeks a return to normalcy on both the earthly and the heavenly planes: "They changed their coffins and interred them separately, upon which the sunlight shone forth, and there was a difference between day and night."[64] The reference to distinguishing between day and night seems to refer as well to the proper or natural distinction—and harmony—that must be maintained between the forces of *yin* and those of *yang*.[65]

A reference to lesbian proclivities may perhaps be found in another section, where a young woman is pursued by the emperor. Although he finally prevails and engages in intercourse with her, her thoughts are obviously elsewhere: "The way of husband and wife is the prevailing rule both now and of old time. But for me it is not convenient." Addressing the emperor, she explains, "Thy handmaiden's disposition is adverse to the way of conjugal intercourse," and tries to excuse herself on the basis of her unworthiness for his favors. He ultimately accepts her offer of her sister as a substitute. The sister seemingly has no aversion to married life, as she bears the emperor thirteen children.[66]

Ihara Saikaku, in his preface to *The Mirror of Manly Love*, calls upon the authority of the *Nihonji* to validate homosexuality. Saikaku claims pederasty originated with the obviously phallic "jewel-spear of Heaven." Heterosexual practices, Saikaku points out, arose generations later. There is some basis to this idiosyncratic reading. Shinto cosmogony envisions cosmic genesis initially as a species of spontaneous generation, with the cosmic egg dividing into Heaven and Earth of its own accord. Procreation begins with the seventh-generation pair of siblings Izanami no Mikoto and Izanagi no Mikoto. Prior to their initial act of sexual congress, they wield the "jewel-spear of Heaven" to stir the oceans below, giving birth to the islands of Japan from the drops that fall from its tip.[67] It has been suggested that the incidence of homosexuality in Japan today can be correlated with the continuing influence of Shinto's phallic cult.[68]

A wide variety of sexual practices are mentioned in the early texts, with little indication of any outrage on the part of society. Among "sins" (*tumi*) in need of expiation are listed incest and bestiality.[69] No mention is made of homosexuality. Evaluations of the historical data in combination with modern practices have led to conclusions about the sociological and psychological attitudes of Japanese society concerning sexuality. It has been argued that the idea that sexual love is regarded as "something that does, and should, well [*sic*] naturally and undenied from the hearts of two people has remained the basic norm of the Japanese people to our time."[70] Despite the later influx of Chinese Confucian morality, which "harnessed" sexuality for social and political ends, this Shinto attitude of sexual love as "subject only to the mutual wills of those who share it" seems to have prevailed, at least on some level.[71]

Thus, in judging human behavior, emphasis is placed on what has been termed agent morality rather than act morality. Behavior can be condoned if it is based on "emotional commitment," "the total sympathy of one person for another, . . . the desire to give," and "emotional rapport between individuals."[72] Such a moral code can afford to be flexible in the face of homosexual relationships, provided that the intentions of the parties were pure, regardless of the specific acts engaged in. Hence, honor and self-sacrifice are pervasive motifs in the medieval literature that idealizes affairs between samurai lovers, these being tangible signs of the sincerity of the lovers. The prerequisite for an honorable affair is a "clean" heart (*kokoro*),[73] as opposed to one that is black or ill-intentioned.

The Shinto emphasis on pollution also seems to have a bearing on the incidence of male homosexuality, because women are the primary agents of ritual pollution (*kegare*). Of the three main sources of pollution—childbirth, menstruation, and death—two are exclusive to women.[74] However, the *Nihongi* and the *Kojiki* both link the introduction of death into the world to women, when Izanami dies during childbirth and subsequently pollutes Izanagi. Women are prohibited from participating in most ceremonies and are forbidden access to many sacred places. Women were allowed to ascend Mount Fuji, a revered Shinto site, only after the Second World War, and continued to be barred from the preeminently sacred island of Okinoshima. The exclusion of women from many key Shinto rituals serves to encourage a high degree of male bonding: "Although obviously not homosexual *per se*, the body contact and physical rejoicing in maleness leave plenty of scope for the latent and potential."[75]

The present legal code of Japan bears out the liberality of Shinto with regard to sexual practices. A wide variety of sexual behaviors considered deviant and punishable by other societies are not covered by the penal code, including homosexuality, sodomy, incest, and bestiality. Moreover, the proscription against seduction specifically applies to heterosexual relationships.[76]

Neo-Shintoism

A Shinto revival occurred in eighteenth-century Japan as an important component of the National Learning movement (*kokugaku*). The impetus was a rising tide of nationalism that sought a return to native Japanese roots in reaction against centuries of dominance by Chinese Confucianism and Buddhism. Renewed interest in native Japanese literature sparked scholarly reevaluations of the *Kojiki* and the *Nihongi*. These offer some insight into changing attitudes toward sexuality.

One enthusiastic adherent of the Neo-Shinto program was Miyahiro Sadao (1797–1858), a *Kokueki honron*, a village official who characterized himself as a "potato-digging village official." Being primarily interested in improving the agricultural economy, Miyahiro championed a revival of Shinto's phallic fertility cults:

> From the beginnings of the two support *ōmikami*, Izanagi no mikoto and Izanami no mikoto, down to the birds and beasts who receive no instruction, the intercourse of male and female is a way, like nature, that has been transmitted to us. Since the procreation of descendants is a great enterprise, it must be revered.[77]

The key element in Miyahiro's argument is the sacredness of heterosexual intercourse: "a religious activity reenacting the archetypal event, and agricultural work must be seen as a comparable sacred moment."[78] Following out this line of thought, his strong objection to sending boys to monasteries may be read as an attempt to end the "unnatural" practices associated with monastic life, which constituted a waste of sexual potential. Consistent with Shinto phallic worship, the penis (*dankon*) was seen by Miyahiro as an instrument (*dogu*) of sacred dimensions: "Could the *musubi no kami* have made a useless organ [*fuyō no ibutsu*] in the body of man? . . . It was out there to be used . . . and, in truth, it is a tool by which to honor the generation [*seisei*] of descendants."[79] Any attempt to prevent this use of "the kami's utensil" constituted a potential sacrilege.[80] Harootunian contends that, under the influence of Shinto, Miyahiro recast bad behavior—the requirements established by Confucian codes of loyalty and filiality for securing proper conduct—in the language of religious transgressions and restricted it to violations of the division of labor, which meant acting against the endowment of one's basic character. Losses (*sonmō*) to the realm derived directly from 'human hearts' that behaved incorrectly; "bent" conduct polluted the heart and body and defiled the household and realm. . . . Because such acts of unethical conduct violated the intention of the spirits, they risked eradicating their blessings.

Echoing Chinese views of cosmic correspondence, an intimation of lingering Confucian values, the end result of the proscribed activities was natural disaster.[81]

    Motoori Norinaga (1730–1801), a leader of the Shinto revival, propounds a more flexible view when discussing the role of love in ancient poetry. He expresses compassion for those who fall afoul of moral conduct in the pursuit of love, whether adulterers or monks:

> Love, of all things in life, is the most difficult to suppress in spite of every effort to control it. And man, even with the realization that conduct contrary to the dictates of his own mind is evil, is helpless to control it; of this there are numerous instances. . . . If one searches the bottom of one's heart it is impossible not to find love there, especially the type of love forbidden by man. And try as one might to suppress it, there will be only melancholy and bewilderment in one's heart.[82]

Motoori's remarks may be closer to the infinitely forgiving spirit of Shinto revealed in the *Kojiki* and the *Nihongi* than Miyahiro's rigid dictates.[83] One might even speculate that homosexuality was to be included in "the type of love forbidden by man." The feelings of the human agent are made the focal point of any moral judgment that is to be made about the agent's actions. The heart (*kokoro*) is the heart of the matter.

Conclusions

The foregoing analyses seem to indicate that the difference between Chinese and Japanese attitudes toward homosexual practices is rooted in their respective religious traditions. Although heterosexual activity is deemed natural in both cases, Japanese Shinto also evidences a primal fear of pollution, which is absent from the Chinese view. This fear may in turn have encouraged homosexual activity among males as a means of avoiding the woman's polluting presence, a position clearly evident in the samurai's disdain of women as mere vessels of conception. Consequently, homoeroticism was more readily accepted within Japanese society. The devaluation of and indifference toward women paradoxically freed them as well to practice lesbianism discreetly.

In contrast, despite periods during which homosexuality was openly practiced, the Chinese tend to be less tolerant of such proclivities. From a religious standpoint, heterosexual intercourse was a reenactment of and participation in the cosmic interchange of Heaven (*yang*) and Earth (*yin*), imbuing it with special significance. This significance could be interpreted in terms of individual health and longevity (as in the case of the Taoists) or in terms of the continuance of family and society (as with the Confucians). The priority given to procreation by Confucianism made male homosexuality less acceptable than lesbianism. Taoism was equally amenable to female homosexuals due to the inexhaustibility attributed to *yin* energy.

Notes

1. Drawing upon this poetic image, an anonymous seventeenth-century work entitled *Records of the Cut Sleeve (Tuan-hsiu-pien)* surveys male homosexuality through fifty famous cases spanning Chinese history.

2. R. H. Van Gulik, *Sexual Life in Ancient China: A Preliminary Survey of Chinese Sex and Society from ca. 1500 B.C. till 1644 A.D.* (Leiden: E. J. Brill, 1974), p. 92.

3. Wing-tsit Chan, *A Sourcebook in Chinese Philosophy* (Princeton, N.J.: Princeton University Press, 1963), p. 316.

4. See Van Gulik, p. 207.

5. Such is the report of Ch'ing scholar Chao I (1727–1814), as noted by Charles Humana and Wang Wu, *Chinese Sex Secrets: A Look Behind the Screen* (New York: Gallery Books, 1984), p. 114.

6. Van Gulik, p. 163.

7. Matteo Ricci, *Fonti Ricciane*, ed. Pasquale M. D'Elia (Rome: 1942–49), vol. 1, p. 98; as cited by Jonathan D. Spence, *The Memory Palace of Matteo Ricci* (New York: Elisabeth Sifton Books, Viking Press, 1984), p. 220.

8. Quoted by C. R. Boxer, ed., in *South China in the Sixteenth Century: Being the Narratives of Galeote Pereira, Fr. Gaspar da Cruz, O.P., Fr. Martin de Rada (1550–1575)* (London: Hakluyt Society, 1953), pp. 16–17, and cited by Spence, p. 221. Spence also includes an illuminating discussion of the cultural factors behind the sweeping condemnation of such Chinese practices by visiting Westerners throughout his chapter "The Third Picture: The Men of Sodom," pp. 201–231.

9. Spence, p. 220.

10. A passage in the *Classic of the Plain Girl (Su-nü-ching)* documents this point. When the Yellow Emperor questions the Plain Girl about those who choose celibacy, she replies: "This is wrong. Heaven and Earth have their opening and closing, Yin and Yang develop from each other. Man is modeled after Yin and Yang and embodies the sequence of the four seasons. If one should resolve to abstain from sexual intercourse, one's spirit will not develop since the interchange of Yin and Yang will then come to a halt." Cited by Van Gulik, pp. 137–138. Although compiled in the Ming dynasty, it is obviously based on much older texts, going back even as far as the Han.

11. See Ricci's eight-point defense of celibacy, which includes the following: "The members of my humble society [the Jesuits] retain all their seed, and do not plant it out in the fields. If you doubt the wisdom of this, how much more should you question throwing it away into a ditch or a gutter." *The True Meaning of the Lord of Heaven (Tianzhu shiyi)*, p. 615, in *Tianxue chuhan*, vol. 1; cited by Spence, pp. 228–229.

12. See, for example, illustrations in Michel Beurdeley, *Chinese Erotic Art*, trans. Diana Imber (Hong Kong: Chartwell Books, 1969), pp. 168, 174, 176, 179. Van Gulik cites chapter 9 of the *Tung-hsüan-tzu*, on "The Posture of the Gobbling Fishes," as an example of a case where lesbian activity is encouraged in the name of procreativity; p. 274.

13. Van Gulik cites a short story entitled "The Mandarin Duck Girdle," included in Feng Meng-lung's *Hsing-shih-heng-yen* (1627), pp. 266–267.

14. The character of Mrs. Fan in Li Yü's *Lien-Hsiang-pan*, quoted by Beurdeley, p. 175. In Chinese culture, butterflies symbolize conjugal bliss.

15. K'ung Tzu, *Great Learning (Ta Hsüeh)*, trans. Sandra A. Wawrytko and Charles Wei-hsun Fu, *Ching*, 7.

16. Li Yü, *The Flesh Prayer Mat*, as quoted by Van Gulik, p. 305.

17. The first rankings of offenses are drawn from the *Table of Merits and Demerits to Warn the World (Ching-shih-kung-kuo-ko)*, whereas

the last is taken from another text. Both date from the Yüan dynasty, a period during which such lists flourished, particularly among Confucian groups. Van Gulik attributes this new-found concern for strict sexual morality to an attempt on the part of the Chinese to protect their women from the Mongol conquerors; pp. 245–250.

18. Chu Hsi, *Chu Tzu yü-lei*, 96:13a; in *Reflections on Things at Hand: The Neo-Confucian Anthology Compiled by Chu Hsi and Lü Tsu-ch'ien*, trans. Wing-tsit Chan (New York: Columbia University Press, 1967), p. 163.

19. Wang Yang-ming, *Instructions for Practical Living and Other Neo-Confucian Writings by Wang Yang-ming*, trans. Wing-tsit Chan (New York: Columbia University Press, 1963), p. 49.

20. Brian E. McKnight, *The Quality of Mercy: Amnesties and Traditional Chinese Justice* (Honolulu: University of Hawaii Press, 1981), pp. 60, 139 n. 13, 142 n. 34.

21. Shen Defu, *Bizhou zhai yutan (Casual Writings from the 'Worn Brush' Studio)*. Shen lived during the Ming dynasty and was also a friend of Matteo Ricci. See Spence, p. 227.

22. Van Gulik states "the idea alone that women abandoned their sacred duty of propagating the family and went to live in self-contained communities where they were not subject to the control of male relatives, was abhorrent to the Confucianists," p. 267.

23. Van Gulik, p. 48.

24. Bao Ruo-Wang, with Rudolph Chelminski, *Prisoner of Mao* (New York: Penguin Books, 1976), pp. 188–190.

25. "The Criminal Law of the People's Republic of China (1979)," pt. 1, chap. 3, sec. 5, art. 43, in *The Criminal Law and the Criminal Procedure Law of China* (Beijing: Foreign Languages Press, 1984), p. 21.

26. This data has been drawn from conversations with a Chinese student currently studying in the United States. He also reported that the government is becoming alarmed at the rise of lesbianism among young Chinese women, a phenomenon he attributed to an appalling lack of sex education in the schools.

27. Mantak Chia and Michael Winn, *Taoist Secrets of Love: Cultivating Male Sexual Energy* (Santa Fe, N.M.: Aurora Press, 1984), p. 57.

28. See Ko Hung, *Nei-p'ien*, chap. 6; cited by Van Gulik, p. 94.

29. Van Gulik, p. 47.

30. All quotations from the *Tao Te Ching* are taken from the translation of Charles Wei-hsun Fu and Sandra A. Wawrytko, to be published in *A Sourcebook in Taoism* for the Greenwood Press series on Resources in Asian Philosophy and Religion.

31. Wang Pi, *Wang Pi*, as translated by Fu and Wawrytko, for inclusion in *A Sourcebook in Taoism*.

32. Sima Chengzhen, *Seven Steps to the Tao: Sima Chengzhen's Zuowanglun,* trans. Livia Kohn (Nettetar: Steyler Verlag, 1987), p. 99.

33. Chuang Tzu, *The Complete Works of Chuang Tzu,* trans. Burton Watson (New York: Columbia University Press, 1968), p. 225.

34. Jolan Chang cites Desmond Morris in *The Tao of the Loving Couple: True Liberation Through the Tao* (New York: E. P. Dutton, 1983), p. 31.

35. Jolan Chang, *The Tao of Sex: The Ancient Chinese Way to Ecstasy* (New York: E. P. Dutton, 1977), p. 26.

36. Chia and Winn, p. 206.

37. Van Gulik, p. 48.

38. See Chia and Winn, p. 206, as well as Mantak Chia and Maneewan Chia, "Helpful Hints for Lesbian Couples," in *Healing Love Through the Tao: Cultivating Female Sexual Energy* (Huntington, N.Y.: Healing Tao Books, 1986), p. 283.

39. To sample the complete array of cultural options in this regard, see Nicholas Bornoff, *Pink Samurai: Love, Marriage & Sex in Contemporary Japan* (New York: Pocket Books, 1991).

40. Bernard Rudofsky, *The Kimono Mind,* as cited in *The Catalogue of Everything Japanese* (New York: Quill, 1984), p. 196.

41. Edwin O. Reischauer, *The Japanese Today: Change and Continuity* (Cambridge: Harvard University Press, 1988), p. 175.

42. Tamba no Yasuyori, *Ishinbo,* as quoted in Michael Beurdeley, Shinobu Chujo, Motoaki Muto, and Richard Lane, *Erotic Art of Japan: The Pillow Poem* (Hong Kong: Leon Amiel Publisher, n.d.), pp. 35–36.

43. See Tamagami Takuya, *Genji monogatori hyōshaku* (Tokyo: Kadokawa shoten, 1964–69), vol. 1, p. 292. Also Earl Miner, "The Heroine: Identity, Recurrence, Destiny," in Andrew Pekarik, ed., *Ukifune: Love in "The Tale of Genji"* (New York: Columbia University Press, 1982), p. 71.

44. Beurdeley et al., p. 264.

45. Josef Franz Schütte, *Valignano's Mission Principle for Japan,* trans. John J. Coyne (St. Louis: Institute of Jesuit Sources, 1980), p. 245, as cited by Spence, p. 225.

46. Ihara Saikaku, *The Mirror of Manly Love,* as quoted by Beurdeley et al., pp. 153–154. There has been considerable speculation as to how these remarks are to be interpreted. Because Saikaku had earlier written lavish depictions of heterosexual love, some critics contend that this work was either satirical in intention, calculated to appeal to a lucrative market, or a means of pleasing highly placed pederasts. See Donald Keene, *World Within Walls: Japanese Literature of the Pre-Modern Era, 1600–1867* (New York: Grove Press, 1976), p. 189.

47. Francis Xavier, as quoted by Joseph-Marie Cros, *Saint François, sa vie et ses lettres* (Toulouse and Paris: 1900), vol. 2, p. 12; cited by Spence, p. 224.

48. Schütte, p. 350, as cited by Spence, p. 225.

49. Philip Rawson, *Oriental Erotic Art* (New York: A & W Publishers, 1981), p. 153.

50. Kittredge Cherry, as quoted by Bornoff, p. 439. Bornoff also reports that a 1985 international lesbian conference held in Japan drew few Japanese participants.

51. The all-female acting troupe has been revived in the Takarazuka Young Girls Opera, founded in 1914. Strict prohibitions against sexual conduct are imposed on the young actresses, at least with regard to contact with men. Their enthusiastic audiences range from adolescent girls to middle-aged women by "offering all the shades of romance without ever darkening them with the threatening shadow of a penis"; Bornoff, p. 444.

52. Takeo Doi, *The Anatomy of Dependence,* trans. John Bester (Tokyo: Kodansha International, 1973), p. 113.

53. Doi goes on to compare Sigmund Freud's theory of homosexual feelings with that of the Japanese novelist Natsume Sōseki in his work *Kokoro:*

> The frustration or conflicts arising from *amae* bring about all kinds of psychological difficulties. Even where it is satisfied through love, friendship, or the affection between master and pupil, it allows no peace of mind. The satisfaction is temporary and invariably ends in disillusionment. For in a modern age of "freedom, independence, and self," the sense of solidarity with others that comes from *amae* is ultimately no more than a mirage. (pp. 120–121)

54. Bornoff, pp. 440–442.

55. See Bornoff's account of a 320-page comic, *"La Nuit Magic,"* by female artist Yumiko Igarashi; pp. 447–448. In the course of the tale, the oppressed heroine emerges as a "fully liberated bisexual sadomasochist" who ultimately returns to her stereotypical office job "a new woman."

56. Marguerite Yourcenar, *Mishima: A Vision of the Void,* trans. Alberto Manguel (New York: Farrar, Straus & Giroux, 1986), pp. 3, 18.

57. Yukio Mishima, as quoted by Jean-Claude Courdy, *The Japanese: Everyday Life in the Empire of the Rising Sun,* trans. Raymond Rosenthal (New York: Harper & Row, 1979), pp. 120–121.

58. Bornoff, p. 428.

59. Ibid., p. 437.

60. Jean Herbert, *Shinto: At the Fountain-head of Japan* (New York: Stein & Day, 1967), p. 21.

61. Herbert, p. 69. He also quotes Motoori Narinaga on this point: "If a system of morals were necessary, men would be inferior to animals, all of whom are endowed with the knowledge of what they ought to do, only in an inferior degree to men"; *Spirit of Renewal (Nahobi no mitama)*, trans. Hans Stolte, Monumenta Nipponica, vol. 2 (1939).

62. Takie Sugiyama Lebra, *Japanese Patterns of Behavior* (Honolulu: University of Hawaii Press, 1976), p. 18.

63. Bornoff, p. 13.

64. W. G. Aston, trans., *Nihongi: Chronicles of Japan from the Earliest Times to A.D. 697* (Tokyo: Charles E. Tuttle Company, 1978), bk. 9, "Jingo," p. 238.

65. Compare this incident to Chuang Tzu's observation: "When the yin and yang go awry, then heaven and earth see astounding sights"; p. 294.

66. Aston, *Nihongi*, bk. 7, "Keikō," p. 190.

67. Saikaku's argument is moot if one insists on a "pure" Shinto basis, that is, one purified of Chinese elements. Many scholars have identified the opening passages of both the *Kojiki* and the *Nihongi* as the interpolations of scholars trained in Chinese culture. Donald L. Philippi emphatically states: "The native mythology must have begun with Izanagi and Izanami." Their ancestry was invented, Philippi argues, for purposes of political expediency. See Donald L. Philippi, trans., *Kojiki* (Tokyo: University of Tokyo Press, 1968), p. 397.

68. See Bornoff's chapter "The Realm of the Sexless," pp. 426–451.

69. Philippi, *Kojiki*, bk. 2, chap. 93. The strongest condemnations are reserved for incest. The practice, especially between sisters and brothers, seems to have been common among *kami* (as in the case of the primal pair) as well as the imperial family. Punishment usually took the form of exile. In contrast, other early societies summarily executed incestuous partners.

70. John C. Pelzel, "Human Nature in the Japanese Myths," in Takie Sugiyama Lebra and William P. Lebra, eds., *Japanese Culture and Behavior: Selected Readings*, rev. ed. (Honolulu: University of Hawaii Press, 1986), p. 23. Pelzel states: "At no point do the myths picture sexual love as in conflict with social 'good,' or as conditioned by the requirements of society. Kinsmen are not shown as having anything to do with one another's marriages, let alone love affairs, and there is no suggestion that the community need judge sexual relations."

71. Pelzel, p. 24.

72. Ibid., pp. 24–26.

73. Ibid., p. 26.

74. Bornoff reports a curious, but significant, indicator of the extent to which this gynophobia prevails in modern Japan—a cartoon depicting the Japanese flag as a "polluting woman soaking into a background of pristine male purity like a menstrual stain," p. 14.

75. Bornoff, p. 428.

76. *The Japanese Legal Advisor: Crimes and Punishments* (Rutland, Vt.: Charles E. Tuttle Company, 1970), pp. 129, 131.

77. Miyahiro in Ono Takeo, *Kinsei chihō keizai shiryō* (Tokyo: Yoshikawa Kyōbunkan, 1958), vol. 5, p. 267; as quoted by H. D. Harootunian in *Things Seen and Unseen: Discourse and Ideology in Tokugawa Nativism* (Chicago: University of Chicago Press, 1988), p. 298.

78. Harootunian, p. 299.

79. Miyahiro, from *Nihon shisō taikei*, vol. 51, *Kokugaku undō no shisō*, eds. Haga Noboru and Matsumoto Sannosuke (Tokyo: Iwanami shoten, 1971), p. 295, as cited by Harootunian, p. 300.

80. Harootunian, p. 300.

81. Ibid, p. 302.

82. Motoori Norinaga, *Observations from Long Years of Apprenticeship to Poetry (Sekijōshishuku-gen)* in *Sources of Japanese Tradition*, comps. Ryusaku Tsunoda, William Theodore de Bary, and Donald Keene (New York: Columbia University Press, 1971), p. 537.

83. On this point Betty B. Lanham writes: "In Japan, folklore intended for children has occasionally been altered to encompass this ethical precept [the request for forgiveness or an apology]; for instance, a translated version of *Little Red Riding-Hood* (Shōgakukan 1965) portrays the fox with tears in his eyes asking for forgiveness. Such a request provides the means for reinstatement within the group; acceptance of the apology is expected. In the United States, the 'loss of face' accompanying an apology appears to prevent its use and thus also the potential readjustment that may be possible." "Ethics and Moral Precepts Taught in Schools of Japan and the United States," in Lebra and Lebra, eds., pp. 290–291.

Bibliography

Aston, W. G., trans. 1978. *Nihongi: Chronicles of Japan from the Earliest Times to A.D. 697*. Bks. 7 and 9. Tokyo: Charles E. Tuttle Company.

Bao Ruo-Wang, with Rudolph Chelminski. 1976. *Prisoner of Mao*. New York: Penguin Books.

Beurdeley, Michel. 1969. *Chinese Erotic Art*. Translated by Diana Imber. Hong Kong: Chartwell Books.

Beurdeley, Michel, Shinobu Chujo, Motoaki Muto, and Richard Lane. N.d. *Erotic Art of Japan: The Pillow Poem*. Hong Kong: Leon Amiel Publisher.

Bornoff, Nicholas. 1991. *Pink Samurai: Love, Marriage & Sex in Contemporary Japan.* New York: Pocket Books.

The Catalogue of Everything Japanese. 1984. New York: Quill.

Chan, Wing-tsit. 1963. *A Sourcebook in Chinese Philosophy.* Princeton, N.J.: Princeton University Press.

Chang, Jolan. 1977. *The Tao of Sex: The Ancient Chinese Way to Ecstasy.* New York: E. P. Dutton.

————. 1983. *The Tao of the Loving Couple: True Liberation Through the Tao.* New York: E. P. Dutton.

Chia, Mantak, and Maneewan Chia. 1986. *Healing Love Through the Tao: Cultivating Female Sexual Energy.* Huntington, N.Y.: Healing Tao Books.

Chia, Mantak, and Michael Winn. 1984. *Taoist Secrets of Love: Cultivating Male Sexual Energy.* Santa Fe, N.M.: Aurora Press.

Chu Hsi. 1967. *Reflections on Things at Hand: The Neo-Confucian Anthology Compiled by Chu Hsi and Lü Tsu-ch'ien.* Translated by Wing-tsit Chan. New York: Columbia University Press.

Chuang Tzu. 1968. *The Complete Works of Chuang Tzu.* Translated by Burton Watson. New York: Columbia University Press.

Courdy, Jean-Claude. 1979. *The Japanese: Everyday Life in the Empire of the Rising Sun.* Translated by Raymond Rosenthal. New York: Harper & Row.

The Criminal Law and the Criminal Procedure Law of China. 1984. Beijing: Foreign Languages Press.

Doi, Takeo. 1973. *The Anatomy of Dependence.* Translated by John Bester. Tokyo: Kodansha International.

Harootunian, H. D. 1988. *Things Seen and Unseen: Discourse and Ideology in Tokugawa Nativism.* Chicago: University of Chicago Press.

Herbert, Jean. 1967. *Shinto: At the Fountain-head of Japan.* New York: Stein & Day.

Humana, Charles, and Wang Wu. 1984. *Chinese Sex Secrets: A Look Behind the Screen.* New York: Gallery Books.

The Japanese Legal Advisor: Crimes and Punishments. 1970. Rutland, Vt.: Charles E. Tuttle Company.

Keene, Donald. 1976. *World Within Walls: Japanese Literature of the Pre-Modern Era, 1600–1867.* New York: Grove Press.

Lebra, Takie Sugiyama. 1976. *Japanese Patterns of Behavior.* Honolulu: University of Hawaii Press.

Lebra, Takie Sugiyama, and William P. Lebra, eds. 1986. *Japanese Culture and Behavior: Selected Readings.* Rev. ed. Honolulu: University of Hawaii Press.

McKnight, Brian E. 1981. *The Quality of Mercy: Amnesties and Traditional Chinese Justice.* Honolulu: University of Hawaii Press.

Pekarik, Andrew, ed. 1982. *Ukifune: Love in "The Tale of Genji."* New York: Columbia University Press.

Philippi, Donald L., trans. 1968. *Kojiki.* Tokyo: University of Tokyo Press.

Rawson, Philip. 1981. *Oriental Erotic Art.* New York: A & W Publishers.

Reischauer, Edwin O. 1988. *The Japanese Today: Change and Continuity.* Cambridge: Harvard University Press.

Sima Chengzhen. 1987. *Seven Steps to the Tao: Sima Chengzhen's Zuowanglun.* Translated by Livia Kohn. Nettetar: Steyler Verlag.

Spence, Jonathan D. 1984. *The Memory Palace of Matteo Ricci.* New York: Elisabeth Sifton Books, Viking Press.

Takuya, Tamagami. 1964–69. *Genji monogatori hyōshaku.* Vol. 1. Tokyo: Kadokawa shoten.

Tsunoda, Ryusaku, William Theodore de Bary, and Donald Keene, comps. 1971. *Sources of Japanese Tradition.* New York: Columbia University Press.

Van Gulik, R. H. 1974. *Sexual Life in Ancient China: A Preliminary Survey of Chinese Sex and Society from ca. 1500 B.C. till 1644 A.D.* Leiden: E. J. Brill.

Wang Yang-ming. 1963. *Instructions for Practical Living and Other Neo-Confucian Writings by Wang Yang-ming.* Translated by Wing-tsit Chan. New York: Columbia University Press.

Yourcenar, Marguerite. 1986. *Mishima: A Vision of the Void.* Translated by Alberto Manguel. New York: Farrar, Straus & Giroux.

Contributors

Robert M. Baum is an assistant professor of history and comparative studies in the humanities at the Ohio State University. He is currently completing a book on the history of Diola religion in precolonial Senegambia. He is the cochair of the American Academy's Consultation on Religion in Africa.

José Ignacio Cabezón received a Ph.D. in Buddhist Studies from the University of Wisconsin, Madison. Currently an assistant professor at Iliff School of Theology, he has previously taught at Carleton College, Trinity College in Hartford, Conn., and the Ohio State University. He has published both scholarly articles on Buddhism and translations of Tibetan Buddhist texts, and is the editor of *Buddhism, Sexuality and Gender* (Albany: SUNY Press, 1992).

Denise and John Carmody are both on the staff of the University of Tulsa, he as Senior Research Fellow, she as chair of the Department of Religion. Denise received her Ph.D. from Boston College, John from Stanford University. They have coauthored dozens of books, including *Ways to the Center: An Introduction to the World Religions,* 4th ed. (Belmont, Calif.: Wadsworth, 1993).

Khalid Duran, of Moroccan origin, received his Ph.D. from the Free University of Berlin. He has worked at the Islamic Research Institute in Islamabad and the German Institute of Near and Middle Eastern Studies. He has taught at Temple University, American University, and the University of California, Irvine. Currently an Associate Scholar with the Foreign Policy Research Institute in Philadelphia, he is the author of *Islam und politischer Extremismus* (Hamburg: 1986).

Marvin M. Ellison is professor of Christian ethics at Bangor Theological Seminary. He received his M.Ph. and Ph.D. from Union Theological Seminary in New York. Ordained in the Presbyterian Church (U.S.A.), he is the author of *The Center Cannot Hold: The Search for a Global Economy of Justice* (Lanham, Md.: University Press of America, 1983).

Lewis John Eron, the associate rabbi at Temple B'nai Abraham in Livingston, N.J., received his rabbinical degree from the Reconstructionist Rabbinical College and his Ph.D. from the religion department of Temple University, with a dissertation on "Ancient Jewish Attitudes Towards Sexuality: A Study of Ancient Jewish Attitudes Towards Sexuality as Expressed in the Testaments of the Twelve Patriarchs."

Arvind Sharma, professor of comparative religion at McGill University, received his Ph.D. from Harvard. He is the editor of *Women in World Religions* (Albany: SUNY Press, 1987) and is currently editing two sequels: *Religion and Women* and *Today's Woman in World Religions.*

Arlene Swidler, adjunct professor of religious studies at Villanova University, received an M.A. in English from the University of Wisconsin and an M.A. in theology from Villanova University. She coedited (with Walter Conn) and contributed to *Mainstreaming: Feminist Research for Teaching Religious Studies* (Lanham, Md.: University Press of America, 1985).

Sandra A. Wawrytko teaches in the Department of Philosophy, Asian Studies Program, San Diego State University. She received her Ph.D. from Washington University, St. Louis. She is the coeditor of *Buddhist Ethics and Modern Society* (Westport, Conn.: Greenwood Press, 1991).